D1271292

Hitler Sites

ALSO BY STEVEN LEHRER

Wannsee House and the Holocaust
(McFarland, 2000)

HITLER SITES

A City-by-City Guidebook (Austria, Germany, France, United States)

Steven Lehrer

McFarland & Company, Inc., Publishers
Jefferson, North Carolina, and London

Acknowledgments

I wish to thank the following for their help: Annette Samaras and Margret Schulze, Ullstein Bilderdienst, Berlin; Heiner Wessel, Berlin; Dr. Erich Rabl, Höbarth Museum, Horn, Austria; Anne Störmer, *Der Spiegel*, Hamburg; Thomas Fritsch and Christiane Schaup, Anton Plenk Verlag, Berchtesgaden; Angelika Obermeier and Dr. Richard Horn, Bayerische Staatsbibliothek, Munich; Yolande Merten, *Berliner Morgenpost*, Berlin; Nicola Hofstetter and Sabine Simonis, SV-Bilderdienst, Munich; Hans Peter Stiebing, Berlin; Martina Caspers, Bundesarchiv, Koblenz; Norbert Ludwig, Bildarchiv Preussicher Kulturbesitz, Berlin; Samuel V. Daniel, Library of Congress, Washington, D.C.

ISBN 0-7864-1045-0 (illustrated case binding : 50# alkaline paper)

Library of Congress cataloguing data are available

British Library cataloguing data are available

©2002 Steven Lehrer. All rights reserved

*No part of this book may be reproduced or transmitted in any form
or by any means, electronic or mechanical, including photocopying
or recording, or by any information storage and retrieval system,
without permission in writing from the publisher.*

Manufactured in the United States of America

Cover photograph: Hitler at the window of his room, Hotel Deutscher Hof, Nuremberg — from *Adolf Hitler: Bilder aus dem Leben des Führers* (1936).

*McFarland & Company, Inc., Publishers
Box 611, Jefferson, North Carolina 28640
www.mcfarlandpub.com*

CONTENTS

INTRODUCTION

Vast bookshelves groan under the weight of books on Adolf Hitler, the Third Reich, and the Holocaust. New Hitler biographies appear as regularly as crocuses, and universities are creating entire departments devoted to Holocaust studies. But anyone who wishes to inspect specific sites associated with Hitler immediately encounters a problem.

Standard guidebooks do not include most of these sites. An American visiting Germany or Austria has difficulty locating them because Germans and Austrians do not want to talk about Hitler at all. Even mentioning him is considered impolite. Although many guidebooks do describe the concentration camps, Germans themselves become quite annoyed if an American inquires about Dachau, Buchenwald, or Bergen Belsen. Clerks in German bookstores, even stores selling only travel books, can become downright rude when an American asks for a guidebook that includes the camps, and even nastier if the subject of Hitler arises.

Nevertheless, our curiosity about Hitler is eminently legitimate. The more we know about him, one hopes, the less likely such a person will ever again rise to power, at least by popular vote, as Hitler did in Germany.

There is no better way to learn about Hitler's warped character and the origins of his murderous impulses than to see the tenements, slums, and shelters in which he was forced to seek refuge because of his unwillingness to work. Wandering the streets of Vienna in 1909, freezing, penniless, homeless, hungry, filthy, emaciated, louse-infested, Hitler learned to hate. Winston Churchill described him as "a maniac of ferocious genius, the repository and expression of the most virulent hatreds that have ever corrupted the human breast."

How cruel was Hitler? The concentration camps, with their gas chambers and crematoria, are one example. Another is the execution chamber in Berlin's Plötzensee Prison. Here Hitler had the conspirators in the July 20, 1944, plot to assassinate him slowly strangled as they hung by piano wire from hooks. The chamber has been preserved as a monument, hooks and all. Hitler ordered another resistance leader, Carl Goerdeler, a former mayor of Leipzig, beheaded at Plötzensee with a handheld ax.

How was Hitler able to do what he

did? Who helped him? Travel to the little Austrian town of Leonding, a suburb of Linz. Here, in a churchyard cemetery, adjacent to one of Hitler's boyhood homes, the grave of his parents is still lovingly tended, bedecked with flowers and candles. In European cemeteries, families must pay to maintain graves. When the family dies out, the remains are disinterred and discarded. The exceptions are *Ehrengräber*, honored graves, the graves of famous people. Hitler's parents' grave falls into this category. Thus, no one should be surprised that the majority of high Nazi and SS officials came from Austria, not Germany.

Visits to sites in Vienna, Berlin, and Leonding, as well as many others described in this book, can furnish insights into Hitler and Nazi Germany that are difficult to obtain in any other manner. The visitor comes away with a more profound understanding of who and what Hitler really was.

A NOTE ON GERMAN ORTHOGRAPHY

In 1998 the German government announced official changes to the writing and spelling of the German language. The *Brockhaus Encyclopedia* (2001) notes (in German; translation by author):

"The new official *Rechtschreibung* [right spelling] was introduced August 1, 1998. Until 2001 schools will not regard use of the old rules as an error. The new Rechtschreibung is already being taught in many schools, with the exception of those in Schleswig-Holstein, where a popular vote in 1998 mandated retention of the old rules. The Federal Constitutional Court decided, July 14, 1998, that introduction of Rechtschreibung is constitutional."

Among these changes was the abandonment of the German "double s" character, written as ß. According to the new rules, ß is to be replaced with "ss." Hence this book uses "ss" for the spelling of sites formerly spelled with ß.

I

AUSTRIA

In 1889 Adolf Hitler was born in Braunau am Inn, a small Austrian town on the German border, and he grew up in rural Austria and Linz. His abject poverty in Vienna severely embittered him. He left in 1913 but returned triumphantly 25 years later as a conqueror.

UPPER AND LOWER AUSTRIA

Höbarth Museum
Horn (Lower Austria, 73 km northwest of Vienna)

In a quiet corner of this museum are multiple objects that belonged to Maria Anna Schicklgruber, Hitler's paternal grandmother. Among them are a decoratively painted armoire, a butter churn, andirons, a wool stand, a rake, and an ox yoke. (A spinning wheel disappeared during the Second World War.) The objects came from a house at 13 Strones, which belonged to businessman Johann Weissinger, who found the objects and stated that they were "property of the father of our Führer and Reich Chancellor Adolf Hitler." The mayor of the town of Heinreichs (Lower Austria, 38 km northwest of Horn) vouched for their authenticity.

Hitler himself had no interest in his relatives in this area, called the Waldviertel. He never went to see his grandmother's artifacts, though a rumor circulated that he would. But the Nazis published an expensive book about them, with Hitler's express permission. After the war Grandmother Schicklgruber's property was lost and forgotten until it surfaced in Munich and was returned to the museum in Horn.

The objects are of interest today because they indicate Maria Anna Schicklgruber's prosperity. A decoratively painted armoire was a rarity among Waldviertel peasants in the early nineteenth century. Only a well-to-do, upper-crust farmer could afford such luxury. In no case would one be found in the home of the average peasant. Obviously Maria Anna Schicklgruber occupied a prominent position in her little world.

Sigmund, Maria Anna. Des "Führers" Grossmutter und deren exquisite Möbel. *Die Presse* (Vienna). April 26, 1999.

5

Maria Anna Schicklgruber's armoire (Höbarth Museum).

Döllersheim
(Lower Austria, Zwettl district)

Maria Anna Schicklgruber, Hitler's paternal grandmother, was buried in the Döllersheim cemetery. After Hitler became German chancellor in January 1933, and before he annexed Austria in April 1938, his fans often organized festivities in nearby Strones, at the birth house of his father, Alois. The town of Gross-Poppen made Hitler an honorary citizen. In Döllersheim, the "Führer's father-city," Hitler supporters planted a "Hitler oak" and named the main square "Alois-Hitler Place." In the Döllersheim cemetery, officials placed a memo-rial stone, the "honored grave of the Führer's grandmother." Maria Anna Schicklgruber's original tombstone had disappeared many years earlier.

According to the Döllersheim parish records, Hitler's father, Alois, surnamed Schicklgruber, was illegitimate. Alois's father was probably not Jewish, as Hitler's critics claimed.[1]

Hitler never came to visit Döllersheim. In June 1938, shortly after he annexed Austria, Döllersheim was turned into an artillery proving ground. A total of 1428 families, 45 communities, and 7 businesses had to be relocated. In 1943 the entire area was destroyed, though according to official plans it was to be retained. Historians believe that Döllersheim was destroyed because Hitler's forebears — including his uncertain paternal grandfather — stemmed from this region.

After World War II, soldiers continued to use Döllersheim as a training ground. While researching his book *Explaining Hitler*, Ron Rosenbaum visited Döllersheim:

It was still a shock to see it, or what was left of it, when we finally found it. We'd been traveling — snowplowing really — for about five miles into the *verfallen* world, on a road lined with barbed wire and marked conspicuously with frequent signs warning unsuspecting motorists about the hidden danger of venturing into the seemingly innocent pastoral landscape. There were unexploded shells lurking beneath the snowy fields.... A small sign on the side of the road announced "Döllersheim." As we pulled to a halt, we could see, up the snowy slope of a small hill, the pale ruins rising out of the deep drifts; a maimed Stonehenge of worn stone walls standing alone without buildings. Less a ghost town than an archaeological ruin. Rising over the bare ruined choirs of the parish church was one lonely, relatively intact rectangular wall. Into the top of it were inset two stone-arched window frames, empty of glass, eyeless sockets through the vacancies of which the snow-clouded sky stared.

Beyer, Beppo. *Allentsteig: Waldviertler Dörfer mit Vergangenheit und ohne Zukunft. Die Presse* (Vienna). March 19, 1997.
Rosenbaum, Ron. *Explaining Hitler.* Random House. New York 1998.
Schubert, Peter. *Schauplatz Österreich: Topographisches Lexikon zur Zeitgeschichte in drei Bänden.* Verlag Brüder Hollinek. Vienna 1976.
Sigmund, Maria Anna. *Allerseelen auf dem Friedhof Döllersheim. Die Presse* (Vienna). November 2, 1998.

Braunau am Inn (Upper Austria)

On April 20, 1889, Adolf Hitler was born in this little town on the border between Austria and Germany. His yellowish, peeling birth house, 15 Salzburger Vorstadt, is a few hundred yards from a bridge over the Inn River, linking Braunau with the Bavarian town of Simbach. In 1889 the birth house was an inn, the *Gasthof Pommer.*

Braunau played no further role in Hitler's life. The town was a short posting for Adolf's father, Alois Hitler, a customs inspector. The family moved when Adolf was still an infant. Hitler passed through again only once, in 1938, on his way to annex Austria to the German Reich. Afterward the Reich took possession of all sites in Austria associated with Hitler's life, among them the *Gasthof Pommer.* The building has now reverted to its former owners.

On the centenary of Hitler's birth, officials placed a block of granite from the former Mauthausen concentration camp outside the house and inscribed in the stone: "For peace, freedom and democracy, never again fascism, millions of dead admon-

Hitler's birth house, Braunau am Inn (Upper Austria).

ish." Nothing on the stone states why it stands in front of the house, and there is no other plaque or marker explaining the building's significance.

Hitler's birth house is now a school for handicapped children. Many Germans visiting the mineral baths in Bavaria come to see the house, and it attracts other foreign tourists as well. There is talk in Braunau of making the house "a site of reconciliation."

Meanwhile, town officials have been trying to prevent "Internet Defamation." One Web site with Braunau in its title has been selling toy Nazi soldiers. Additional sites are offering up "German personalities," mainly Hitler in every conceivable uniform, sitting, standing, strutting, and raising his hand in the Hitler greeting. Other German personalities in the on-line catalogues are Hermann Göring, Joseph Goebbels, Rudolf Hess, and Ernst Röhm.

The mayor of Braunau, Gerhard Skiba,

Left: **Storm troops gather at Hitler's birth house.**
Right: **Stone placed outside birth house on the centenary of Hitler's birth. "For peace, freedom and democracy, never again fascism, millions of dead admonish."**

has asked for legal action against the Web sites. The vendor of the toy Nazi soldiers maintained that he was selling highly prized collectibles, some worth as much as 10,000 DM. But publicly displaying Nazi symbols, such as banners, signs, and greetings, is illegal in Germany and Austria. Government officials are currently bringing charges against the toy merchant.

Adolf Hitlers Geburtshaus als "Stätte der Versöhnung"? Die Presse. February 23, 2000.
Frank, Michael. Braunau wehrt sich gegen Internet-Angebote. *Süddeutsche Zeitung.* August 12, 2000.
Schmemann, Serge. Where Hitler's story began: Birthplace alive with ghosts. *New York Times.* April 20, 1989, p. 1.

Leonding
(Upper Austria, district of Linz)

From 1899 to 1905 Adolf Hitler lived here in a little house at 16 Michaelsberg-strasse. He attended the local school until his mother, Klara, moved with her two children to Linz. Hitler's father, Alois, by this time was retired, and died in Leonding.

On March 13, 1938, as German troops marched into Austria, Hitler visited the graves of his parents in the Alte Pfarrkirche churchyard, adjacent to his boyhood home. These graves are still lovingly tended and are always bedecked with flowers and candles.

Lambach
(Upper Austria, Wels district)

In 1896–97 Hitler, who was living in nearby Leonding, attended the second and third grades at the Lambach school. Lambach is situated on the left bank of the Traun River. In the Middle Ages, when boats could not pass beyond the Traunsee, Lambach was a transshipment point for salt from Halstatt, destined for Vienna and Bohemia. The Benedictine monastery in Lambach, founded in the eleventh century, assumed its present form between 1640 and 1725.

As a choirboy Hitler first saw the swastika at the monastery. The abbot Theodrich Hagen (1859–72) had adopted the swastika for the monasterial insignia.[2]

Schubert, Peter. *Schauplatz Österreich: Topographis-ches Lexikon zur Zeitgeschichte in drei Bänden.* Verlag Brüder Hollinek. Vienna 1976.

Linz
(Upper Austria)

In 1905 Klara Hitler and her children moved to this city, first to a small apartment on the third floor of Humboldtstrasse 31, then to more spacious quarters at Blüten-strasse 9, in the suburb of Urfahr.

On March 12, 1938, Hitler spoke to enthusiastic crowds from the balcony of the city hall. To thank the town for his happy boyhood years in Linz, the Führer promised to make it the cultural center of the Third Reich.

Linz is indeed a lovely city. It is the capital of Upper Austria, built on both banks of the Danube, at a point where the valley opens out. Urfahr, on the left bank, is connected to Linz by three bridges. Hitler himself sketched plans for another bridge; his drawing still exists. Hitler's plans for Linz included one of the largest, best-endowed art museums in the world. Hitler had visited Italy in 1938, and the Italian

Top: Hitler's boyhood home in Leonding. *Bottom:* Grave of Hitler's parents in Leonding.

Top: Gasthof Leingartner, where Hitler family stayed in Lambach. *Bottom:* Benedictine monastery in Lambach, across the street from Gasthof Leingartner.

museums had greatly impressed him. His new museum for Linz, he announced, would outstrip both the Uffizi and the Louvre. He commissioned architect Albert Speer to prepare blueprints of the painting gallery. A second architect, Roderich Fick, was to design the entire complex, called the *Führermuseums.* The complex would include the Linz Opera, a first-run movie theater, a theater for operettas, the art gallery, a triumphal arch, and a library. The art museum was to replace a railroad administration building. Hitler wanted his nineteenth-century paintings, which he had been accumulating since 1933, to form the core of the collection. Works from all epochs and parts of Europe would be added, many stolen from Jewish collectors.

Top left: Chapel of Lambach monastery, where Hitler sang as a choirboy and for a short time dreamed of becoming a priest. *Top right:* Hitler's first swastika, the Lambach monasterial insignia. *Bottom right:* Humboldtstrasse 31, Hitler's first boyhood home in Linz. *Bottom left:* Blütenstrasse 9, Hitler's second boyhood home in Linz.

Sankt Pölten
(Lower Austria)

On October 6, 1920, Hitler traveled from Munich to Sankt Pölten to speak at a National Socialist meeting in a local auditorium, Die Stadtsäle.

Members of the Social Democratic Party, led by a local assemblyman named Heinrich Schneidmadl, broke up the meeting and got into a bloody street fight. Schneidmadl extricated Hitler from the melée, and Hitler returned to Munich by train.

Schubert, Peter. *Schauplatz Österreich: Topographisches Lexikon zur Zeitgeschichte in drei Bänden.* Verlag Brüder Hollinek. Vienna 1976.

Grundlsee
(Steiermark, Liezen district)

A businessman named Castiglione, who had made a fortune during the German inflation of 1923, built a villa in this town. In 1945 the villa became the hiding place for Hitler's private library. The SS was supposed to destroy these books, but Allied troops were able to capture them with the aid of the German resistance movement.

Mönichkirchen
(Lower Austria, Neunkirchen district, 75 km south of Vienna)

During the Balkan campaign ("Spring Storm," April 6, 1941, to June 1, 1941), the Aspangbahn tunnel housed Hitler's special train and field headquarters, *Amerika*, which Albert Speer describes:

For reasons of safety, the train was drawn by two heavy locomotives and had a special armored car with light antiaircraft guns following behind the locomotives. Soldiers all muffled up stood on this car ... prepared to use the guns. Then came Hitler's car, the central portion of which formed

Hall in Sankt Pölten, where Hitler delivered one of his first speeches.

a large salon. The walls were paneled in rosewood. The concealed illumination, a ring running around the entire ceiling, threw a bluish light that gave a corpse-like look to faces; for that reason the women did not like staying in this room. Of course there was a kitchen, and compartments for Hitler's personal needs: a bedroom, a lavishly equipped bath, wardroom, anteroom, and servants' room. Attached directly to this car was the "command car," which was provided with multiple means of communication with the outside world. In addition it contained a military map room, and thus could serve as a moving Führer's headquarters. Immediately after that came the car with Hitler's permanent escort, consisting of more than twenty men. Then came the guest cars ... then two first class sleeping cars, a press car, and a baggage car. A second special car with antiaircraft guns brought up the rear of the train.[3]

The Balkan campaign began when the Italians attacked Greece from their Albanian base, October 28, 1940. After early Italian successes the Greeks counterattacked and penetrated deeply into Italian Albania. To forestall the defeat of his ally Mussolini, Hitler ordered German military intervention (Order No. 18 of November 12, 1940) and an attack on Greece (Order No. 20 of December 13 for Operation "Marita"). At the same time, a coup d'etat in Yugoslavia brought down the government of Prince Paul, who was friendly to Germany. Hitler thereupon determined to "smash Yugoslavia militarily and as a state" (Order No. 25). Because German troops had entered Bulgaria, Great Britain landed 58,000 soldiers in Greece before April 24, 1941. The Wehrmacht overran Greece and Yugoslavia by April 30. Crete remained the last British stronghold, but the Germans drove the defenders out after a very bloody air attack. Ultimately, the Balkan campaign delayed Hitler's Russian invasion by several weeks. Had the Russian invasion begun earlier, German troops might have captured Moscow and deposed Stalin before the first flake of snow fell on the Smolensk Road.

Schubert, Peter. *Schauplatz Österreich: Topographisches Lexikon zur Zeitgeschichte in drei Bänden.* Verlag Brüder Hollinek. Vienna 1976.

Speer, Albert. *Spandau. The Secret Diaries.* Translated by Richard and Clara Winston. Pocket Books. New York 1977.

Zentner, Christian, and Friedemann Bedürftig, eds. *The Encyclopedia of the Third Reich.* English translation edited by Amy Hackett. Macmillan. New York 1991.

Klesheim Palace (Schloss Klesheim, district of Salzburg)

This palace lies north of Salzburg. Johann Fischer von Erlach built it for the archbishop of Salzburg, Johann E. Graf Thun, in 1700–1709. The imposing main facade of the elegant baroque building has double approach ramps leading up to an arcaded entrance portal and overlooks an extensive terrace. There are couchant stags by Josef Anton Pfaffinger on either side of the approach ramps. A gallery runs around the great hall of the palace, which, like the other rooms of state, is richly decorated with stuccowork. Extending in the direction of Salzburg are parterres with lawns and flowers.

In 1940–41 the building was modernized for Hitler's guests. Among other conferences Hitler was here for a meeting with Benito Mussolini, April 22–23, 1944. The two dictators discussed the Italian contribution to the war effort and German influence in Italy. Klesheim Palace is presently in the hands of the Salzburg provincial government. In recent years it has frequently been the scene of summit meetings among the major powers. The palace now houses a hotel and restaurant training school.

Moser, Erich Peter. *Salzburg. City and countryside.* Rudolf Krey, Gmbh, Vienna (undated).

Schubert, Peter. *Schauplatz Österreich: Topographisches Lexikon zur Zeitgeschichte in drei Bänden.* Verlag Brüder Hollinek. Vienna 1976.

Klesheim palace, Salzberg, where Hitler met with guests.

VIENNA

Schillerplatz (first district).
The Academy of Fine Arts.

The academy rejected Hitler in October 1907 after he submitted a portfolio of drawings and took a grueling two-day examination. The Academy rejected him again in October 1908 without even permitting him to take the examination. Hitler had rendered architectural perspectives competently, but people and animals in his drawings were out of proportion, poorly drawn, and vastly out of scale with the backgrounds. He drew

Drawing by front soldier Hitler, "Ardoye in Flanders," summer 1917. Note that the church tower leans to the right. Leaning buildings are a characteristic of Hitler art.

human figures, in particular, with flagrant disregard for anatomy or accurate animation. Moreover, buildings, especially towers, tended to lean. "Test drawing unsatisfactory," wrote the examiner.

Had the academy accepted Hitler, and had he become an architect, the world might have heard very little of him. The academy building, one of the most important to be designed by the architect Theophil Hansen, opened in 1877. Just past the entrance, one passes a splendid assembly hall, with copies of friezes from the Parthenon on its walls, antique statuary, and rows of columns that give the impression of an antique temple. Anselm Feuerbach painted the ceiling frescoes, which Hitler mooned over, even as Reich chancellor.

Hamann, Brigitte. *Hitlers Wien*. Piper Verlag. München 1996.

The Ring (Ringstrasse)

The architecture of this magnificent boulevard impressed Hitler as "enchant-ment from the *Thousand and One Nights*." The Ring, he gushed, was "the most beautiful street that had ever been built on old fortifications, with buildings, certainly in eclectic styles, but designed by able, determined architects who did not create mediocrities."

Opened in 1865, the Ring is a splendid, four-kilometer-long, circular avenue around the inner city. It was the most important piece of Viennese municipal renovation since the Middle Ages. Until 1857 medieval walls compressed Vienna, a narrow, dark, overfilled place. The suburbs, forming a gentle embankment around the walls, were separated from the city center by a 450-meter-wide meadow belt, used as a parade field, exercise area, and park.

After Emperor Franz Joseph ordered the walls demolished, the inner city was not united with the suburbs until 1890, with construction continuing for another decade. By then Vienna was an archetypical modern metropolis, the expression of an imperial might that had withered long before. As Hitler remarked in a speech in 1929, the

Academy of Fine Arts, Vienna, which rejected Hitler in 1907 and 1908.

Ring was really a political statement, "the huge, overwhelming, splendid middle point of a central authority, conferring legitimacy on a monarchy already being torn asunder by destructive forces.... But the little man arriving in the big city would have the feeling that here lived the king, the imperator."

The Ring's architectural high points are its public buildings in various historical styles: the Hellenistic Parliament, the neogothic votive church and city hall, the renaissance Burgtheater, court opera, stock exchange, and university. Among these structures were the fanciest hotels in town and the palaces of the nobility and newly rich industrialists.

Hamann, Brigitte. *Hitlers Wien.* Piper Verlag. München 1996.

The Court Opera (now called Staatsoper)

Performances of Wagnerian operas here captivated Hitler during his early years in Vienna.

Initially almost no one liked the Court Opera. One critic wrote that it resembled "an elephant lying down to digest its dinner," and another called it a "sunken box." Even Emperor Franz Joseph found the building "a trifle low" (Hoffman, 1998). The Opera did in fact have a squatting ap-

pearance because the city's development had raised the street level three feet. But the two architects who had designed the Opera were not consoled. One, Eduard van der Null, hanged himself in 1868, leaving a destitute widow. Her friends instituted a fund-raising drive, rescuing her from lifelong penury. The other architect, August von Siccardsburg, died two months after van der Null — of heartbreak, the Viennese claimed. Hitler often told the stories of the two unlucky men, along with his own.

"I was so poor, during the Viennese period of my life, that I had to restrict myself to only the best performances. This explains that already at that time I had heard *Tristan* thirty or forty times, and always from the best companies," Hitler remarked. He spent two kronen for standing room at the opera and was infuriated that young officers attending only to flirt with nubile ladies paid ten heller, a 98 percent discount. And there was no possibility of moving into an empty seat at the first intermission, as there is in American opera houses. Even today Viennese ushers with the mien of SS concentration camp guards will summarily eject the hapless spectator from a seat he has not paid for.

Most annoying to Hitler and his friend August Kubizek were the claques. Singers would rent claques for performances, buying

Court Opera, Vienna, where Hitler attended many performances of Wagner's operas.

their sycophants standing-room tickets and paying them besides. At almost wholly inappropriate moments, the claques would begin to applaud vigorously. During one performance of *Tannhäuser* Hitler angrily shushed a group of toadies and when one would not remain silent, punched him in the ribs.

The Opera was badly damaged during World War II, but the exterior has now been entirely restored. The interior looks considerably more modern than it did in Hitler's time.

Hofmann, Paul. *The Viennese: Splendor, Twilight, and Exile.* Anchor Press. Doubleday. New York 1988.
Kershaw, Ian. *Hitler. 1889–1936: Hubris.* Norton. New York 1998.
Kubizek, August. *Adolf Hitler, Mein Jugendfreund.* Leopold Stocker Verlag, Graz, and Stuttgart. 6th edition 1995.

Parliament Building

The young Hitler often watched with considerable disgust the indecorous proceedings in this august building.

The architect Theophil Hansen designed the Parliament, his *chef d'oeuvre*, completed in 1883, which he modeled after the temples of Greek antiquity. The statues of ancient historians lined the steps. "A Hellenic wonderwork on German soil," Hitler commented. What went on inside the place was another matter.

One day Hitler surprised Kubizek by taking him on a visit to Parliament. The imposing chamber made an instant impression on Kubizek. The classic beauty and harmony of the space made him think of a concert hall, well suited to performance of a choral work, an opera, or sacred music.

Hitler quickly disabused the overawed Kubizek of his stately first impression: "The man who sits over there helplessly, ignored by everyone, swinging the bell back and forth, is the president. The other worthies perched on their high chairs are the ministers. In front of them, bowed over their little desks, are the stenographers, the only people doing anything. I feel for the stenographers, but I assure you that these industrious individuals have no real significance. Before them on the benches are supposed to be all the representatives of the countries and kingdoms in the Austrian empire. But most of the representatives are really out for a walk."

As Kubizek watched, one representative began a speech. The other representatives demonstrated their disinterest by leaving

Parliament, Vienna, where Hitler watched with disgust the indecorous proceedings.

the chamber. But later, when a debate began, things became livelier, as Kubizek wrote:

Musically speaking, the solo of the Herr Representative had barely ended when the orchestra came in.

The representatives flooded into the chamber, screaming loudly, one interrupting the other, the president swinging the bell. The representatives answered him by raising and slamming down the lids of their desks. Others were whistling, and in the middle of this undignified spectacle a babel of words was flying through the chamber — German, Czech, Italian, God knows what other languages — mostly curses.

I looked at Adolf. Was this not the best moment to leave? But what was wrong with my friend? He jumped up, balling his fingers into fists, his face burning with agitation. I preferred to sit still, as I had no idea at all what the commotion was about.

Cristol, Pierre, et al. *Vienna*. Alfred A. Knopf. New York 1994.
Kubizek, August. *Adolf Hitler, Mein Jugendfreund*. Leopold Stocker Verlag, Graz, and Stuttgart. 6th ed. 1995. The quotes above are from this book.

Burgtheater

Hitler marveled at this masterpiece of the architects Gottfried Semper and Karl von Hasenauer, built (1874–88). He copied their design for a theater he intended to build in Linz, right down to Semper's grand stairway and renaissance style. As late as 1940, Hitler talked about using Semper's old plans for a new Reich Opera in Berlin, "the most beautiful and best possible."

Kubizek, August. *Adolf Hitler, Mein Jugendfreund*. Leopold Stocker Verlag, Graz and Stuttgart. 6th ed. 1995. The quote above is from this book.

Heldenplatz (first district)

This "place of heroes" furnished the splendid stage for Hitler's first great speech in Vienna. He chose the Heldenplatz partly for its huge size, but also because of its tradition, especially for German nationalists. The "heroes" were the heroes in the nineteenth-century wars of liberation against Napoleon, the seventeenth-century heroes in the war with the Turks, and the unknown soldier, whose monument is still part of the Heldentor, the heroes' gate, that separates the Heldenplatz from the Ring.

In 1908 Hitler was considering renovating the Heldenplatz. According to Kubizek, Hitler wanted to connect the court museums on the opposite side of the ring with the Heldenplatz, thus making the Heldentor a centerpiece. On the opposite side of the Heldenplatz from the imperial palace (Hofburg), Hitler wanted to build two mighty triumphal arches. Kubizek wrote that in the gigantic new Heldenplatz Hitler envisioned "an ideal spot for mass marches," where the marchers would "feel a great, monumental impression."

In fact, these ideas for the Heldenplatz were not Hitler's own. He had filched them from Gottfried Semper. Semper's plans had never come to fruition, and Hitler had simply read about them.

On March 15, 1938, Hitler spoke from the balustraded balcony of the newest part of the Hofburg, the neue Burg, facing the Heldenplatz. Before 250,000 wildly cheering Viennese, the Führer proclaimed the "homecoming of Austria" into the German Reich. In the meantime, the Gestapo was hunting down political opponents and Jews.

Hamann, Brigitte. *Hitlers Wien*. Piper Verlag. München 1996.

Kärtner Ring 16 (first district). Hotel Imperial

Originally the palace of Duke Philipp of Württemberg, the building became a

Top: Heldenplatz, Vienna, where Hitler spoke from balcony (center) to deliriously happy crowds in 1938. *Left:* Heldenplatz balcony. *Right:* Hotel Imperial. Hitler showed himself to crowds from his balcony here in 1938.

hotel in 1872–73. In March 1938, just after he annexed Austria, Hitler stayed here and showed himself to adoring crowds from the balcony of his room. Later he received Vienna archbishop Theodor Innitzer. He promised the archbishop to remain loyal to the church and to work together with him to bring about a "religious springtime," which could also extend to Germany. No press announcement about the meeting was ever made, and Hitler, needless to say, did not keep his promises.

Neuer Markt (first district). Kaisergruft

Under this plain stucco building is the crypt housing the remains of the rulers of imperial Austria. In 1940, after overrunning France, Hitler had the coffins of the son of Napoleon I and his mother, Duchess Maria Louise, removed from the crypt and brought to Paris to win over the French people. Since then, Count Franz Josef Karl has lain near his father Napoleon in the Invalides.

Marxergasse 17 (third district). The Sofiensäle

Built in 1838, this was originally the first Russian steam bath in Vienna, then a dance hall. On March 22, 1912, author Karl May gave a lecture here entitled "To the Forefront of the Ranks of Noblemen." In the audience of 3,000 sat Hitler, wearing borrowed shoes.

The 70-year-old writer was quite a scandalous character. Journalists had discovered that the youthful May had been imprisoned for fraud and theft. Worse, he had never seen the foreign lands he described in his wildly popular books.

May was famous for his stories of cowboys, Indians, and the American west that are still best-sellers in German-speaking countries. The historian Gordon Craig has called May "a one-man dream factory in an age that did not yet know cinema, radio, or television." Men as diverse as Hitler and Albert Einstein were ardent fans. But May's talk on that March night was devoted to praising the peace movement, to which he had dedicated his book, *And Peace on Earth.*

The 68-year-old pacifist Bertha von Suttner, whom May venerated, attended the lecture as an honored guest in the first row. She had called May a "spiritual comrade in matters of peace," defended him against all criticism, and said of him, "We spiritual workers hold the ladder which humanity must climb to attain nobility."

Bertha von Suttner had clearly inspired the title of May's lecture. As a convinced Darwinist, she believed in the upward march of human progress, toward the good and noble, toward peace and the abolition of war.

Although the audience expected to hear another thrilling tale of May's celebrated Indian hero, Winnetou, May's unexpected topic nevertheless delighted them. Afterward, many people congratulated May on the street outside. Suttner remarked that there was "a demonstration of reverence for May and a protest against the slander campaign to which May had been subjected."

The newspaper reporters who attended were far less enthusiastic. According to the Neue Freie Presse, the talk "for those listeners who were not enthusiastic May readers was a severe test of patience." The Fremdenblatt was more blunt and wrote that May's lecture was a "deadly bore."

Hitler, an enthusiastic May fan, was completely enchanted, both by the talk and by Karl May himself. Hitler called May a "splendid, complete human being, who accurately describes the most distant parts of the earth." May's writings were "immensely appealing to young people," said Hitler. In answer to the criticism that May had never seen the places he described in his novels, Hitler said that the descriptions "speak for May's genius, since they were far more realistic than those of other research travelers."

Sofiensäle, Vienna, lecture hall where Hitler listened to a speech by Wild West novelist Karl May in 1912.

When May died 10 days after his talk in the Sofiensäle, the controversy he generated only grew. May's death devastated the young Hitler, who elevated the author to a cult figure. Even as reich chancellor, Hitler found time to reread the 60 volumes of May's writings. In 1943, despite the paper shortage, Hitler had 300,000 copies of May's novel *Winnetou* distributed to his soldiers, although May's hero was non–Aryan, that is, a "red skinned" Indian. Hitler also recommended the stories to his generals, whom he faulted for lack of imagination. May's books, wrote architect and later defense minister Albert Speer, "stirred Hitler the way a philosophic text or the Bible moved others." May served as "proof that everything is possible," that it was not necessary "to know the desert to direct troops on North African battlefields." A person with "imagination and sensitivity can know more of a foreign people's psychology than someone who has studied the same people in the flesh," just as May could "understand the soul, customs, and living conditions of Bedouins and Indians." Karl May proved that it was "not necessary to travel in order to know the world," a reassuring thought to Hitler, who had never set foot outside Europe.

Speer advised historians, when attempting to portray Hitler as the supreme commander, to take into account Karl May's influence, especially in the character of Winnetou. Hitler considered Winnetou the model company commander and an exemplary man. From this "heroic figure," young people could learn truly what "noble courage" was.

Sadly, Hitler absorbed every aspect of May except his pacifism.

Craig, Gordon A. *The Germans.* New American Library. New York 1983.

Hamann, Brigitte. *Hitlers Wien.* Piper Verlag. München 1996.

Speer, Albert. *Spandau. The Secret Diaries.* Translated by Richard and Clara Winston. Pocket Books. New York 1977.

Währinger Strasse 21 (9/18 district)

Anatomical Institute, University of Vienna, opened 1896. (Vienna Morgue) In September 1938 Britain and France had ceded part of Czechoslovakia, the Sudetenland, to Hitler at Munich (see Führerbau and Munich Accords). Before annexing the rest of Czechoslovakia in 1939, Hitler had a few corpses sent to the Anatomical Institute and maintained that they were Germans murdered by Czechs. There was no "peaceful solution" to Czech aggression, Hitler announced, as he proceeded to roll into Prague. Bombs severely damaged the institute during World War II, and it was rebuilt after the war.

Weihburggasse 3 (first district). Stadtkrug

A popular tavern that Hitler frequented during his Vienna years. From October 1937 to February 1938 the Stadtkrug became a favored meeting place for important Austrian Nazis and emissaries from the Third Reich. During World War II the Stadtkrug was supposed to be closed, but Hitler intervened and it remained open.

Simmeringerhauptstrasse. Zentralfriedhof (Central Cemetery)

Grave of Geli Raubal (1908–31).

Geli was Hitler's niece and mistress, daughter of Hitler's half sister, Angela Raubal, who in 1925 became Hitler's housekeeper in Berchtesgaden. Angela brought along Geli and another daughter, Friedl. Hitler became deeply enamored of Geli, a pretty blond girl with a pleasant singing voice. In 1929 Hitler rented a large apartment in Munich, Prinzregentenplatz 16, and installed Geli in one bedroom. Soon Hitler was seen everywhere with Geli. He became intensely possessive and discouraged her hopes for an operatic career. The relationship became stormy when Geli heard rumors that Hitler intended to marry Winifred Wagner, the widow of Siegfried Wagner and daughter-in-law of composer Richard Wagner. At the same time, Hitler suspected Geli of dallying with his chauffeur, Emil Maurice. Quarrels between Hitler and Geli became louder and more frequent.

In the summer of 1931, to escape Uncle Adolf's tyrannical domination, Geli announced her intention to move to Vienna. Hitler angrily forbade her to go. On September 17, as he was about to leave for Hamburg, Hitler and Geli had a violent quarrel. Distraught, Geli wandered around the apartment all day, carrying a dead canary she intended to bury. The next morning, September 18, Geli was found shot to death, Hitler's 6.35 mm Mauser pistol at her side. The official verdict was suicide. But not everyone was satisfied.

Some people believed a furious Hitler murdered Geli. Others said that Heinrich Himmler had her killed because she was an embarrassment to the Nazi Party. But speculation about Geli's death was dangerous. Indeed, Father Bernhard Stempfle, the publisher of the anti–Semitic *Miesbacher Anzeiger,* who helped Hitler edit *Mein Kampf,* may have talked too much. In 1934, after the Night of the Long Knives, Father Stempfle was found dead in a forest near Munich with three bullets in his heart.

Hitler sent Geli's body, after a cursory autopsy, to Vienna's Central Cemetery for burial before the story of her death hit the newspapers. Hitler bought a prestigious grave and marker facing the cemetery's Luegerkirche (church). But in 1946, when Hitler was no longer around to pay for upkeep of the grave, cemetery authorities exhumed Geli's remains, placed them in a

plain zinc coffin, and interred them in a paupers' field. They marked the site with a wooden cross, which has since disappeared.

An amateur sleuth, Hans Horvath, has been trying for years to have Geli exhumed for a detailed postmortem. Horvath wants to know if Geli's nose was broken in a quarrel with Hitler, as the *Munich Post* wrote in 1931. Horvath also wants to determine if Geli might have been pregnant, since there were rumors that she was carrying either the child of Hitler or of a Jewish Viennese music teacher. Knowledge of the pregnancy might have caused Hitler to fly into a murderous rage. Professor Johann Szilvassy, an expert on forensic medicine at the University of Vienna, has agreed to do the autopsy.

Using an old diagram and a metal detector, Horvath has identified the site of Geli's grave. She lies in a desolate corner of the cemetery, overgrown with weeds. But the city has not permitted exhumation because, they claim, there has not been a request from a relative.

Geli's remains may soon disappear forever. If a plan to redesign the Central Cemetery is carried out, all bodies in unmarked graves will be dug up and dumped into a huge pit to make space for a "cemetery of the future."

Rosenbaum, Ron. Hitler's Angel. *Vanity Fair.* April 1992, p. 180.
Snyder, Louis L. *Encyclopedia of the Third Reich.* McGraw-Hill. New York 1978.

HITLER'S LODGINGS IN VIENNA

Stumpergasse 29 (sixth district)

Hitler lived in this building (second stairway, third floor, apartment 17) from February to November 1908. This was Hitler's first long stay in Vienna, a city that he came to loathe.

Hitler and his friend from Linz, the music student August Kubizek, sublet a room in the apartment of Maria Zakreys. In his book Kubizek begins the chapter "Stumpergasse 29" with a description of his arrival at the train station in Vienna:

As I stood helpless among all the noise and bustle … Adolf appeared, with the air of a well-habituated big city dweller. He wore a heavy dark winter coat, dark hat, carried a walking stick with an ivory grip, and looked almost splendid. He was obviously overjoyed at my arrival, greeted me warmly, and according to custom, gave me a light kiss on the cheek.

The first problem was the transport of my trunk, which was quite heavy, thanks to the concerns of my mother. I was already looking for a porter when Adolf grasped one of the grips. I took hold of the other and we crossed the Mariahilferstrasse. People were everywhere, a frightening commotion and horrible noise, so that it was impossible to understand a word. But impressive electric arc lamps lit the plaza in front of the station as bright as day. I can still remember how happy I was when Adolf quickly turned into a side street, the Stumpergasse. Here it was quiet and dark. Adolf stopped before a fairly new building on the right side of the street, number 29. As far as I could tell, it was a very beautiful building, well kept and attractive, perhaps too elegant for young people like us. But Adolf walked through the entrance and across a narrow courtyard. The back of the building was decidedly more modest. There was a dark stairway leading to the third floor. Many doorways opened onto the corridor. Number 17 was the correct one. Adolf opened the door. An evil odor of petroleum struck me, which is still inseparably associated in my mind with this apartment. We were standing in a kitchen. The landlady was not at home. Adolf opened a second door. In the room he inhabited burned a small oil lamp. I looked around. Newspapers were what I saw first; they lay all over the room, on the table, on the bed. The place looked dispiriting and impoverished.

Hitler, who had grown up in a scrupulously hygienic house, suffered mightily in Frau Zakrey's rooms, as Kubizek wrote: "There was a single faucet in the corridor, from which eight different tenants were

Stumpergasse 29, in 1908 Hitler's first home in Vienna.

forced to draw water in buckets and pitchers. There was one dirty toilet for the entire floor, with a door that was almost impossible to open. And bugs were everywhere! "Every night Hitler went on a bug hunt and "in the morning had a specimen pierced with a needle."

After Kubizek published his book in 1953, all Hitler biographers accepted Stumpergasse 29 as Hitler's first Viennese address. But in 1996 Brigitte Hamann wrote that, in fact, the correct address was Stumpergasse 31, second stairway, apartment 17 in the cellar. In a footnote Hamann writes that she obtained this information from the StLA Meldeamt. She attributes the number 29 to Kubizek's error.

Hitler did no work at all, soon ran short of money, and moved out in the middle of the night.

Viennese Medizinalrat[4] Dr. Albert Krassnigg tells the following story:

According to the account of my father's friend (he was a teacher and after 1945 a parliamentary representative from Lower Austria) his mother sublet a room to Hitler for a few months in 1909. Hitler didn't pay his rent for two months, vanished, and left behind a shabby little trunk. When much later the lady opened the trunk, it contained only three bricks. In April 1938, after the Anschluss [annexation of Austria], SS men visited and asked the elderly lady whether she remembered Hitler. She told them the truth, and there were no further consequences.

Hamann, Brigitte. *Hitlers Wien.* Piper Verlag. München 1996.

Kubizek, August. *Adolf Hitler, Mein Jugendfreund.* Leopold Stocker Verlag, Graz and Stuttgart. 6th edition 1995.

Felberstrasse 22

Hitler lived in apartment 16 in this building, across the street from the Westbahnhof, a railroad station. Though he was here for nine months, there are no reliable witnesses to his activity. Marie Rinke, a young woman, remembered speaking to him, and was favorably impressed. Some historians believe that during his months in Felberstrasse Hitler became an obsessed anti–Semite.

Close to his room was a kiosk that sold tobacco and newspapers. Hitler probably

Felberstrasse 22, Hitler's second home in Vienna.

bought from this kiosk the trashy rags he read so eagerly in nearby cafes. Most likely one of them was a racist periodical, *Ostara.*

Ostara was the brainchild of a warped former Cistercian monk, Adolf Lanz, who called himself Jörg Lanz von Liebenfels. Lanz was full of homoerotic ideas about a struggle between the heroic, creative blond race, and a race of dark "beast-men" who preyed with animal lust on blond women, destroying humankind and its culture.

In a postwar interview Lanz claimed that he recalled Hitler when he lived in Felberstrasse. According to Lanz, Hitler had visited him and requested back copies of *Ostara.* Because of Hitler's shabby appearance Lanz let him have the copies gratis and gave him 2 kronen besides. Skeptical historians wonder how Lanz knew the young tatterdemalion he encountered was indeed Hitler, since more than a decade was to elapse before Hitler became even a local Munich celebrity.

When he could no longer afford the Felberstrasse apartment, Hitler moved again.

Kershaw, Ian. *Hitler. 1889–1936: Hubris.* Norton. New York 1998.

Sechshauserstrasse 58

Hitler moved to this tenement (second floor, room 21, apartment of Mrs. Antonia Oberlechner) August 22, 1909. The apartments have no running water; there is a single faucet for each floor and an outhouse in the back. The building was last used to house poor Turkish immigrants and is now boarded up.

By September 16, 1909, Hitler had left the building after paying no rent, failing to fill out the necessary police registration form, and leaving no forwarding address. His savings used up, he lived in the street, sleeping on park benches and in flophouses until late December. In perhaps the supreme irony of history, within a quarter century

Left: Sechshauserstrasse 58, Vienna tenement where Hitler lived before he drifted into the streets in 1909. *Right:* Sechshauserstrasse 58, interior, single faucet for tenants on floor.

this penniless vagrant was to be the absolute ruler of Germany and, six years later, most of Western Europe.

Simon Denk Gasse 11 (ninth district)

After 1938 the Viennese newspapers wrote expansive articles about an apartment in this building that Hitler supposedly occupied in 1909. Nazi officials adorned the building entrance with a wreath and a large Hitler picture. An honor guard of Hitler youths stood at attention by the front door. Illustrated newspapers carried photos of the entryway on their front pages. *How the Ostmark Experienced Its Freedom*, a Nazi picture book, had a photo of Simon Denk Gasse 11 captioned "The poor home of the Führer during his Viennese years." The reader got the impression that Hitler had lived here and nowhere else.

In fact, there is no proof that Hitler ever resided at this address. In 1938 the Nazi Party archives confiscated the original address reports that Hitler had filed with the police. Obviously, government officials were trying to prevent research into Hitler's Viennese past. But modern historians have not suffered because the party archives retained the original records of Hitler's addresses, and the Viennese police kept copies. There is no reference in these records to Simon Denk Gasse 11.

Hamann, Brigitte. *Hitlers Wien.* Piper Verlag. München 1996.

Kastanienallee 2 (thirteenth district). The Meidling Asylum for the Shelterless

(Meidling station; take the S3 train from Karlsplatz) Viennese Jews generously funded the privately financed homeless shelters, which Hitler was soon to know well. Among these philanthropists were Baron Rothschild, Baron Königswater, and Baron Epstein. A prominent lawyer, Dr. Moritz Singer, was director of the Association of Viennese Soup and Tea Establishments; these provided to the poor, at cost, vegetables and a little-known drink, cocoa with milk. Jewish philanthropists paid for children's homes, orphanages, warming rooms, and thousands of daily meals and stipends for needy students. But these charitable acts did not shield the donors from anti–Semitism. Jewish philanthropy, according to one Christian socialist paper, was simply another way of making money: "It is interesting that the people who fund the workers' shelters always own breweries, and our comrades, thankful for the gifts or loans of money, are dependent on alcohol for years afterward." The Association for the Shelter of the Homeless ran this establishment. The Court book dealer, Herr Künast, served as director of the association, which received money from many prominent donors, such as the operatic composer

Karl Millöcker.[5] Indeed, the association was supported almost exclusively with private funds. It distributed clothing and money while it helped the needy find work.

The huge Meidling shelter, which opened in 1908, was located adjacent to the Meidling cemetery, a few blocks from Schönbrunn palace. The shelter offered a warm roof, food, showers, and baths to 1,000 persons nightly. In contrast to the old city shelter and the notorious workhouse, the Meidling shelter was quite popular. During the winter hundreds of homeless waited night after night in long lines for admission. Many were turned away when the beds filled up. Guards on duty all night long intervened at once in any disturbance. Outside, people spent the night on the sidewalk in front of the building, hungry and freezing, hoping for a chance to be admitted the next night. The newspapers always reported when, at the Meidling shelter's door, another child froze or starved to death, a severely ill person died, or someone committed suicide.

Hitler entered the Meidling shelter just

Kastanienallee 2, Vienna, homeless shelter where Hitler lived in winter 1909.

before Christmas 1909, having hit rock bottom. He was thin and bedraggled. He wore filthy, lice-infested clothes. His feet were sore from endless wandering.

He was lucky to be admitted quickly, especially since the Association for the Shelter of the Homeless was then in a severe cash crunch. The city of Vienna had just reduced its contribution to the association from 50,000 kronen to 30,000 kronen annually. As one newspaper, *Die Arbeiterzeitung,* wrote mordantly:

Month after month the beggar's sack is passed uselessly around Vienna, which has the social obligation to help. The fact that in March more than 3,000 children — 100 daily — sought admission to shelters does not touch the gentlemen at all. They are not their children, after all; other children may starve and die.... [It was] the disgrace of Vienna that no money was available for this important duty. For princely receptions, for organizing the hunt, there was always money, as there was for banquets and booze ... but Vienna has no money to prevent any citizen of this city from spending the night out of doors, to prevent women and children from being denied entrance to shelters — for that we have no money. This disgrace must come to an end.

The cash shortage was aggravated by the overfilling of hospitals so that many of the sick sought admission to the shelters. In another article, "The Vienna hospital disgrace," the *Arbeiterzeitung* raged that mothers with feverish or injured children were turned away from hospital after hospital.

But those admitted to the Meidling shelter found order and strictly hygienic conditions. A ritual accompanied acceptance: The "house father" received the anonymous arrivals and gave them each a ticket, which entitled them to enter the delousing room, the bathrooms, and washrooms. The sick got emergency attention. While the homeless persons washed, their clothes were cleaned and deloused. Then they went to a window and were given free soup and bread. With the ringing of the sleep bell, the dormitories were opened. Cots stood side by side. By nine the next morning everyone had to leave.

Besides providing a bed and first aid, the shelter had an important social function. The homeless inhabitants helped one another. The old hands gave the novices vital advice, for example, which shelter or warming room was desirable, where to find a job, what ploys to use when begging. At night the huge dormitories became bazaars. Tailors and shoemakers plied their trades for small amounts of money or cigarettes. There was a flourishing market in tobacco, schnapps, and many other items. Most desired were shelter admission cards for additional nights because the free lodging was only supposed to be provided for a week. Specialists, however, had their methods: they obtained cards from other places and sold them on the black market.

Hitler stayed two months in Meidling, on and off. In the shelter he befriended another homeless man, a Berliner named Reinhold Hanisch. Hitler and Hanisch were not always able to get Meidling admission cards and so were forced to go from shelter to shelter. Sometimes the two men wandered to the Erdberg district, to the privately financed warming rooms of the Jewish baron Königswater, which were open at night. During the day Hitler, sorry looking and depressed, trooped with other homeless men to a convent in Gumpendorferstrasse, where nuns ladled out soup. Hanisch took Hitler with him to shovel snow, but without an overcoat Hitler did not last at this very long. Hitler tried carrying bags for passengers at the Westbahnhof, but his appearance probably frightened off prospective customers. Finally, Hitler obtained the munificent sum of 50 kronen from his aunt, Johanna Pölzl, and bought an overcoat from the government pawnshop.

On February 9, 1910, Hitler left Meidling for the relative luxury of the Männerheim in Meldemann Strasse. His worst days in Vienna had come to an end, just as the problems of the Meidling shelter reached crisis proportions. On April 3, 1910, there was a riot in Meidling when 200 homeless people who had been refused admission to the overfilled shelter tried to storm the building, and the police had to intervene. Indignant and scornful, the *Arbeiterzeitung* wrote, "Vienna's disgrace has now become eternal, rich Vienna's disgrace. Night after night, hundreds must slink into miserable hovels. Instead of shelter, there are only police sabers for these people."

Hamann, Brigitte. *Hitlers Wien.* Piper Verlag. München 1996.

Wurlitzergasse 89. Homeless shelter

Historians once believed that Hitler might have slept here from time to time. The building, opened in the summer of 1910, currently houses homeless immigrants and a nursing school.

Meldemann Strasse 27 (Twentieth district, Brigittenau). Männerheim

This men's shelter is located near the Danube banks in an industrial district. Part of the district, Leopoldstadt, had the largest concentration of Jewish families in Vienna. The Männerheim was considerably more luxurious than other homeless shelters in Vienna.

The seven-story building opened in 1905 and was managed by the city of Vienna. Financing came from the private Kaiser Franz Joseph I Jubilee Fund for People's Housing and Welfare, to which many Jews contributed, above all Baron Nathaniel Rothschild and the Gutmann family.

When the first blueprints and drawings of the Männerheim were shown at an art exhibition, they caused a sensation. There were no cavernous dormitories; instead there were 544 individual rooms for guests, impeccable hygienic conditions, and many common rooms, to make possible "education and fellowship."

Brigittenau was chosen for the Männerheim because of conditions in the district. Brigittenau, on the city's periphery, had many businesses with a need for workers and thus the most growth of any part of Vienna. From 1890 to 1910 the population had increased from 37,000 to 101,000. Many of the newcomers were single young men who worked in the factories. Because there was no affordable housing, these men, called *Bettgeher*, were forced into the overfilled shelters.

The purpose of the new Männerheim was to reduce the number of *Bettgeher*, thus protecting the tender morals of Brigittenau's guest families. As Prince Carl Auersperg, director of the Jubilee Fund, said on the occasion of Emperor Franz Joseph's visit to the Männerheim in 1905, "In particular, the Männerheim will demonstrate that it is ... possible to help persons seeking a place to sleep. A home can be provided for single workers in the dreary, overfilled poor neighborhoods. The home will furnish not only cheap accommodations, but also the opportunity to care for the body and spirit."

The Männerheim charged only two-and-a-half kronen per week for a room.

Meldemann Strasse 27 Vienna men's shelter, where Hitler lived from 1910 until he left for Munich in 1913.

A skilled or unskilled worker earning 1,000 kronen yearly could easily afford this modest rent.

The Viennese praised the Männerheim as a "fairy tale of heavenly accommodation on earth" and a "marvel of elegant economy." Emil Kläger, a Viennese journalist, pretended to be homeless and spent one night in the home. He wrote, "A large electric arc lamp, which hangs over the entrance, serves as a beacon for stumbling people. The Männerheim makes a strong impression, in comparison to the little houses and plain factory buildings nearby. I open the front door and stand, astounded, in a vestibule that would not disgrace a good hotel. Pleasant warmth envelops me."

Kläger paid 30 kreuzer and without difficulty obtained an entrance card for one night. He first sought out the dining room: "I was surprised by the elegance of the room, illuminated by two arc lamps. The walls were covered to half their height by blue-green tiles.... I saw respectable roast pig with trimmings, which cost 19 Kreuzer according to the card. A complete lunch is 23 Kreuzer, a soup with trimmings 4 Kreuzer ... all quite good."

Next, Kläger observed the guests: "Every moment the door opens and a person enters in bad clothing and a bag under his arm. Most of these people look unspeakably tired.... In the evening until about 11:30 there is lively, but not noisy, fellowship."

Inspecting the premises, Kläger found much to admire. "Right next to the dining room there is a spacious, nicely laid out reading room, which has two divisions, one for smokers, one for non-smokers. Here there are daily newspapers and a pretty library, which is for the guests. Most of the books are light novels and popular science. There are also writing desks, with the necessary writing implements." There was entertainment on Sunday afternoons, in the form of concerts and lectures. In the basement were a shoemaker, a tailor, a trunk storage room, bicycle rack, and a shoe polishing room.

The hygienic conditions were first rate. A house physician provided free care for minor illnesses. As in all shelters there was a delousing room for new arrivals. Next to the washrooms were shaving stands and a bathroom with 16 showers, 25-foot baths, and 4 bathtubs. A bath cost 25 heller, about a quarter of the price in a public bath. These amenities prevented disease. Though there was an outbreak of cholera in 1910, the Männerheim was spared.

The bedrooms on the upper floors were opened at eight in the evening. The occupants had to vacate them by nine the next morning. The bedrooms were laid out in long rows of tiny individual cubicles, each measuring 1.4 by 2.17 meters. They contained a bed, a little table, a clothing locker, and a mirror. The bed linen of long-term guests was changed weekly, of overnight guests daily, as in a hotel. Each bedroom had a door and a light fixture. This was probably the first room Hitler ever had with electric illumination.

Although the population of the Männerheim was constantly changing, the average age and social level remained constant. Roughly 70 percent of the men were between 14 and 35 years old. Laborers and apprentices made up 70 percent of the residents, who were metal workers, locksmiths, lathe operators, metal molders, coachmen, clerks, waiters, gardeners, and temporary workers. Also in residence were unemployed men, a few penniless aristocrats, unsuccessful artists, divorced men, and men who had gone bankrupt. Eighty percent of the men had an annual income of less that 1,200 kronen and thus were not required to pay income tax.

The origins of the inhabitants of the Männerheim reflected the ethnic diversity of the Austro-Hungarian Empire. Almost half, 43.5 percent, came from Lower Austria and Vienna, 23 percent from Bohemia and Moravia, 11.6 percent from Hungary. Between 2 and 3 percent of the men came from Upper Austria (among them Hitler), Galicia, Silesia, Slovenia, Croatia, Bukovina, Salzburg, Dalmatia, and Bosnia. Of the men who were not citizens of the empire, 4.5 percent came from Germany, 1.3 percent from Italy, and 0.9 percent from Russia.

The sometimes difficult relations among the ethnic groups in the empire as a whole, a land with five major religions and a dozen languages, is illustrated by an event in the Männerheim. In August 1909 there was friction between German nationalists and Austrian Czechs.[6]

A Hungarian photographer with a police record, Wilhelm Mandl, caused a commotion by throwing a stone in a washbasin and was arrested. For years Mandl had shuttled between the Männerheim and the homeless shelters. Mandl was a Jew, three years older than Hitler, and was described in newspaper accounts as an aggressive German nationalist. Thus, even the strictly disciplined Männerheim was not much different from the empire of which it was a tiny part, the "Babylon of peoples."

The managers of the Männerheim, first Johann Kanya and, after June 1910, Robert Schaffer, were formidable disciplinarians. They lived on the premises and demanded obedience, cleanliness, and quiet. Women's visits were strictly forbidden. Occupants were punished with expulsion for the slightest infraction.

Although another homeless shelter was built in Wurlitzergasse, there were never enough beds to go around. Vienna had almost 80,000 Bettgeher and even more homeless. In 1911, in the Männerheim, 514 of the 560 guests had been in residence for more than a year. Newcomers gained admission only with difficulty. Usually, no one would voluntarily give up his room. Hitler

and Reinhold Hanisch were lucky to find housing in the Männerheim.

On hearing that Hitler could paint, Hanisch proposed that Hitler should paint scenes of Vienna. Hanisch would peddle the paintings and the two would share the proceeds. With some of 50 kronen he had received from his aunt Johanna, Hitler bought paint and brushes. In the safe, clean Männerheim, he copied watercolors from other pictures. Hanisch then hawked Hitler's output, primarily to Jewish picture frame dealers. For the first time in his life Hitler was earning his own living.[7]

Hitler soon became lazy. Hanisch was able to sell the pictures faster than Hitler could paint them and had to nag Hitler to work harder. As Hanisch became more and more annoyed, Hitler insisted he could not paint to order; he had to be in the right mood. After one big sale Hitler disappeared from the Männerheim for a few days, returning when he ran out of money.

The two finally had a falling out. Hitler painted a large picture of the Parliament, then accused Hanisch of withholding 50 kronen from the sale price and 9 kronen more for a watercolor. The matter came to the attention of the police, who jailed Hanisch briefly, not for cheating Hitler but for using the false name of Fritz Walter. Hanisch disappeared from Hitler's life, though Hitler continued to make a living by selling his paintings.

The pleasant day room in Meldemann Strasse, where Hitler painted and occasionally harangued the other occupants with political diatribes, looks much as it did in Hitler's time. Hitler lived in the Männerheim until he decamped for Munich in 1913.

Hamann, Brigitte. *Hitlers Wien*. Piper Verlag. München 1996. Emil Kläger's descriptions of the Männerheim are from this book.

Keegan, John. *The First World War*. Alfred A. Knopf. New York 1999.

Kershaw, Ian. *Hitler. 1889–1936: Hubris*. Norton. New York 1998.

II

GERMANY

Before we look at specific sites in Germany, it is useful to know something about Hitler's German architects and the fate of their buildings.

After Hitler became reich chancellor in 1933, a small group of German architects worked on his huge building program until World War II forced a halt. Hitler called his buildings "words of stone," which were meant to be "eternal." Munich, Nuremberg, Linz, and Hamburg, but above all, Berlin, were to be rebuilt as "Führer cities." They would contain architecture that was "gigantic," "monumental," "overpowering," "smashing."

More than half a century after the war, Germans are still debating whether to raze these monuments to Hitler's megalomania or declare them protected landmarks. In the meantime, upkeep of some of the structures has been quite lax. A prime example is the Berlin Olympic Stadium, parts of which are in danger of collapse.

"We will use granite," Hitler averred, so that stone monuments to the Nazi movement would be like cathedrals in the millennia to come. Indeed, some of his buildings still make powerful impressions.

Examples are the Führerbau in Munich (actually a matched pair of buildings) and the Zeppelin Tribune (Führertribune) in the Reich Party district of Nuremberg.

For decades the study of Nazi architecture was taboo in many colleges. But there has been a recent upsurge of interest. In the wake of Albert Speer's memoir, *Inside the Third Reich* (1969), books about the history of Hitler's buildings have been published.

Students of architecture are now studying the leading architects of the period. Werner Durth, an architect and sociologist in Darmstadt, has written two well-received books on this subject.

Born after World War II, Durth was annoyed by the 12-year lacuna, 1933–45, in histories of German architecture. But he was not content to occupy himself with Albert Speer's book and diaries. In 1978 Durth began his own researches into the Nazi architectural past.

Durth discovered that Nazi architects were eager to escape the influence of the despised, avant-garde, "100 percent Bolshevik" Bauhaus. Here are some of the most prominent architects:

- Julius Schulte-Frohlinde. Declaring that "Jews and Marxists" were "destructive wire-pullers," Schulte-Frohlinde was architect for Robert Ley, head of the German Labor Front.[8] Schulte-Frohlinde built mammoth training schools that looked like fortresses. They were called Ordensburgen — order fortresses — and were meant to produce Ordensjunker — order nobles — a new generation of Nazi functionaries. The German Army (Bundeswehr) now uses the fortresses, located at Sonthofen (106 kilometers S.W. of Munich), Crössinsee (Pomerania, N.E. Germany), and Vogelsang (Eifel Mountains, near Frankfurt am Main). Schulte-Frohlinde's buildings still have the statuary Hitler liked: nude, muscular torchbearers, draped in flowing capes. In 1952 Schulte-Frohlinde built a new city hall in Düsseldorf.

- Hanns Dustmann had an even more stellar career than Schulte-Frohlinde. Dustmann had been an office manager for Bauhaus founder Walter Gropius. On the evening of January 30, 1933, just after Hitler became chancellor, Dustmann reported to party functionaries as "SS man Dustmann." As Reich architect and "honor-dagger-carrier" of the Hitler Youth, Dustmann was appointed professor by Hitler himself, who commissioned him to build a colossal *Volk* museum and a gigantic Langemarck hall for Berlin.[9] After the war Dustmann became house architect for the Victoria Insurance Company. He built more than 30 buildings for banks and other financial institutions, including Allianz, the giant German insurance company, which is only now paying the claims of many Holocaust victims.[10]

Hitler at the dedication of Ordensburg Sonthofen, April 1936. On the far left is Robert Ley, head of the German Labor Front (Bildarchiv Preussischer Kulturbesitz).

- Friedrich Hetzelt was an architect of Carinhall, Hermann Göring's famous "hunting lodge" near Berlin. Hetzelt also designed the Berlin offices of Reinhard Heydrich. After the war Hetzelt built an opera house and theater in Wuppertal.

- Herbert Rimpl built the Hermann Göring Works, a slave-labor-mining and smelting operation, and was an armament expert who received secret commissions in the occupied territories. After the war he built the Federal Criminal Justice Building in Wiesbaden.

- Friedrich Tamms, a specialist in bunkers and flak towers,[11] as well as pithy propaganda, became the highly decorated chief architect of Düsseldorf and secured commissions for some of his old colleagues. One was Carl Piepenburg, who was Albert Speer's first assistant during the building of Hitler's Reich Chancellery. Piepenburg also designed the Führerbunker under the chancellery garden.

- Helmut Hentrich, who had drawn up plans for a facade of square double pillars for one of Hitler's Berlin buildings, used the same plans after the war for the offices of the Trinkaus Bank

- Cäsar Pinnaus, who laid out the rooms in the Reich Chancellery, was able to use his 1940 plans in 1980 when he built the headquarters of the Rhein-Westfall Banking Group in Münster.

All of these men were close associates of Albert Speer. A middling architect, Speer was nonetheless a striver, who became a Nazi Party member in 1931, party architect in 1932, and, after 1935, stage builder and lighting director for the Nuremberg party rallies. Architecturally, Speer was Hitler's second choice, after Paul Ludwig Troost (1878–1934). In Munich Troost had designed the Führerbau, the German Art Museum (*Haus der Kunst*), and the Nazi Temple of Honor, which were completed after his death.

The big day for Speer's associates came on January 30, 1937, when Hitler appointed Speer inspector general of buildings for Berlin. But many other people were quite distressed because they knew Speer was about to begin erecting pretentious, colossal monstrosities. Even Speer's own architect father told his son, "You've all gone completely crazy."

Speer and his colleagues met for meals at Horcher's, a popular Nazi watering hole (and the setting for the first act of Carl Zuckmayer's play *The Devil's General*). In 1941 and 1942, they were still meeting here as concentration camp inmates from Flossenbürg and Neuengamme were laboring in granite quarries to produce building materials. But the Russian winter of 1941, which stopped the German invasion in front of Moscow, and the catastrophic defeat of the German Sixth Army at Stalingrad a year later, brought Hitler's building program to an abrupt end.

After the war the victors demolished many buildings associated with the Third Reich. In 1946 the Russians tore down the new Reich Chancellery. In 1947 the Americans dynamited Troost's Munich Temple of Honor. In 1987 the British demolished Berlin's Spandau prison, a nineteenth-century brick building, after the suicide of its last war-criminal prisoner, Rudolf Hess. A shopping center has replaced the prison.

The victors' worry that these places were "contaminated" and could serve as cult sites for neo–Nazis has been amply borne out. The few remaining walls from Hitler's Obersalzberg buildings in Berchtesgaden, his mountain retreat, pull in 300,000 tourists yearly. But the victors simply did not have enough time to demolish everything Hitler had built, though they did try.

On May 13, 1946, the Allied Powers declared that all buildings and monuments of "military and National Socialist character" would be completely destroyed and eliminated by January 1, 1947, with the exception of "objects with material utility for the populace or of great architectural value." Of these, only offensive parts would be removed.

But the time for Allied elimination of all Nazi buildings quickly passed, and the responsibility fell into the hands of German officials. On grounds of "worth" and "utility" they spared Hitler's buildings but removed blatant Nazi ornamentation.

Only the imperial eagle was taken from the Führerbau in Munich, where the Munich Accords had been signed in September 1938. From the finance ministry and court buildings, the excisions were even less noticeable. The stone eagles were left in place, with the exception of the swastikas, which were chiseled from the claws.

Authorities treated some gewgaws even more curiously. A four-and-a-half-meter tall, nine-ton imperial eagle perched from 1940–1962 on the main building at Berlin's Tempelhof Airport. When American officials needed the eagle's pedestal for a radar antenna, they put the eagle's torso in storage and sent the head, which weighed 136 kilograms, to the U.S. Military Academy at West Point. A few years later the Air Force presented the head to the Berliners. Since 1985 the head has sat on a concrete pedestal, part of a monument to the 1948 Berlin Airlift.

The British used the Berlin Reich Sport Field for their headquarters. They meticulously polished the bronze Nazi eagle and held the queen's birthday parades on the enormous May Field. To the inscriptions on the wall of the clock tower hall, which praise "blood sacrifices" and commemorate the "long gray rows" of Langemarck, the British added "God save the Queen."

The Japanese have been even less squeamish about Nazi buildings than the British because of the long, unbroken Japanese relationship with the Germans. The Japanese-German Center in Berlin is a partial reproduction of Hitler's Reich Chancellery. Cäsar Pinnau's design for the interior of the Japanese building resembles his 1940 Reich Chancellery interior.

When German governmental agencies moved into former Nazi buildings, they usually made no alterations. For example, the Bavarian Economic Ministry took over a Wehrmacht building that the U.S. Army had used as a PX for its Munich command. The Economic Ministry made no effort to remove Nazi decorations from the facade. A warrior's bust still sits over the main entrance, and coalscuttle Wehrmacht helmets form part of the window gables.

Durth, Werner. *Deutsche Architekten*. Vieweg-Verlag. Braunschweig/Wiesbaden 1989.

Durth, Werner, and Niels Gutschow. *Träume in Trümmern*. Vieweg-Verlag. Braunschweig/Wiesbaden 1989.

Krüger, Karl Heinz. Die Entnazifizierung der Steine. *Der Spiegel* 4:64–81, 1989.

Schmidt, Heiner. Prora-Koloss mit Zukunft. *Hamburger Abendblatt*. October 2, 2000.

MUNICH: CITY CENTER

"Munich is the city closest to my heart. Here as a young man, as a soldier, and as a politician I made my start," said Hitler. Indeed, Munich was the first German city he lived in after leaving Austria. He returned to Munich after serving in the German Army in World War I.

In postwar Munich Hitler encountered an obscure political group that he molded into the Nazi Party. He made his first grab for power, the so-called Beer Hall Putsch, in Munich in 1923. During this same period he gathered around him many of the people who would play key roles in his regime and share the guilt for his crimes. Industrial-scale mass murder began in Dachau, a concentration camp in a Munich suburb.

Hitler's personal life, such as it was, centered around Munich. Geli Raubal, his niece and, some say, the only woman he ever loved, was found shot to death in his Munich apartment in 1931. Eva Braun met Hitler in Munich and married him on the penultimate day of his life.

Munich was the site of Hitler's greatest diplomatic triumph, the Munich Accords of 1938, with England's Neville Chamberlain, France's Edouard Daladier, and Italy's Benito Mussolini. A nearly successful attempt on Hitler's life occurred in Munich in 1939, and the city was the center of one of the few German anti–Nazi resistance movements, the White Rose.

Hitler had grandiose plans for rebuilding Munich, which he called "The Capital of the Movement." He intended to create two "avenues of splendor," east-west and north-south, intersecting in a square that would put to shame St. Peter's Square in Rome and the Place de la Concorde in Paris.

Along the new avenues Hitler wanted to construct monumental buildings, arcades, galleries, an opera house, and a gigantic "column of the movement." To handle the traffic, an autobahn ring, a new train station, and new subways would be built. The planned completion date was 1945.

The builders dug only 590 meters of a new north-south subway tunnel before the war ended the entire endeavor. After the war the tunnel was closed off, except for a section used to cultivate mushrooms. When Munich began digging its new subway, the north-south tunnel was included in the line between Marienplatz and Harras.

Munich suffered grievously during the war. Between 1940 and 1945, 70 air raids, 61,000 tons of high explosives, and 3.5 million incendiary bombs reduced one of Europe's fabled cities to a heap of rubble. Six thousand Germans died during the raids, and 15,000 others were injured. More than half of the town's buildings were flattened

completely or so severely damaged that they were razed, leaving 265,000 people homeless.

Deming, Brian, and Ted Iliff. *Hitler and Munich: A Historical Guide to the Sights and Addresses of Munich Important to Adolf Hitler, His Followers, and His Victims.* Verlag A. Plenk KG. Berchtesgaden, Germany ca. 1986.
Rosenbaum, Ron. *Explaining Hitler.* Random House. New York 1998.

North Side of Prielmayerstrasse Northwest of Stachus. Justizpalast

The Nazis held many trials of dissidents in this ornate, four-story building, including the trials of Father Rupert Mayer and the White Rose conspirators.

The White Rose was a small group of anti–Hitler students at Munich's Ludwig-Maximilian University. They began their activities in 1942. Nazi officials pitilessly liquidated them in 1943.

The three founding members of the White Rose-Hans Scholl, Alexander Schmorell, and Christoph Probst — were medical student–soldiers. Scholl had been a medic in France and lived close to the university. Schmorell was half–German, half–Russian and had arrived in Munich from the Urals at age four. Probst was married with two children. The three men were deeply ashamed of the Nazi atrocities and were determined to oppose the regime.

Sophie Scholl, Hans's twenty-one-year-old sister, came to Munich to study biology and philosophy and joined the group. Sophie had found out accidentally that her brother and Schmorell were producing literature to incite opposition. Another medical student, Willi Graf, and a few other students also joined. But Inge Scholl, the sister of Hans and Sophie, never learned of the clandestine activity until after her siblings' arrest.

The young students found a supporter on the university faculty, Kurt Huber, who was Sophie's philosophy professor. Huber had a lame right leg, trembling hands, and problems speaking. He disdained the Nazis, but his wife had enrolled him in the party without his knowledge to increase his salary. An authority on folk music, he had lost a good appointment in Berlin when he rejected the absurd Nazi idea that only music in a major key was natural for Teutonic peoples. Huber's lectures in Munich were laced with subtle digs aimed at the regime.

The conspirators met at Hans Scholl's apartment on Franz-Joseph-Strasse 13, the architect's studio of Hans's friend Manfred Eickemeyer, on Leopoldstrasse 38, and occasionally at the home of Schmorell's father in Harlaching, a section of Munich. Their first pamphlet, printed in late May 1942, "Leaflets of the White Rose," gave the group its name. Hans Scholl later told the Gestapo that White Rose was the name of a Spanish novel he had read, though no such book was ever published.

"Nothing is more unworthy of a cultured people than to allow itself, without resistance, to be 'governed' by an irresponsible ruling clique motivated by the darkest instincts," the first White Rose pamphlet began. Germans should offer passive resistance to "the atheistic war machine."

There were 800 words of text, typed, double-spaced, with quotes from Goethe, Schiller, and other giants of German culture. At the end was a request that readers copy the message and pass it on. Scholl and Schmorell mailed the pamphlet to professors, teachers, clergy, even hotelkeepers and restaurateurs. They selected addresses from city directories and phone books and included people as far to the north as Hamburg in their mailing list.

The next circular carried a harsher message, imploring Germans to sabotage the war effort, as well as Nazi festivals and gatherings. By the fourth mailing, the cry had become quite emphatic: "For Hitler and his followers there can be no punishment on this earth which will expiate their crimes…. An example must be made of them so that nobody will have the slightest inclination to attempt any such thing ever again." The text concluded, "We will not be silent. We are your bad conscience. The White Rose will not leave you in peace."

In July 1942 the army sent the medical students to the eastern front, where they spent four months. By the time they came back to Munich for more training, they were more determined than ever to defy Hitler. The disillusionment of the Wehrmacht troops, along with the murders and atrocities they had witnessed, deepened the students' commitment. Moreover, the Gestapo had arrested Robert Scholl, Hans's and Sophie's father, because he had mentioned to a secretary that the war was already lost.

Hans Scholl, Alexander Schmorell, and Willi Graf were able to raise some money for the White Rose from anti–Hitler individuals and groups outside of Munich. They were also able to enlist Professor Kurt Huber to help write their fifth pamphlet, "Leaflets of the Resistance Movement in Germany." They dropped the "White Rose" moniker, and Huber, who was quite conservative, insisted on a text that was much less communistic in tone than Scholl and Schmorell had wanted. Shorter and punchier, the message was that the defeat of Germany was imminent: "No pack of criminals can possibly achieve a German victory. Break with National Socialism while there is still time." After a plea for "reasonable socialism" and a European federation of nations, the pamphlet concluded, "Freedom of speech, freedom of religion, protection of the individual citizen against the arbitrary actions of authoritarian states-these are the foundations of the New Europe. Support the Resistance Movement! Circulate the leaflets!"

The students produced the pamphlets on a duplicating machine in Manfred Eickemeyer's Leopoldstrasse studio. They mailed their leaflets from many different cities to give the impression that they were a huge organization.

One night in February 1943 Schmorell, Graf, and Hans Scholl went around Munich with stencils and paint, smearing "Down with Hitler," "Hitler the mass murderer," and "Freedom" on every blank wall they could find. Next day shocked Nazi officials set Putzfrauen to work scrubbing off the graffiti but were unable to identify the culprits.

In the meantime the war had taken a catastrophic turn. Because of Hitler's ill-considered refusal to withdraw his troops, 330,000 German soldiers were lost at Stalingrad, the entire Sixth Army. The German public was shocked. The White Rose conspirators gained tremendous confidence in their cause and produced their fatal sixth pamphlet.

Scholl and Schmorell intended the text for fellow students and the university community, whom they addressed as *co-militants*. "The eyes of Germany are upon us! The nation looks to us to break the National Socialist terror in 1943 through the power of the spirit as once before the Napoleonic terror was broken in 1813.... The dead of Stalingrad call to us!"

Hans and Sophie Scholl distributed the leaflets much more boldly than ever before. On Thursday morning, February 18, 1943, with classes in session, the Scholls brought a suitcase stuffed with leaflets into the university main corridor and left them in little piles throughout the building. They dropped the last ones from a gallery above the main floor.

A janitor, Jacob Schmid, who was a Nazi Party member, saw the papers come fluttering down. Immediately suspicious of treasonous student activity, Schmid raced up the steps to the gallery, shouting, "Halt! You're under arrest!" and collared the unre-

sisting Hans and Sophie. A few minutes later they were in Gestapo headquarters in the former Wittelsbach Palace.

At first, Gestapo officials were not certain that they had caught the right people. Hans and Sophie had not tried to defend themselves or flee. But then the investigators found outlines for pamphlets and other incriminating material in Hans's apartment. Hans and Sophie immediately confessed.

The interrogators pitied the beautiful Sophie. They told her that if she would admit to being misled, to blindly and ignorantly following her brother, the court might agree to a prison term. She knew exactly what she was doing, Sophie replied indignantly.

Four days later came the trial. The notorious Judge Roland Freisler arrived from Berlin especially for the occasion.[12] Freisler bombastically sentenced Hans, Sophie, and Christoph Probst to death. The three were sent to the guillotine the same day. Four other conspirators were executed a few days later.

In 1946 the janitor Jakob Schmid was sentenced to five years hard labor for turning in the Scholls. The court characterized the 61-year-old Schmid as a "little party official who saw his big opportunity and did not want to pass it up."

Johann Reichardt was the executioner who beheaded Hans and Sophie Scholl, as well as 3,005 other people during the 12 years of the Third Reich. In November 1945 the Bavarian Ministry of Justice decided to retain Reichardt in the job he had performed since 1924. But the ministry reassigned him to Landsberg Prison, where, until March 1947, he dispatched Nazi war criminals with a noose. Reichardt died in retirement.

Deming, Brian, and Ted Iliff. *Hitler and Munich: A Historical Guide to the Sights and Addresses of Munich Important to Adolf Hitler, His Followers, and His Victims.* Verlag A. Plenk KG. Berchtesgaden, Germany ca. 1986.

Preis, Kurt. *München unterm Hakenkreuz.* F. A. Herbig Verlagsbuchhandlung. München 1989.

Maxburgstrasse at Herzog-Max-Strasse, Southeast Corner

This main synagogue site is now a park. A congress of German rabbis was gathering in Munich on June 8, 1938, when the Nazis demanded that the synagogue be vacated in 24 hours. Emanuel Kirschner, a singing instructor at the Royal Bavarian Music Academy, held a final service. Kirschner had participated in the dedication of the synagogue 51 years before. The next day, demolition of the structure began. Some parts were brought down with dynamite. Two weeks later the site was a parking lot.

In 1969 a stone monument was erected, with inscriptions in Hebrew and German. The Hebrew reads:

Remember this, the enemy mock you
They burned down your shrine
They demolished the house of your name
They burned down all the houses of God in this
    land.

The German reads, "Here stood the main synagogue of the Israelite congregation, built from 1883–87, which was demolished in the time of the Jewish persecution. On November 10, 1938, the synagogues in Germany were burned down."

Neuhauserstrasse at Kapellenstrasse. Father Rupert Mayer's Crypt

Father Mayer was one of the most articulate, persistent, and respected Germans to oppose Hitler. Pastor of St. Michael's Church (Neuhauserstrasse at Ettstrasse), Mayer became a thorn in the Nazi eye one night in 1923. The square-jawed priest limped to the podium in the Bürgerbräukeller and spoke to the audience about a topic dear to Hitler's heart: "Can a Catholic be a National Socialist?" Hitler, raised as a Catholic, tithed regularly to the Church until he came to power. He never renounced his Church affiliation and advised his many Catholic associates to remain Church members.[13]

The audience greeted Father Mayer with a rousing cheer. The priest was famous for his patriotism, his moving sermons, and his selfless devotion to the welfare of the poor. But if his listeners expected a blessing, Mayer quickly disabused them.

"You have applauded me too soon," said Father Mayer, "because I will tell you clearly that a German Catholic can never be a National Socialist."

The crowd was stunned. They drove Mayer from the stage with hoots and boos. SA Brownshirts struggled to protect the priest as he left the Bürgerbräukeller.

Mayer's background provides few clues to the origins of the eloquent stand he made against the Nazis. He was born in Stuttgart in 1876, the son of a prosperous merchant. Young Rupert surprised his family by becoming a priest in 1899 and a Jesuit a year afterward.

The Church sent Mayer to Munich in 1912, after he had been a priest in Swiss, Austrian, and German towns. In a short time he was recognized for his efforts on behalf of laborers and the poor.

In 1914, at the onset of World War I, Mayer volunteered to serve as a chaplain on the battlefield. So brave was he under fire that he was awarded the Iron Cross First Class, the first chaplain ever so honored. In 1916 a shell wound of his left leg led to amputation. Even wearing a prosthesis, he limped for the rest of his life.

Mayer was back in Munich in 1917, delivering inspirational sermons in St. Michael's Church and holding Sunday mass for travelers in railroad stations. He was a whirlwind of benevolent activity, leading religious societies, working with the handicapped, raising money for the poor, and helping to care for the victims of the influenza epidemic in the winter of 1918–19.

Mayer loathed Hitler's extreme views and anti–Semitism. Hitler, said Mayer, was a "rabble rouser who doesn't treat the truth too exactly."

Understandably, the relationship between the two men was never good. Mayer opposed Hitler's November 1923 Beer Hall Putsch, and the putschists blamed the priest for their failure. When Mayer hurried to the Feldherrnhalle to help the wounded putschists and comfort the dying, they gave him dirty looks and refused his ministrations.

After Hitler became chancellor in 1933, Mayer continued to oppose him. In one sermon the priest said(Deming and Iliff, ca 1986): "[The Nazis] love to tell [me], "You should be happy. In Spain they would have put you to the wall long ago." But I very quietly say this: I've looked death in the eye hundreds of times already. I'm used to it. That is not so bad. But when someone kills a person spiritually, when [the soul] is destroyed before the world, I can think of nothing more terrifying." Even though Mayer voiced only religious, not political, views, by 1936 the Nazis had had a bellyful. They forbade Mayer to speak in public, then to preach at all. The police arrested him on June 5, 1937, but church authorities arranged for his release by silencing him.

Mayer obeyed and kept his mouth shut but quickly discovered *qui tacet consentit.*[14] Unwilling to let anyone think that the Nazis had made him buckle under, he convinced his superiors to let him preach again.

Retribution was swift. In July 1937, in room 211 (now room 248) of the Justizpalast, the regime tried Mayer for preaching illegally and incarcerated him in Landsberg Prison, the same place Hitler was jailed after the 1923 Beer Hall Putsch.

Church officials were distressed, and did not hide their dismay. On July 4, 1937,

Cardinal Michael Faulhaber of Munich spoke out for Mayer in St. Michael's (Preis, 1989): "I use this festive opportunity to declare publicly that the Catholics of Munich are upset and dismayed, indeed embittered, at the arrest of Father Mayer. His continued imprisonment burdens Catholics deeply.... I call the arrest of Father Rupert Mayer an inflammatory sign of the times." Mayer got out of prison in May 1938, after the warden urged him to moderate his views in public. Mayer replied that he was too old to change and contemptuously left his Iron Cross First Class behind in his cell.

Just after Hitler invaded Poland in September 1939, the Nazis arrested Mayer again for illegal preaching. This time they sent him to Sachsenhausen concentration camp, where his health deteriorated.

Not wanting Mayer to die a martyr, the authorities moved him to Ettal monastery, south of Munich, where he was confined until war's end. Left totally isolated, Mayer said he felt like he was among the living dead. American troops freed him in May 1945.

Mayer returned to the ruins of St. Michael's Church in Munich, where he tried to help the citizens of the shattered city. On November 1, 1945, All Saint's Day, while leading mass, Mayer had a stroke. He stood mumbling, "the Lord, the Lord," until congregants carried him to a hospital. He died a few hours later.

Mayer was buried in Pullach, a Munich suburb. On May 23, 1948, as 300,000 people lined the route, his remains were transferred to the Bürgersaal on Neuhauserstrasse, 200 meters west of St. Michael's. Many people have visited Mayer's crypt, including Pope John Paul II, who prayed there on May 3, 1987.

Deming, Brian, and Ted Iliff. *Hitler and Munich: A Historical Guide to the Sights and Addresses of Munich Important to Adolf Hitler, His Followers, and His Victims.* Verlag A. Plenk KG. Berchtesgaden, Germany ca. 1986.

Preis, Kurt. *München unterm Hakenkreuz.* F. A. Herbig Verlagsbuchhandlung. München 1989.

Altheimer Eck 19, the "Poison Kitchen."

Journalists of the *Munich Post*, which was published at this location, were among the first to focus critical attention on Hitler. They ridiculed him, investigated him, and wrote articles on the Nazis' murderous criminal behavior. Ron Rosenbaum described the *Munich Post*'s 12-year struggle in his book, *Explaining Hitler.*

The first *Munich Post* articles on Hitler in 1921 were the result of an anti–Hitler Nazi faction, which published a pamphlet entitled "Adolf Hitler, Traitor." The pamphlet questioned Hitler's source of income ("Just what does he do for a living?") and wondered whether he might be Jewish. After the *Munich Post* published the text of the pamphlet, Hitler sued the newspaper for libel and won a verdict of 600 marks.

In 1931, when Geli Raubal, Hitler's niece and mistress, was found shot to death, the Munich Post raised questions about Hitler's role in her demise and wondered whether Hitler had broken her nose in a quarrel. The article caused Hitler so much anguish that he was on the verge of shooting himself.

At almost the same time, the Munich Post published an exposé under a banner headline: "Warm brotherhood in the Brown House," followed by the subtitle, "Sexual life in the Third Reich."[15] The article pointed out that although the Nazis condemned homosexuality, it was rife among them. A case in point was the head of the SA Brownshirts, Ernst Röhm, who boasted that homosexuality had been unknown in Bavaria until he arrived but that he'd been working to make rapid and lasting changes in that situation. The author of the *Munich Post* article made clear that he was not de-nouncing homosexuality, merely the Nazis' hypocrisy.

The *Munich Post* did not overlook the many murders that the Nazis were committing. One reporter, Rudolf Goldschagg, who extensively chronicled the slaughter, insisted to his son that Hitler was not a crazy killer. "My father did not think Hitler was crazy," Rolf Goldschagg told Ron Rosenbaum. "He always referred to him as a political criminal."

In March 1933, after the Nazi takeover of Bavaria was complete, Hitler avenged himself on the poison kitchen. SA Brownshirts raided the Munich Post, destroyed its offices, dumped trays of broken type into the street, and dragged reporters and editors off to jail.

Altheimer Eck 19 no longer exists as a street address because the street was renumbered after the war. Today there is a printing shop in the space the *Munich Post* once occupied. A plaque on the wall explains how in 1934 the shop moved in when the address was still Altheimer Eck 19, but it makes no mention of the *Munich Post*.

Rosenbaum, Ron. *Explaining Hitler.* Random House. New York 1998.

Ettstrasse 2. Police Headquarters

During the Beer Hall Putsch, some policemen were dispatched against the putschists from here.

Neues Rathaus (City Hall)

On November 9, 1938, Hitler was here, attending a meeting of party leaders, when he heard that a Polish Jew, Herschel Grynszpan, had assassinated Ernst von Rath, third secretary of the German embassy in Paris. Hitler immediately ordered Security Police Chief Reinhard Heydrich to destroy all Jewish places of worship in Germany and Austria. In fifteen hours the Nazis had burned 101 synagogues and demolished another 76. Roving bands wrecked 7,500 Jewish-owned stores. The pillage went on through the night, and next day the streets were covered with broken glass; hence the name *Kristallnacht.* The final blow that shattered Jewish economic life in Germany came on November 12, when Reichsmarschall Hermann Göring issued a ban on all Jewish business activity.

Corneliusstrasse 12

The second Nazi Party headquarters was in a building on this site in 1923, at the time of the Beer Hall Putsch. The original building no longer exists.

Petersplatz 8. Cafe Neumayr, a Hitler Favorite

Hitler came to Monday evening gatherings here in the early 1920s. He liked to test new ideas on his cronies. A six-story building has replaced the old cafe.

Tal 54–55. Nazi Party Birthplace

On September 12, 1919, Hitler, still a soldier, was commanded to attend a gathering of the German Workers' Party (DAP) at the little Sterneckerbräu beer hall, then located in this six-story building. Hitler was initially indifferent to the assignment, believing that the DAP was merely another group that "sprang out of the ground, only to vanish silently after time." But a brochure he received at the meeting caught his interest, and when he got an announcement of another meeting, he went. Although Hitler was contemplating forming

his own party, his army superiors, desirous of helping the DAP, ordered him to join. A few months later, Hitler had an office in a former taproom of the Sterneckerbräu beer hall, complete with a light, telephone, table, chairs, a bookcase, and two cupboards.

Thierschstrasse 15

This was the third Nazi Party headquarters. The party moved out before Hitler came to power.

Deming, Brian, and Ted Iliff. *Hitler and Munich: A Historical Guide to the Sights and Addresses of Munich Important to Adolf Hitler, His Followers, and His Victims.* Verlag A. Plenk KG. Berchtesgaden, Germany ca. 1986.

Thierschstrasse 41

Hitler Sublet a Room Here Until 1929. A statue of the Virgin Mary gazes heavenward from a niche in the second floor of the building. Hitler moved to Thierschstrasse in March 1920, after his discharge from the army at the end of World War I. A visitor described Hitler's room as "drab and dreary beyond belief, akin to a back bedroom of a decaying New York tenement." Another visitor recalled, "The room itself was tiny. I doubt it was nine feet wide. The bed was too wide for its corner and the head projected over a single narrow window. The floor was covered with cheap, worn linoleum with a couple of threadbare rugs, and on the wall opposite the bed there was a makeshift bookshelf, apart from the chair and rough table, the only other piece of furniture in the room." (Deming and Iliff, ca 1986).

The room was the coldest in the house. According to the landlord, "Some lodgers who've rented it since got ill. Now we only use it as a storeroom; nobody will have it any more."

Thierschstrasse 41, Munich, where Hitler lived from 1920 until 1929.

Hitler's reading material consisted of newspapers and books, many of them popular editions of history, geography, Germanic myths, and especially, war (including the indispensable Clausewitz).

Deming, Brian, and Ted Iliff. *Hitler and Munich: A Historical Guide to the Sights and Addresses of Munich Important to Adolf Hitler, His Followers, and His Victims.* Verlag A. Plenk KG. Berchtesgaden, Germany ca. 1986.
Kershaw, Ian. *Hitler. 1889–1936: Hubris.* Norton. New York 1998.
Toland, John. *Adolf Hitler.* Doubleday. Garden City, N.Y. 1976.

Herzog-Rudolph-Strasse 1

Site of synagogue burned down on Kristallnacht, November 9, 1938. A five-story postwar building has replaced the synagogue. Above the entrance is a marker that reads, "Here stood the Synagogue *Ohel Jakob* which on 9 November 1938 was destroyed at the direction of the National Socialists."

Maximilianstrasse 14

This five-story building was the office of Gustav von Kahr, the Bavarian commissioner in 1923. Kahr had dictatorial powers on account of the state of emergency. Hitler supporters and government loyalists confronted each other here during the Beer Hall Putsch.

Platzl 9. Hofbräuhaus

This well-known beer hall was the site of the Nazi Party's first mass meeting, October 16, 1919. The party, still called the German Workers' Party, attracted 70 people to the gathering. Hitler spoke and began to establish his reputation as an orator.

On February 24, 1920, Hitler addressed another meeting at the Hofbräuhaus. He outlined the party's 25-point program, including a demand to treat all Jews as aliens. There were many hoots and raspberries as he spoke, but at the conclusion the crowd of 2,000 gave him a roaring ovation.

On August 13, 1920, Hitler publicly denounced the Jews. He demanded "the removal of Jews from the midst of our people."

One of Hitler's speeches at the Hofbräuhaus roused his listeners to a frenzy. A ferocious altercation then broke out between supporters and opponents, who began smashing furniture and heaving beer steins. Somehow Hitler managed to finish his talk.

Today the Hofbräuhaus is still a beloved beer garden, but it has no memorials to its most famous orator.

Deming, Brian, and Ted Iliff. *Hitler and Munich: A Historical Guide to the Sights and Addresses of Munich Important to Adolf Hitler, His Followers, and His Victims.* Verlag A. Plenk KG. Berchtesgaden, Germany ca. 1986.

MUNICH: BRIENNER STRASSE CORRIDOR

Haus der Deutschen Kunst (Art Museum)

Located on the north side of Prinzregentenstrasse, at the south end of the Englischer Garten, this was Hitler's first major Munich building project. In 1933, with great pomp, Hitler laid the cornerstone for this ugly building, designed by his favorite architect, Paul Ludwig Troost. The Führer solemnly declared Munich the "capital city of German art" and whacked the cornerstone with a ceremonial hammer. The hammer broke. Troost died of pneumonia a few months later.

The Haus der Deutschen Kunst opened on July 18, 1937. Because of the rows of pillars along the facade, Munich wags called it the "Athens Train Station" and the "Munich Art Terminal." The exhibits included no abstract art, which Hitler hated. Most contemporary artists, the Führer opined, painted "malformed cripples and cretins, women who inspire only disgust, men who are more like wild beasts, children who, were they alive, must be regarded as cursed by God." After 1945 an American officers'

club displaced the paintings. In 1955 the club moved out, and the paintings moved back in.

Northeast Corner Ludwigstrasse and Schönfeld Strasse

This three-story renaissance building is now the home of the Bavarian State Archives. It housed the Bavarian War Ministry in 1923 and was captured by Ernst Röhm during the Beer Hall Putsch, November 1923. Otto von Lossow, the Bavarian military boss, had his headquarters here.

Ludwigstrasse at Galeriestrasse

This four-story building has a walkway arcade facing the Hofgarten. The Cafe Heck, a Hitler favorite, was here. It was the old party cafe, where Hitler met his comrades after his release from Landsberg Prison in 1924. According to Albert Speer, the place was furnished with plain wooden chairs and iron tables. When the weather was pleasant, Hitler would eat at the tables set out in the Hofgarten. He continued to patronize the Cafe Heck after he came to power. Sometimes late at night, Speer received a call from

Haus der Deutschen Kunst, Hitler's first major building project in Munich.

an aide at Hitler's apartment, "The Führer is driving over to the Cafe Heck and has asked that you come too." Speer had to drag himself out of bed, with no prospect of getting back to sleep before 2 or 3 A.M. Hitler had a stock apology for the nocturnal summons: "I formed the habit of staying up late during our days of struggle. After rallies I would have to sit down with the old fighters, and besides my speeches usually stirred me up so much I would not have been able to sleep before early morning."

Odeonsplatz. Feldherrnhalle, an Important Landmark of the Nazi Era

Friedrich von Gärtner had built this open, colonnaded arcade (1841–44, 66 ft. high), modeled on the Loggia dei Lanzi in Florence. Among the statues of Bavarian Feldherrn (supreme commanders) is Gen-

eral Johan von Tilly (1559–1632), who fought in the Thirty Years War. A Bavarian Army Memorial commemorates the Franco-Prussian War (1870–71). In 1905 W. Ruemann designed the two lions on the steps.

During the Beer Hall Putsch, November 9, 1923, police fired on the putschists here and brought the putsch to its bloody finale. After Hitler came to power, he placed a bronze plaque on the east side of the Feldherrnhalle, in memory of the men who died in the putsch. On Hitler's orders, people passing the plaque had to give the Nazi salute. Many citizens found this requirement onerous, and would bypass the plaque by using Viscardigasse, behind the Feldherrnhalle. Viscardigasse became known as "Shirker's alley."

"We are determined to make this a holy day for the German nation for the future and all time," Hitler said of the putsch anniversary. Every November 9, the Nazis staged a parade along the streets the putschists followed. The whole route was

Feldherrnhalle. Nazi troops gather to honor fallen comrades.

lined with smoking funeral urns. Hitler and his cronies marched to the boom of muffled drums. Concealed loudspeakers blared out the names of the dead along with inspirational music.

Brienner Strasse 8

The Carlton Tea Room was a Hitler favorite after 1933. Albert Speer described it as a bogus luxurious place with reproduction furniture and fake crystal chandeliers. Hitler liked it because other patrons left him undisturbed and did not bother him with applause or requests for autographs, as was the case elsewhere in Munich. There is now a five-story building on the site.

Brienner Strasse at Maximilianplatz

This park is a memorial to the Nazis' victims. The Gestapo office was across the street.

Brienner Strasse at Türkenstrasse

Site of Munich Gestapo headquarters in the former Wittelsbach Palace. An office building is now on

Top: Hitler speaks at the Feldherrnhalle on the anniversary of the Putsch, mid–1930s. *Bottom:* Nazi plaque on east side of Feldherrnhalle, commemorating men who died in the Beer Hall Putsch.

the site. The White Rose conspirators, including Hans and Sophie Scholl, were questioned and incarcerated here. There is a memorial plaque on the southwest corner, on which is inscribed the following:

Here stood the Wittelsbacher Palais built in 1848 by Friedrich von Gärtner.
1848–1868: Seat of Ludwig I.
1887–1919: Residence of Ludwig III.
1919: Meeting place of the Action Committee of the People's Republic.
In the Nazi period it was the headquarters of the Gestapo. Destroyed by bombs, 1944.

A stone lion, a replica of one of the lions from the front of the Wittelsbach Palace, is on the north side of the block facing Gabelsbergerstrasse.

Türkenstrasse 17

In 1923 the police barracks was here, replaced today by a parking lot. The red brick entrance to the barracks remains, inscribed "The Glorious Royal Bavarian Infantry, Bodyguard Regiment, 1814–1919." At the time of the Beer Hall Putsch, Hans Ritter von Seisser, chief of the Bavarian police, had his office in the building. Seisser was one of three men in control of the Bavarian government.

Brienner Strasse 45, Between Arcisstrasse and Karolinenplatz

The Brown House, the office of the Nazi Party, stood on this grass-covered plot of land. The building was flattened in World War II and never rebuilt.

The three-story structure dated from 1828 and was originally called the Barlow Palace. In 1930 the Nazi Party bought the building with money from German industrialists. Between 1933 and 1935 a tunnel

Top: The Brown House, home of the Nazi party after 1930. *Bottom:* Hitler consoles the widow of a putsch victim, November 9, 1935. The Brown House is in the background.

was built connecting the Brown House with the nearby Führerbau.

Hitler's office was on the second floor. The office had tall windows looking out on the Königsplatz, red-brown walls, a bust of Mussolini, a painting of Frederick the Great, and a First World War battle picture.

Hitler was not in the Brown House very often. He liked to sleep late in the morning and might or might not appear around noon. Persons who wanted to see him sometimes waited for many hours. His intimates knew they had a better chance of meeting up with him after 4 P.M. at the Cafe Heck.

Rath, Florian. Eine Zeitzeuge erinnert sich an das Leben mit den Bunkern. Immer wenn der Kuckuck schrie. *Süddeutsche Zeitung*, April 23, 1999.

Weyerer, Benedikt. Wie die Nazis ihren Aufstieg finanzierten. Eine Hand wäscht die andere. In der Müchner Zentrale flossen erhebliche Summen aus Industriekänalen zusammen. *Süddeutsche Zeitung*, December 4, 1998.

Arcisstrasse 12. Führerbau. Meiserstrasse 10. Nazi Administration Building

Paul Ludwig Troost designed the Führerbau, one of a pair of identical buildings. The second building, across Briennerstrasse at Meiserstrasse 10, was a Nazi administration building and now houses the Bavarian State Graphics Collection. Tunnels connect the two buildings.

In the notorious 1938 Führerbau meeting at Arcisstrasse 12, British prime minister Neville Chamberlain's acceptance of Hitler's territorial demands has provided a chestnut of today's political rhetoric.[16]

Everybody knows that Chamberlain was the man at the airport with the umbrella, waving his scrap of paper with Hitler's signature and telling the world

Top: Führerbau, Munich, where Hitler signed 1938 agreement with British prime minister Neville Chamberlain. *Bottom:* Führerbau, central hall, 65 feet high and 100 feet wide. At each end of the building are two grand staircases.

that there would be "peace in our time." Ever since, "Munich" has signified appeasement, a lack of gumption in foreign affairs.

The story is familiar enough. Hitler wanted the rich military and industrial resources of the Sudetenland, a German-speaking area of Czechoslovakia abutting the

Führerbau balcony.

edge of railings lining the cliffs," wrote Harold Nicolson in his diary. Frantic to avoid spilling British blood "in a faraway country" because of "people of whom we know nothing," Chamberlain flew to Munich to placate Hitler.

Unfamiliar to most people is the fact that Hitler was taking the biggest gamble of his life. If he had lost, his opponents would have arrested and shot him. Winston Churchill tells the story in *The Gathering Storm*.

In 1938 the Czechs had one of the strongest fortifications in Europe, an almost impregnable mountain fortress line facing Germany's eastern frontier. Defending this line were 1.5 million Czech soldiers, equipped by a highly organized, powerful industrial machine. The huge French Army on Germany's western border was partly mobilized, and, though reluctantly, the French ministers were ready to honor their treaty to defend Czechoslovakia.

reich. On September 27, 1938, he sent Wehrmacht troops to the Czech frontier and gave the Prague government an ultimatum: cede the Sudetenland to Germany or be invaded. Statesmen believed a general European war would invariably result. France was bound by treaty to defend Czech sovereignty, and Britain would have to follow France. The Soviet Union also had an agreement to defend Czechoslovakia if France stepped in first. In London workers dug trenches in the parks, while children tried on gas masks. "We feel we are on the very

Behind the brash front that Hitler presented to the British and French governments was a German officer corps profoundly alarmed by their Führer's schemes. Ludwig Beck, chief of the Wehrmacht General Staff, was convinced that Hitler had finally gone too far, and Beck intended to resist.

Like Hitler, Beck and his Wehrmacht colleagues were convinced that "Germany needed more room for living" and also recognized that this "could only be obtained through war." But Beck believed that Germany was not sufficiently prepared for a war, certainly not on two fronts. German military strategists since Carl von Clausewitz in the early nineteenth century had dreaded being crushed in a two-front war.

After Hitler invaded Austria in March, and with an attack on Czechoslovakia looming, Beck sent the Führer a memo. The memo argued with detailed facts that Hitler's actions would lead to catastrophe and destruction of the reich. Beck wanted a promise that there would be no more reckless military adventures. Hitler did not respond to Beck's memo, and in July there was a personal confrontation between the two men.

Hitler, the most incorrigible military adventurer since Napoleon, was not about to forswear use of the army. The army was an instrument of the state, said the Führer, and he was head of the state; therefore, the army must obey him.

Beck immediately resigned, though his formal request to be relieved of his command went unanswered.[17] To replace Beck, Hitler chose General Franz Halder, but the army's opposition to military adventures was far from over. The Wehrmacht high command respected and trusted Beck. They disdained the military talents of the World War I corporal Hitler and feared the hostile forces arrayed against them. Between 30 and 40 combat-ready Czech divisions stood poised on Germany's eastern frontier, while the French Army, with odds of eight to one, pressed against the reich's western border. Facing France were 13 German divisions, only 5 of which were composed of first-line troops.

Beck asked the cautious, conspiratorial foreign office state secretary, Ernst von Weizsäcker, to make inquiries in London. An emissary relayed Beck's message: "Bring me solid proof that England will fight if Czechoslovakia is attacked, and I will finish off this regime."

The British disdained the inquiry.

They had not yet learned the difference between Beck, a Prussian general, and Hitler, the Bavarian corporal. As one of the leaders of the German resistance movement, Carl Goerdeler, commented, "Chamberlain rescued Hitler."

Beck did not give up. As Halder testified after the war: "By the beginning of September, we had taken the necessary steps to immunize Germany from this madman. At this time, the prospect of war filled the great majority of the German people with horror."

Involved in the plot to overthrow Hitler were generals Beck, Halder, Karl von Stülpnagel, Erwin von Witzleben (commander of the Berlin garrison), General Georg Thomas (controller of armaments), General Graf Brockdorff-Ahlefeldt (commander of the Potsdam garrison), and Wolf Heinrich Graf von Helldorf, in charge of the Berlin police. The plotters, called the *Wehrkreis* (defense circle), informed the commander in chief, General Walther von Brauchitsch, who approved.

The logistics of the plot were simple. As a part of troop movements against Czechoslovakia and regular military routine, the plan was to hold a single armored division near Berlin so that it could reach the city in one night's march. General Erich Hoepner commanded the chosen division, the third armored division, stationed south of Berlin. His secret mission was to occupy Berlin, Hitler's chancellery, and the important Nazi ministries on a given signal. For this purpose the plotters added Hoepner's division to General Witzleben's command.

Graf von Helldorf made detailed arrangements to arrest Hitler, Hermann Göring, Joseph Goebbels, and Heinrich Himmler. "There was no possibility of a hitch," Halder testified. "All that was required for a completely successful coup was Hitler's presence in Berlin."

Hitler arrived in the capital from Berchtesgaden on the morning of September 14. In the afternoon Halder learned of the Führer's arrival and went to consult Witzleben. The plotters decided to strike at eight that evening.

But at 4 P.M., according to Halder, Witzleben received a message that Chamberlain was flying to Berchtesgaden to see Hitler. "If Hitler had succeeded in his bluff," Halder told Witzleben, Halder "would not be justified, as chief of staff, in calling it." The coup was postponed.

The Berchtesgaden meeting produced no conclusive results. Undaunted, Chamberlain returned to Germany on September 22. He met with Hitler at Bad Godesberg, near Cologne, and presented to the dictator a British-French proposal: The parts of the Sudetenland with 50 percent or more German population should be ceded to Germany. The Czech government accepted this plan only after being warned that, if they did not, they could not count on Britain and France to come to their aid.

Hitler rejected the proposal. He said he could not trust promises of the Czech government, and German troops would occupy the Sudetenland by October 1. He demanded that the Czech government accept his terms by September 28.

The German general staff was profoundly alarmed. Their own invasion plan, *Fall Grün* (case green), indicated that the Czech army, even if fighting without allies, could hold out for three months. Germany would need to maintain covering forces on the Polish and French borders, as well as on the Baltic and North Sea coasts. A quarter million more soldiers would be required in Austria to prevent popular uprisings and a possible Czech offensive. Worst of all, the German generals believed, within three months Czechoslovakia's allies would enter the war, spelling *finis Germaniae*.

On September 27 Admiral Erich Raeder, chief of the German Admiralty, met with Hitler at 10 P.M. Dreading the worst,

Hitler and Admiral Erich Raeder review the fleet. In September 1938 Raeder begged Hitler not to invade Czechoslovakia.

Raeder appealed vehemently to Hitler to back down. Raeder's fears were confirmed a few hours later by news that the British fleet was mobilizing.

Churchill, with his visceral loathing of Hitler, nevertheless expresses a sneaking admiration for the Führer's steely resolve: "The strain upon this one man and upon his astounding will power must at this moment have been most severe. Evidently he had brought himself to the brink of a general war. Could he take the plunge in the face of an unfavorable public opinion and the solemn warnings of the Chiefs of his Army, Navy, and Air Force?"

In his diary Joseph Goebbels recorded the stress on Hitler. The Führer was "very nervous and irritable," Goebbels wrote, a result of the "burden on his nerves." But the generals were even more distraught, Goebbels sneered, and "again naturally their pants are full."

Finally Hitler blinked. At 2 A.M. German radio broadcast an official denial that Germany would mobilize, and at 11:45 A.M. the official German news agency gave a statement to the British press denying mobilization.

On September 28 Hitler agreed to a third meeting, this time with Chamberlain, Italian duce Benito Mussolini, and French prime minister Edouard Daladier in Munich on September 29. Cheering crowds greeted the four men as they arrived in a city decked with flags and banners.

Thousands of Munich's citizens gathered at the Königsplatz at noon to watch the statesmen enter the Führerbau, which had just been finished. The severe yellow stone structure lacked any ornamentation, except for a bronze eagle on the facade. The central hall was 65 feet high and 100 feet wide. At each end of the building were two grand staircases. The conference room, where the diplomats were to meet, had leather-covered walls and an imposing marble fireplace crowned by a portrait of Otto von Bismarck.

One observer described the meeting (*Der Spiegel*, 1988): "There was no methodical program. The unguided discussion was laborious and confused, and seeing that it was hampered by the need for a double translation, it took a great deal of time. It continually changed its aim. It stopped every time a contradiction appeared. The atmosphere grew thick and heavy."

Mussolini became de facto chairman because he was the only delegate fluent in English, French, and German. Czech was not needed. The two representatives from Czechoslovakia were forced to wait in an adjacent room.

"Actually the whole thing was a cut-and-dried affair," said Hermann Göring, who also attended. "Neither Chamberlain nor Daladier was the least bit interested in sacrificing or risking anything to save Czechoslovakia…. We got everything we wanted, just like that." Hitler received permission for a five-stage German occupation of the Sudetenland beginning October 1 and ending October 10.

On September 30, 1938, just before leaving Munich, Chamberlain went to Prinzregentenplatz 16, Hitler's apartment. He handed Hitler a document containing the solemn promise that Germany and Britain would never go to war with each other. Hitler signed. Chamberlain waved this worthless piece of paper triumphantly on the tarmac in London, just after stepping off his plane.

The rest of Czechoslovakia quickly fell to pieces as other parts sought independence. On March 15, 1939, threatened with invasion, Emil Hacha, the new Czech president, "asked" Germany to intervene. The German Army rolled into Prague, and Czechoslovakia ceased to exist.

The loss of Czechoslovakia was an unmitigated disaster. Britain and France were immediately deprived of 21 regular Czech army divisions, 16 second-line divisions already mobilized, and the Czech mountain fortress line. This fortified barrier alone had tied down 30 German divisions, the main strength of the mobile, fully trained German Army. As Albert Speer noted:

The Czech border fortifications caused general astonishment. To the surprise of experts a test bombardment showed that our weapons would not have prevailed against them. Hitler himself went to the former frontier to inspect the arrangements and returned impressed. The fortifications were amazingly massive, he said, laid out with extraordinary skill and echeloned, making prime use of the terrain. "Given a resolute defense, taking them would have been very difficult and would have cost us a great many

Top: Führerbau, third-floor conference room, September 29, 1938. From left to right (front row only), British prime minister Neville Chamberlain, French premier Edouard Daladier, Hitler, Mussolini, Italian foreign minister Count Ciano. A portrait of Bismarck is partly visible over the fireplace (Archiv Preussischer Kulturbesitz). *Bottom left:* Führerbau, third-floor conference room today. The leather-covered walls and imposing marble fireplace remain. The portrait of Bismarck over the fireplace has been removed. *Bottom right:* Führerbau, armoire with busts of soldiers, women, and Hitler.

lives. Now we have obtained them without loss of blood."

Germany also gained control of the Skoda Works, the second largest armaments maker in Central Europe (Krupp in Essen was the largest). In 1938 Skoda's production was the equivalent of the entire British arms industry.

The situation of the Western Allies vis-à-vis Hitler had taken a disastrous turn. The annexation of Austria in March had brought 6,750,000 Austrians into the reich, the Munich agreement another 3,500,000 Sudetens, over 10,000,000 workers and soldiers. Germans now acknowledged their Führer as an authentic genius.

Yet in 1945, contemplating suicide in his Berlin bunker, 12 meters underground, Hitler lamented his "lost opportunity" and railed against the dead Chamberlain: "The fellow spoiled my entrance into Prague."

"The war should have been started in 1938," Hitler added. Then it would have been won "easily and quickly." But the Western Allies "accepted everything. Like weaklings, they gave in to all my demands."

The Führerbau survived the war unscathed. In June 1945 the U.S. Army made the building the central collecting point for art the Nazis had stolen. By December 1945, 18,376 artworks had arrived. Four American army officers directed a staff of 107 German civilian employees, who photographed, stored, and catalogued the art with the intent of restoring the works to their rightful owners. In 1949 the army transferred the central collecting point to the German *Treuhandverwaltung für Kulturgut*.

The Führerbau is today a music conservatory. A thick cluster of trees screens the two entrance porticos from the Königsplatz, the royal square where Hitler had ostentatiously placed his headquarters. The plush carpets have been removed from the two grand staircases.

Room 105, the former conference room, contains a grand piano and folding chairs, used for recitals and concerts. Nothing about the Führerbau indicates that it was the site of a world-historical event.

Under the building is a six-to-nine-meter-deep labyrinth of passageways, air raid bunkers, and storerooms for large quantities of food, which would have enabled the occupants to hold out for months. Wine cellars and a special chamber for poultry and game held delicacies that ordinary Germans could only dream about.[18]

Hitler's bathtub, covered with dirt, is in one basement room. Shortly before Germany capitulated in 1945, the tub was removed from Hitler's apartment in Prinzregentenplatz and brought to the Führerbau.

Eleven million file cards with names of Nazi Party members were kept in green steel cabinets in the cellar of Meiserstrasse 10. In 1945 Hitler wanted the cards destroyed. They were sent to a paper mill near Munich, but before they could be mulched, the American army found them and moved them to the Berlin Document Center. The green steel cabinets today hold art reference material.

Special tours of the cellars and passageways can be arranged through the Central Institute for Art History, Meiserstrasse 10, telephone 28 92 75 62 or 28 92 75 84.

Badewanne mit schmutziger Geschichte. *Berliner Morgenpost*. October 29, 1998.

Churchill, Winston. *The Gathering Storm. The Second World War.* Vol 1. Houghton Mifflin. Boston 1948.

Deming, Brian, and Ted Iliff. *Hitler and Munich: A Historical Guide to the Sights and Addresses of Munich Important to Adolf Hitler, His Followers, and His Victims.* Verlag A. Plenk KG. Berchtesgaden, Germany ca. 1986.

"Der Griff nach dem letzten Grasbüschel." München 1938: Hitlers Triumph über die Westmächte — Der Schacher um die Tschechoslowakei. *Der Spiegel*. 39:51–60, 1988.

Höfl-Hielscher, Elisabeth. 1945 — Münchner auf Beutezug. Bei der Plünderung des "Führerbaus" kam es zum grössten Gemälderaub der Geschichte. *Süddeutsche Zeitung*. May 5, 2000.

McGrath, Peter. The lessons of Munich. *Newsweek.* October 3, 1988, p. 37.

Rath, Florian. Eine Zeitzeuge erinnert sich an das Leben mit den Bunkern. Immer wenn der Kuckuck schrie. *Süddeutsche Zeitung.* April 23, 1999.

Schmemann, Serge. A Munich Refrain: Peals of Music in Hitler's Hall. *New York Times.* September 30, 1988.

Speer, Albert. *Inside the Third Reich.* Translated by Richard and Clara Winston. Avon Books. New York 1971.

Zsolnay, Robert. Im Reich der Schreibtischtäter. *Süddeutsche Zeitung.* November 26, 1999.

Königsplatz

Square, originally grass, which Hitler had paved with granite stones for parades. Grass now grows between the stones. Some people want to have the stones pulled up; others think they create the appearance of a piazza.

Top: Königsplatz, just after Hitler had it paved over. *Bottom:* Königsplatz with Nazi storm troops, November 9, 1935. The Führerbau is at left, the Temple of Honor, with sarcophagi of men killed in Beer Hall Putsch, center.

Schleissheimerstrasse 34

Hitler's first room in Munich, on the third floor above a tailor's shop. Hitler arrived in Munich on May 25, 1913, and found this room in an ad, placed by Joseph Popp, a tailor. The building was in a seedy district in the north of the city. Hitler's companion, Rudolf Häusler, who had arrived with him from Vienna, shared the tiny room until mid–February 1914. Hitler kept Häusler from sleeping by reading late at night by the light of an oil lamp. The irate Häusler rented an adjacent room until May 1914.

Hitler produced and sold the same architectural watercolors he had painted in Vienna and made a modest living. His landlady, Frau Popp, did not remember a single visitor to his room during the two years he lived on Schleissheimerstrasse.

But the Austrian police looked for him because he had not registered for military service. Having left Austria, he would be subject to a prison sentence if apprehended. On Sunday, January 18, 1914, an officer of the Munich criminal police turned up in Schleissheimerstrasse and gave Hitler a summons to appear two days later in Linz to register. Hitler appealed to the Austrian consulate and followed up with a three-and-a-half-page letter describing his down-and-out state in Vienna and pleading for consideration. Touched, authorities in Linz allowed him to appear in Salzburg and even paid his fare. Doctors judged him too weak to be a soldier and rejected him.[19]

On August 2, 1914, Germany declared

Top: Schleissheimerstrasse 34, Hitler's first room in Munich, 1913. The facade has been renovated since Hitler's time. *Bottom:* Hitler watercolor painted 1914, "Courtyard, old Residenz, Munich." The First World War, which began in August 1914, and the Versailles Treaty, which the victorious Allies imposed on Germany in 1919, made Hitler's rise to power possible. Had there been no war, Hitler probably would have spent his life as an obscure Munich painter of architectural scenes.

war on Russia. Hordes of rapturous citizens, Hitler among them, poured into Munich's Odeonsplatz. They cheered wildly and sang "Die Wacht am Rhein" and "Deutschland über Alles."[20]

A day after the mass gathering in the Odeonsplatz, August 3, 1914, Hitler wrote to Bavarian king Ludwig III, asking to be allowed to serve as an Austrian in the Bavarian Army. According to the law, he should have been returned to Austria for military service. But the deluge of volunteers caused general confusion, which prevailed as Hitler volunteered on August 5 for the First Bavarian Infantry.

He was sent home that day but on August 16 was called to report for duty. The experience left him ecstatic: "To me those hours seemed like a release from the painful feelings of my youth. Even today I am not ashamed to say that, overpowered by stormy enthusiasm, I fell down on my knees and thanked heaven from an overflowing heart" (Kershaw 1998).

Kershaw, Ian. *Hitler. 1889–1936: Hubris.* Norton. New York 1998.
Leser-Frage: Wie wurde Hitler deutscher Bürger. *Berliner Morgenpost.* October 8, 1998.

Löwenbräukeller

On September 14, 1921, the Bavarian League, an organization that supported the German government, was meeting in the Löwenbräukeller. Hitler ordered his storm troopers (Sturm Abteilung, SA), an unruly group of brown-shirted thugs, to break up the meeting. They invaded the hall and pummeled the principal speaker, a Hitler enemy named Otto Ballerstedt. The police interrogated Hitler, who expressed no remorse. "It's all right," he told them. "We got what we wanted. Ballerstedt did not speak." Hitler addressed the beer enthusiasts at the Löwenbräukeller on several occasions after he came to power, especially after Georg Elser tried to assassinate him in the Bürgerbräukeller in 1939.

Löwenbräukeller, Munich beer hall, site of early Hitler speeches and Beer Hall Putsch center.

Deming, Brian, and Ted Iliff. *Hitler and Munich: A Historical Guide to the Sights and Addresses of Munich Important to Adolf Hitler, His Followers, and His Victims.* Verlag A. Plenk KG. Berchtesgaden, Germany ca. 1986.

Blutenbergstrasse 3

The Beer Hall Putsch trial was held here. A postwar schoolhouse has replaced the infantry school building used for the trial.

Blutenbergstrasse 18

In this small two-story building with a balcony Hitler was jailed to await the Beer Hall Putsch trial.

Schellingstrasse 62

Osteria Bavaria, a favorite cafe of Hitler's. Albert Speer, then Hitler's architect, describes a lunch at this restaurant in the early 1930s:

At the usual time, around half past two, I went to the Osteria Bavaria, a small artists' restaurant that rose to unexpected fame when it became Hitler's regular restaurant. In a place like this, one could more easily imagine a table of artists gathered around Lenbach or Stuck, with long hair and huge beards, than Hitler with his neatly dressed or uniformed retinue.[21] But he felt at ease in the Osteria; as a "frustrated artist" he obviously liked the atmosphere he had once sought to attain to, and now had finally both lost and surpassed....

A five-story building on the northeast corner of Schellingstrasse and Schraudolphstrasse has replaced the cafe.

Speer, Albert. *Inside the Third Reich.* Translated by Richard and Clara Winston. Avon Books. New York 1971.
Waite, Robert G. L. *The Psychopathic God: Adolf Hitler.* Basic Books. New York 1977.

Schellingstrasse 56

Schelling Salon, where Hitler often had lunch. This eatery was close to three important locations: the *Völkischer Beobachter* offices, the Nazi Party offices, and Heinrich Hoffmann's photo studio. But one day the restaurant owner cut off Hitler's credit, and thereafter Hitler found more congenial places to dine.

Schellingstrasse 50

This apartment and office building was the location of the Fourth Nazi Party offices (1925–1931), which were in the back of the building. Heinrich Hoffmann, Hitler's personal photographer, had his studio in the front. Hitler met seventeen-year-old Eva Braun here in 1929, when she worked as Hoffmann's assistant. Hoffmann had hired Eva because he thought Hitler would like her. Hoffmann introduced Hitler to Eva as "Herr Wolf," a nickname of which Hitler was fond. Eva always maintained that she did not know Herr Wolf was the famous politico.

There is a sculpture of an eagle in relief over the front entrance of Schellingstrasse 50. The bird's head has been chiseled away.

Schellingstrasse 39

Former *Völkischer Beobachter* offices. The *Völkischer Beobachter* (Volkisch Observer) was the main publication of the Nazi Party. The party acquired it at the end of 1920, and as of 1923 the Eher Press published it daily. In 1921 it bore the subhead "Militant Paper of the Great German National Socialist Movement." It was a political paper for the masses, with oversize format, black and red type, and illustrations. During the 1920s the *Völkischer Beobachter* was, next to party meetings, the most important propaganda medium for disseminating Nazi ideology. Within the party it was regarded as the "connecting link between the Führer and his followers."

The Eher Press director as of 1922 was Max Amann, and the *Völkischer Beobachter's* editor in chief as of July–August 1921 was Dietrich Eckart, until Alfred Rosenberg replaced him in March 1923.

On November 8, 1923, the *Völkischer Beobachter* offices on Schellingstrasse became the command center for the Beer Hall Putsch. The *Völkischer Beobachter* was banned afterward but was reborn in February 1925. Hitler himself was publisher of the paper until April 30, 1933. Its circulation in 1925 was 4,000 copies and increased to 126,000 in 1932. Beginning in February 1927 a Reich edition was printed along with the Bavarian one, and as of March 1930 there was a separate Berlin edition, which lasted a year. In 1933 the *Völkischer Beobachter* established its own editorial office and press in Berlin. After Hitler became chancellor, January 30, 1933, the *Völkischer Beobachter* became a quasi-governmental publication, and its articles had an official character.

The quantity and quality of toilet paper declined drastically after 1941. But Germans discovered that the *Völkischer Beobachter*, printed on soft thin stock, made an acceptable substitute.

The original Schellingstrasse 39 building survives to this day, although it has been given a more modern facade.

Read, Anthony, and David Fisher. *The Fall of Berlin*. Norton. New York 1992.
Zentner, Christian, and Friedemann Bedürftig, eds. *The Encyclopedia of the Third Reich*. English translation edited by Amy Hackett. Macmillan. New York 1991.

Geschwister-Scholl-Platz

Located on the west side of Ludwigstrasse, directly south of Adalbertstrasse, this plaza is named in honor of White Rose conspirators Hans and Sophie Scholl. A matching plaza on the opposite side of Ludwigstrasse is named in honor of Professor Kurt Huber, another participant in the conspiracy. The Scholls were taken into custody in the adjacent university building. There is a bronze relief in the university's main hall memorializing the seven White Rose conspirators who went to the guillotine in Stadelheim prison.

Leopoldstrasse 38

Site where White Rose pamphlets were printed.

Franz-Josef-Strasse 13

White Rose conspirators Hans and Sophie Scholl lived in a house in the courtyard.

Elisabethplatz 4

Hitler took military training here in 1914. When he was called for duty on August 16, he was ordered to report to Recruiting Depot VI in Munich and assigned to the Second Reserve Battalion of the Second Infantry Regiment. In September the army sent him to the Bavarian Reserve Infantry Regiment 16, called the "List Regiment" after its first commander and composed of green recruits. Hitler and his comrades received their basic training in this large public school on Elisabethplatz. The five-story building, erected in 1901 on the corner of Elisabethstrasse, west side of Elisabethplatz, is now a trade school.

The List Regiment received more training at Lechfield, near Augsberg, and, along with Hitler, was sent by train to the battlefields of Flanders on October 21, 1914.

Gentzstrasse 1

Site of Ernst Hanfstaengl's apartment. Hanfstaengl was one of Hitler's most interesting early supporters.

Ernst Franz Sedgwick Hanfstaengl, nicknamed Putzi, was 36 and a Bavarian original when he met Hitler in 1923. Almost six and a half feet tall, with a face like a water sprite and a puckish mien, Putzi was the son of a Munich art dealer father and an American mother. In 1905 Putzi went off to Harvard, met Theodore Roosevelt in Washington, managed a branch of his father's art gallery in New York, started an art school in Greenwich Village, and returned to study history in Munich.

Hitler cultivated Putzi for his worldliness, his access to Munich society, and especially for his piano playing. Putzi was always ready to sit down at the Bechstein grand and bang out Hitler's favorite tunes.[22] Richard Wagner had written most of them: the Rienzi overture, the prelude to the *Meistersinger*, and the finale to *Tristan und Isolde*. "Isolde's Liebestod" was de rigueur during crises in Hitler's life: his 1924 release from imprisonment in Landsberg and the 1931 death of his niece and mistress Geli Raubal. Putzi did not mind whether Hitler sat dreamily listening or marched back and forth whistling and conducting. During election campaigns, Putzi said, he felt like the trainer of a boxer who used music to revive Hitler between rounds.

In November 1923, just after the failed Beer Hall Putsch to take over the Bavarian government, Hitler fled to Putzi's house in Uffing and was arrested there. According to Putzi, Hitler would have put a bullet through his head if Putzi's wife, an American, had not disarmed the future Führer with a jiu-jitsu grip; some historians poohpooh this story.

Hitler biographers have not ignored Putzi, who died at the age of 88 in 1975.

Alan Bullock, Joachim Fest, John Toland, and Ian Kershaw have described Putzi and his front-row seat during Hitler's early rise to power. But recently discovered records show Putzi as a disillusioned, isolated Nazi apostate in the United States during the last years of World War II. In fact, at least one Hollywood director hopes to film Putzi's memoirs, *Between the White House and the Brown House* (1970).

After Hitler came to power in 1933, Putzi's relations with the Nazis quickly deteriorated. Putzi had observed considerable corruption and averred that Hitler was listening to despicable criminals and perverts. "At the rate we're going," Putzi told his son Egon, "we'll have a war-a war in which England and America will be against us. It's dangerous for Germany and for the world."

Putzi's own enemies had tried to frame him for embezzlement. "Well, they failed and I cleared myself completely," he told Egon. "But they are not through. I expect to be fighting for life itself before long. They're certain to get around to liquidating me sooner or later."

The liquidation attempt came in 1936 during the Spanish Civil War. Putzi, the German foreign press chief, was ordered to fly immediately to Spain, supposedly to protect the interests of German correspondents there. In the air the pilot told Putzi he was to parachute over the Red lines between Barcelona and Madrid. Putzi screamed that parachuting was a death sentence. The sympathetic pilot explained that Hermann Göring had given him signed orders just before takeoff.

Suddenly, one of the engines began to fail, and the pilot called back that there was something wrong. With a meaningful look the pilot told Putzi he would be forced to make an emergency landing at a small airfield. Once on the ground, Putzi pretended to call Berlin for instructions and informed the pilot that the Führer had ordered his foreign press chief to return to

Germany. Putzi took the night train to Munich and the next morning took another train to Zurich. Soon he debarked for England.

When war broke out in 1939, the British interned Putzi as an enemy alien. Immediately, Putzi recalled his old connections in America, above all the members of New York's Harvard Club, to which, as a Harvard graduate, he had entrée. There, before World War I, as a young art dealer and branch manager of the family gallery, Putzi had practiced the piano. Nearby, a young Democratic member of the Roosevelt political clan often breakfasted and listened appreciatively. In 1939 the appreciative listener, Franklin D. Roosevelt, was president of the United States.

The interned Putzi wrote a letter to Roosevelt, and soon, through the intervention of J. Edgar Hoover and the FBI, Putzi found himself in the United States. He was installed in a villa in a Washington suburb, and Roosevelt mentioned him favorably to friends. To guard Putzi, the U.S. Army Air Corps sent one of their soldiers, Putzi's son, Sergeant Egon Hanfstaengl, who had fled Germany at the same time as his father. Government officials also sent a Steinway concert grand piano.

Though he downplayed the fact in his memoirs, Putzi occupied himself working for Roosevelt's secret service. He contributed to a psychological profile of Hitler and interpreted Joseph Goebbels's radio propaganda. He correctly perceived the massacre of Polish officers at Katyn as Josef Stalin's crime and inveighed, in vain, against Roosevelt's demand for Germany's unconditional surrender. Putzi argued that this demand could only demoralize German officers, who had hoped to topple Hitler after the disastrous Wehrmacht defeat at Stalingrad.

The German historian Christof Mauch has presented insights into the motivations of the totally isolated Putzi. According to Mauch, Putzi saw the war in Europe as a "world-wide civil war," which, if not contained, could end with "Stalin in Strasbourg." The dissatisfied Wehrmacht officers "needed a signal that they would not be cast into the same kettle as the Nazi thugs."

Putzi's ideas terrified the English. Any contact between anti–Hitler German officers and the Western Allies would be a nightmare for Stalin and would endanger the allied alliance with the Soviet Union. Even more vexing was Putzi's knowledge of just who these officers were, the correctness of which was borne out by their July 20, 1944, attempt to assassinate Hitler.

Putzi's last plan to halt the Russian advance on Berlin was adventurous. In early 1944 he proposed that, before the invasion of France, the Allies should put on the radio a Hitler imitator, who would order all German troops in the West to cease resistance. Roosevelt communicated Putzi's scheme to the OSS, the secret service precursor of the CIA. By now the Normandy landings were already in progress, and the vice director of the OSS, Edward Buxton, explained that "the best time for the radio operation has passed."

Shortly afterward, Roosevelt had to distance himself from Putzi. In late summer 1944, according to Mauch, there was an acute danger that British officials would make public in the United States the names of prominent Nazis who had been interned, Putzi among them. Since the presidential election was only a few weeks off, such a revelation could turn into a political debacle for Roosevelt.

In September 1944 Putzi was flown to England, where he spent a prolonged internment. He was not "de–Nazified" until 1949, in the Bavarian town of Weilheim. According to official records, he was "exonerated."

There is now a postwar building on the site of Putzi's old Munich apartment at Gentzstrasse 1.

Mauch, Christof. *Schattenkrieg gegen Hitler. Das Dritte Reich im Visier der Amerikanischen Geheimdienste 1941–1945.* Deutsche Verlags-Anstalt. Stuttgart 1999.

Toland, John. *Adolf Hitler.* Doubleday. Garden City, N.Y. 1976.

Widmann, Carlos. Play it again, Putzi. *Der Spiegel* 10: 58–64, 1999.

Isabellastrasse 45 (Five-Story Building on West Side of the Street)

Birthplace of Eva Braun (1912–1945). Eva Braun was Hitler's mistress for twelve years and his wife for one day. She was the daughter of a schoolteacher and was working for Hitler's personal photographer, Heinrich Hoffmann, when she met Hitler. She was tall, slender, attractive, and active. She liked to ski, swim, climb mountains, and engage in gymnastics. She posed for nude photos, now owned by the Bildarchiv Preussicher Kulturbesitz, but was a shy person with no particular intellectual attainments.

When his niece-mistress Geli Raubal was found shot to death September 18, 1931, Hitler was devastated. He was surrounded by charming, brainy women but was wary of them. "A highly intellectual man should have a primitive and stupid woman," he told Albert Speer. "Imagine if I had a woman to interfere with my work."

Hitler dominated Eva. He would not permit her to fly or drive a fast car. He made her rich by assigning half the rights of his photographs to her — the other half went to Hoffmann.

At Berchtesgaden Eva stayed in the background. Hitler did not permit her in Berlin until the last two years of her life, when he was away at a military redoubt. Whenever important guests visited, Eva remained out of sight. Very few Germans knew about her. Hitler maintained that he had no private life, and Eva ruefully said of herself, "Ich bin Fräulein kein privates Leben [I am Miss No Private Life]." She often felt miserable and attempted suicide several times.

With the war going badly, Hitler sent Eva to Munich, but she refused to stay there. On April 15, 1945, she arrived at the Führerbunker to share Hitler's fate. "A Germany without Adolf Hitler would not be fit to live in," she declared.

On April 29 Hitler decided to gratify Eva by marrying her. The ceremony was a brief one. Bride and groom asserted that they were of Aryan descent and free of hereditary disease. Walter Wagner, a minor official Goebbels corralled, performed the ceremony. Hitler spent his wedding night dictating his last will and political testament, a ringing denunciation of the Jews. On April 30, at 3:30 P.M., Eva swallowed cyanide and died beside her new husband.

Snyder, Louis L. *Encyclopedia of the Third Reich.* McGraw-Hill. New York 1978.

Hohenzollernstrasse 93

Braun family apartment, a five-story building. In 1929 Eva Braun met Hitler when she was living with her family on the second floor of this building.

Lothstrasse 29

Barracks where Hitler lived after World War I (postwar building now on site). Hitler left Pasewalk Hospital on November 19, 1918, after having been gassed and treated for blindness. On November 21 he moved into this barracks. He was almost 30 years old and had no career prospects. The army had been his home since August 1914, and he was initially unwilling to look around for anything else.

Defeated Germany was in a state of upheaval. A soldier's council ran Hitler's barracks. The minister president of the revolutionary Bavarian government was Kurt Eisner, a radical and a Jew. (Eisner was assassinated the following spring.)

The army assigned Hitler to the seventh Company of the first Reserve Battalion of the second Infantry Regiment. With 14 other members of the company he was ordered to guard the Traunstein prisoner of war camp. The camp held mainly Russians, who were quickly transported elsewhere. Hitler was given gate duty, an easy posting.

On February 20, 1919, Hitler received a new posting, guard duty at the Hauptbahnhof, the main railroad station. His job was to maintain order among the hordes of soldiers passing through the station. He earned an extra three marks a day testing old gas masks. In the meantime communist councils were ruling Bavaria.

By May 1919 Munich was, in effect, under military rule, the communists banished. The city center was packed with barricades, barbed wire, and control points. An "information department" was established to instill in the troops a correct, anti–Bolshevik attitude. In June 1919 Hitler was assigned to the first anti–Bolshevik instruction courses. He was soon giving lectures, such as "Who Bears the Guilt for the World War?" "Peace Conditions and Reconstruction," and "Social and Political-Economic Catchwords." Hitler immediately discovered that he could stir his audiences: "I started out with the greatest enthusiasm and love. For all at once I was offered an opportunity of speaking before a larger audience; and the thing I had always presumed from pure feeling without knowing it was now corroborated; I could 'speak.'" In his speeches a surefire crowd pleaser was denunciation of the Jews. Anti–Semitism was rife, and Hitler's diatribes played to the masses. Jewry was a race, not a religion, Hitler said. Anti–Semitism based on reason must lead to the systematic removal of the rights of the Jews. "Its final aim must unshakably be the removal of the Jews altogether."

In mid–September 1919 Hitler joined the German Workers' Party (DAP), and received membership number 555. This small organization, with a great boost from Hitler's oratorical talents, was soon to become the National Socialist German Workers' Party (NSDAP), called the Nazi Party in English-speaking countries.

On March 31, 1920, Hitler left the army. He gathered his belongings — a coat, cap, jacket, pants, suit of underwear, shirt, socks, shoes, and fifty marks demobilization pay — and moved to a small room at Thierschstrasse 41.

Kershaw, Ian. *Hitler. 1889–1936: Hubris.* Norton. New York 1998.

MUNICH: EAST OF THE ISAR RIVER

Delpstrasse 12

Eva Braun's villa. Eva and younger sister Gretl moved into this villa, which Hitler had acquired for them, on March 30, 1936. Heinrich Hoffmann paid for the house from the huge sums of money he had received as Hitler's photographer. Hitler rarely visited Eva here, even though the villa was thought to be a love nest. But Eva loved the house, because it gave her independence from her parents. Bushes she planted still grow in the garden. Before the war the street was called Wasserburgstrasse. Afterward it was renamed in honor of Alfred Delp, a priest the Nazis murdered in 1945.

Prinzregentenplatz 16

In 1929 Hitler moved out of his little room on Thierschstrasse and into a nine-

Prinzregentenplatz, Hitler's home in Munich from 1929.

room apartment in this building. He gave Geli Raubal, the daughter of his half sister, one room.

Geli's mother, Angela, worked as his housekeeper. Hitler supported Geli and paid for her singing lessons. After Geli's death, September 18, 1931, Hitler had a bust made of her, which he kept in his apartment, surrounded with flowers.

Traudl Junge, one of Hitler's secretaries, described his apartment (Galante and Silianoff, 1989):

I was astonished to find that [Hitler] only had one floor of the house. The ground floor was occupied by the porter and by various offices for guards and policemen. On the second story was the apartment Hitler shared with his housekeeper, Frau Winter, and her husband. Private individuals inhabited all the other floors.

The Führer's apartment was just like any other apartment belonging to a well-to-do bourgeois. In the hall there were pieces of wicker furniture, every window was curtained with flowery material, and the walls of a dressing room were covered in mirrors lit by wall lamps. Everything was in very good taste, and there were thick carpets throughout the apartment. At the end of the corridor, on the left, was a door leading to the rooms where the Winters lived: a kitchen, bathroom, living room and bedroom. This living room doubled as a waiting room for Hitler's ministers when the government was in Munich.

Opposite the front door was the Führer's spacious office and his library. Hitler had a strong preference for large rooms, and later on I often wondered how he could bear living caged up under the low ceilings and tiny windows of his bunker. Next to the library was a bedroom, which was kept locked: it was there that his beloved niece Geli Raubal had killed herself. Hitler had been so upset by her death that no one had been allowed to enter the room since it happened. Eva Braun also had a small room at her disposal, but she used it rarely, and never when Hitler was in Munich. The right wing contained a guest room, which I used as an office whenever I had some typing to do, and between the two was the bedroom where Hitler slept, which I'd never been into.

Benito Mussolini visited Hitler's apartment, September 25, 1937. The two dictators had a one-hour meeting, during which they agreed to establish relations with Japan, support the fascist dictator Francisco Franco in Spain, and oppose the policies of Britain and France. These resolutions strengthened the Axis alliance, formed in 1935.

On September 30, 1939, before he left Munich after signing the Munich Accords (see Führerbau), Chamberlain visited Prinzregentenplatz 16 and presented Hitler with a document pledging that Britain and Germany would never go to war with each other. Hitler signed.

After the war Prinzregentenplatz 16 became a reparations office for Hitler's Jewish victims. It is now Munich's central traffic fines office. Occasional pilgrims, many of the neo–Nazi variety, come to visit Hitler's old apartment.

Galante, Pierre, and Eugene Silianoff. *Voices from the Bunker.* G. P. Putnam's Sons. New York 1989. Rosenbaum, Ron. Hitler's Angel. *Vanity Fair.* April 1992, p. 180.

Rosenheimerstrasse, at Gasteig

Site of Bürgerbräukeller, Hitler's favored beer hall speech venue. The Beer Hall Putsch began here. The Bürgerbräukeller was "an eminently respectable beer hall much frequented by the better class of people." After his release from Landsberg Prison, Hitler made a significant public speech in the Bürgerbräukeller, declaring himself the unquestioned leader of the Nazi Party.

Because the putsch had started in the Bürgerbräukeller, Hitler and the Nazis continued to revere the place. After Hitler came to power in 1933, he held annual ceremonies commemorating the putsch in the Bürgerbräukeller. During one, November 8, 1939, there was an attempt on his life.

On the afternoon of the speech, Georg Elser, a cabinetmaker, entered the Bürgerbräukeller with a box full of dynamite and a timer. Elser had been incarcerated in the Dachau concentration camp because of his communist sympathies and had just been let out.

Elser concealed himself behind a pillar as waiters and party factotums bustled around, preparing for the evening's festivities. When they had left, Elser placed his time bomb inside a pillar, behind a hidden door, which he had prepared a few days before. Because Hitler was scheduled to begin his speech at 10 P.M., Elser set his explosives to go off at 11:20 P.M.

At 10:10 P.M. Hitler launched into his oration, a tirade against the British, who two months earlier had declared war on Germany after the Wehrmacht had invaded Poland. But Hitler, possessed of a sixth sense for personal danger, became suddenly uneasy. At 11:07 P.M. he broke off his talk and rushed to the railroad station for a train to Berlin.

Eight minutes after Hitler left the Bürgerbräukeller, the bomb went off. It killed seven people and injured 63, among them Eva Braun's father.

When his train stopped at Nuremberg, Hitler learned about the huge explosion. He remarked, "Now I am completely content. The fact that I left the Bürgerbräukeller earlier than usual is a corroboration of Providence's intention to let me reach my goal."

Arrested the following day, Elser maintained he had acted alone. Hitler was skeptical and blamed the British secret service.

But Elser did not undergo a public trial. Instead, he was incarcerated in a concentration camp, where he was treated as a privileged person, suggesting to many people that Hitler had arranged the whole assassination attempt. On April 5, 1945, Heinrich Himmler ordered Elser murdered in Dachau, a few days before American soldiers liberated the camp.

From 1945 to 1957 American troops used the Bürgerbräukeller as a service club. In 1958 the Bürgerbräukeller became a beer hall again but was later razed.

Deming, Brian, and Ted Iliff. *Hitler and Munich: A Historical Guide to the Sights and Addresses of Munich Important to Adolf Hitler, His Followers, and His Victims.* Verlag A. Plenk KG. Berchtesgaden, Germany ca. 1986.

Congress Hall of the Deutsches Museum

South side of Ludwigsbrücke on island in the Isar. A Nazi Speech here, January 13, 1943, led to a student protest demonstration, probably the only one during the Hitler era.

The speaker was Paul Giesler, a bad-tempered, fanatic Nazi official, who loved to talk. The 47-year-old Giesler had become the *gauleiter* (Nazi district boss) in Munich, when his predecessor, Adolf Wagner, had a stroke in June 1942.

The occasion for Giesler's speech was the 470th anniversary of Munich's Ludwig-Maximilian University. The organizers were using the museum's congress hall because no lecture hall in the university would accommodate the large audience. But the students quickly became fed up with the carping, boorish, prurient Giesler.

The students were using their studies to escape military duty, Giesler told his listeners. "As for the girls," he continued, "there is no reason why each of them should not make an annual contribution to the Fatherland of a child, preferably a son. Let all girl students with healthy bodies bear children. This is an automatic process and, once started, continues without the least attention."

"Of course," Giesler added, "a certain amount of cooperation is required in these matters. If some of you girls lack sufficient charm to find a mate, I will be glad to assign you one of my adjutants for whose ancestry I can vouch. I can promise you a thoroughly enjoyable experience" (Deming and Iliff, ca. 1986).

Needless to say, Giesler's reception was not a thoroughly enjoyable experience. The angry students began making so much noise that they drowned Giesler out. Even crippled soldiers in the audience joined in the whistling, jeering, and shouting.

Deeply offended, the women in the audience tried to walk out, but SS men obstructed the exits. Fights broke out. A soldier pummeled one of the students. Riot police were summoned to clear the hall.

Naturally the newspapers printed none of this. Articles about Giesler's talk stated only that the *gauleiter* spoke with "a refreshingly warlike spirit." But everyone in Munich quickly heard about what Giesler had said and how the students had reacted. Although members of the anti–Hitler White Rose conspiracy were not present, the outcry against Giesler spurred them to greater resistance efforts of their own.

Deming, Brian, and Ted Iliff. *Hitler and Munich: A Historical Guide to the Sights and Addresses of Munich Important to Adolf Hitler, His Followers, and His Victims.* Verlag A. Plenk KG. Berchtesgaden, Germany ca. 1986.
Preis, Kurt. *München unterm Hakenkreuz.* F.A. Herbig Verlagsbuchhandlung. München 1989.

Stadelheim Prison

South side of Stadelheimerstrasse, a block east of Tegernseer Landstrasse. On June 4, 1922, Hitler was jailed here for five weeks after being charged with inciting a riot. As he was hauled off, he told his friends, "Two thousand years ago the mob of Jerusalem dragged a man to execution in just this way."

In 1934, during the Night of the Long Knives (see Lichterfelde Barracks, Berlin), Ernst Röhm and other members of the SA were incarcerated and shot here. Members of the White Rose, an anti–Hitler group, were jailed and beheaded here in 1943. Adjacent to the prison is a cemetery where some members of the White Rose conspiracy are buried.

The city of Munich places wreaths on the graves annually. In the cemetery there is also a mass grave for 4,092 Nazi victims.

MUNICH: SITES ASSOCIATED WITH THE BEER HALL PUTSCH

During the November 1923 Beer Hall Putsch, Hitler tried but failed to take control of the conservative Bavarian state government and the Weimar government in Berlin. He was already head of the National Socialist German Workers' Party, with 70,000 members the most powerful political party in Bavaria. He and many other Germans viewed the freely elected government of the Weimar Republic as an abomination that the victorious Allies had imposed after the German defeat in World War I. Moreover, Germany was in the throes of catastrophic hyperinflation, and French troops had just occupied the Ruhr. Hitler wrongly believed that the social upheaval these two calamities were causing would assure success for the putschists.

The First World War and the terms of the Versailles Peace Treaty caused the German hyperinflation of 1923 to a great extent. To pay for the war, the kaiser's ministers borrowed gold from Germany's citizens, giving paper notes in return. Repayment, the Germans assumed, would come from the defeated French and English. After all, Otto von Bismarck, the Iron Chancellor, had imposed an indemnity of five billion francs on the beaten French in 1871. This money paid for Bismarck's wars and later financed the rapid postwar growth of Berlin. To meet the vastly greater costs of the First World War, Imperial Finance Minister Karl Helfferich was ready to demand 150 billion marks when the fighting ended. But the Germans lost.

"The hour has struck for the weighty settlement of our accounts," said Georges Clemenceau, the French premier, to German foreign minister Count Ulrich von Brockdorff-Rantzau. The year was 1919. The First World War had ended with an armistice seven months before. The scene was the Hall of Mirrors in France's Versailles Palace, where Louis XIV, the Sun King, had once reigned.

The victorious Allies declared to the representatives of a defeated Germany that there were to be no negotiations. The Germans were simply to receive the terms that the Allies had agreed on.

The reception the vengeful French gave to Brockdorff-Rantzau, a thin, pale professional diplomat with a monocle, must have alerted him to expect the worst. They forced his special train, filled with 180 diplomats and experts preparing to argue the German case, to skulk along at 10 miles an hour. The Germans were thus compelled to see the devastation their armies had inflicted on the countryside of northern France. In Versailles the French housed the German delegation in an isolated hotel surrounded by barbed wire and made them carry their own bags upstairs.

The French terms were harsh. Clemenceau demanded total payment for all of France's war damages, its 5,000,000 dead and wounded, its 4,000 ruined towns, and its 20,000 destroyed businesses. He declared that the Germans must pay up to a hundred years if necessary, with interest. British experts calculated that the Germans owed a total of 800 billion marks, which was more than all the German national wealth.

The Allies summarily rejected a German counteroffer of 100 billion marks without interest. Instead, they demanded an immediate initial payment of $5 billion in gold, along with considerable quantities of coal, chemicals, and shipping, to be delivered by May 1921. The final amount to be paid was left to future negotiations. Winston Churchill called the reparations "a sad story of complicated idiocy." They led to an unending dispute between Germany and the Allies and were a partial cause for the ruinous fall of the German mark.

At first the decline in value of the mark was not precipitous. Between 1918 and the summer of 1921, the mark slid in value from 4.20 to the dollar to 75 to the dollar, a significant descent. But people were more preoccupied with hunger and the shortage of food.

By the summer of 1922 the value of the mark had fallen to 400 to the dollar. On June 24, 1922, right-wing radicals assassinated Walther Rathenau, the millionaire Jewish minister of reconstruction, and shook what little faith anyone had left for prospects of a German recovery. From 400 per dollar the mark sank to 7,000 by the beginning of 1923, and every week it slumped further.

January 1923 was a disaster. The government of Chancellor Josef Wirth collapsed. President Friedrich Ebert, a former saddle maker, tried to build a more conservative coalition that could win the support of big business and deal with the inflation. He selected as chancellor Wilhelm Cuno, the director of the Hamburg-America shipping line. Cuno's elegant manners and appearance disguised temporarily his total inability to help govern a disintegrating Germany. ("Cuno is a fat cigar," Walther Rathenau had once said, "which will have to be smoked some day because of its lovely band.")

The bickering over reparations went on. The Germans asked for a moratorium and delayed their deliveries of raw material, while they tried to negotiate better terms. France's vindictive premier, Raymond Poincaré, refused to tolerate such tactics. In fact, he was anxious for any pretext that would allow the French to claim a violation of the Versailles Treaty and justify an invasion of Germany. "Whatever happens," he had told British prime minister Bonar Law, "I shall advance into the Ruhr on January 15."

When the Germans continued to stall, the French complained formally that the Germans had not delivered half the 200,000 telephone poles due for shipment to France during 1922. The Germans blamed their state governments for the delay, since the governments owned the forests with the trees to be cut down for telephone poles.

The British did not take the French complaint seriously. History had recorded no such political use of wood as the French were making since the Greeks had built a horse outside Troy, said Sir John Bradbury, the British envoy.

Then the French made a new complaint regarding dilatory coal deliveries from the Ruhr. Disregarding British protests, they sent a Franco-Belgian "technical commission" to the Ruhr on January 11, 1923, to investigate the matter.

The French discovered that the German Coal Syndicate had just moved from the Ruhr to Hamburg. The French, who had already sent a few troops to "protect" their commission, followed up with more troops. The German government immediately suspended all reparations deliveries and called on German citizens in the Ruhr to passively resist the French invasion. The French response was to dismiss any Ruhr official who disobeyed them and to arrest anyone who attempted to use force against them. On March 31 French troops fired on a crowd of workers at the Krupp Works in Essen, killing 13. By then the French had put the entire Ruhr under military rule, depriving Germany of its industrial center, the source of 80 percent of its coal, iron, and steel, the means for its economic recovery.

The German mark collapsed. From a rate of 7,000 to the dollar in January, when the French occupied the Ruhr, it slumped to 160,000 by July. The German government, to subsidize the idled Ruhr workers, churned out banknotes. At the Ullstein publishing headquarters on the Kochstrasse in Berlin (where Ullstein is still located), government officials requisitioned the printing presses to produce increasingly worthless paper. One of the owners, Hermann Ullstein, recalled (Friedrich, 1972): "All doors were locked and officials of the Reichsbank were placed on guard. Round the machinery sat elderly women, staring fascinated at those parts of the presses from which the finished products came pouring out. It was the duty of these women to see that the billion mark notes were placed in the right baskets and handed to the officials. They had to keep an eye on every single billion. Officials are so funny sometimes."

Speculators and profiteers became rich, but inflation devastated the average person and had dire psychological effects. Savings of a lifetime evaporated overnight. Insurance policies became worthless. Pensioners and people with fixed incomes were left destitute.

Hitler saw the turmoil roiling Germany as his opportunity to act. By 1923 many Bavarians favored a return of the independence from Germany that Bavaria had enjoyed before German unification in 1871. But Hitler did not want Bavarian independence; instead, he wanted to lead a new right-wing Berlin government, supplanting that of President Friedrich Ebert and Chancellor Gustav Stresemann, who had replaced Wilhelm Cuno.

The Bavarian government's leaders were scornful of the Berlin government, and were themselves plotting the formation of a new nationalist dictatorship in Berlin. Three men controlled the government of Bavaria: Otto von Lossow, head of the Bavarian army; Gustav Ritter von Kahr, general state commissar; and Hans Ritter von Seisser, the Bavarian police chief. These men sympathized with many of Hitler's

views but did not like some of his radical ideas.

On the evening of November 8, 1923, the celebrated Beer Hall Putsch began at the Bürgerbräukeller, where a large group of prominent Bavarians had gathered, among them Kahr, Lossow, and Seisser, as well as Hitler and Erich Ludendorff. The former army general quartermaster, Ludendorff was the man who was mainly responsible for Germany's military policy and strategy in the latter years of World War I. A man with a gluttony for work and a granite character, Ludendorff had won the right to wear the coveted red stripes of the general staff at age 30 in 1895. He had a thick body, a blond mustache over a harsh down-curving mouth, a round double chin, and that bulge at the back of the neck that Ralph Waldo Emerson called the mark of the beast.

When the First World War ended, Ludendorff had hidden in a Berlin boardinghouse, then disguised himself with false whiskers and fled briefly to Sweden. On returning to Germany, he was revered as a war hero. As Hitler's ally, he had agitated against the government in Berlin and given Hitler status.

For half an hour Kahr had been reading a prepared speech to the crowd of 3,000 packed into the Burgerbräukeller, when Hitler made his grand entrance. A clutch of men in steel helmets, Hitler's storm troopers, appeared, and pushed in a heavy machine gun. Hitler materialized, accompanied by two armed bodyguards brandishing pistols. Hitler stood on a chair, and, drowned out by the tumult, he pulled out his Browning automatic pistol and fired a shot through the ceiling.

Hitler announced that the revolution had broken out and 600 armed men surrounded the hall. The Bavarian government was deposed, he shouted, and he would form a provisional Reich government. He requested Kahr, Lossow, and Seisser to follow him into an adjoining room. Reluctantly they complied.

Pandemonium reigned, but Hermann Göring, a former World War I flying ace and Hitler's ally, urged everyone to be calm. "You've got your beer," he said (Kershaw, 1998).

Waving his pistol in the next room, Hitler shouted that no one would leave without his permission. He proclaimed the formation of a new government, himself at the head. Ludendorff, Lossow, Seisser, and Kahr all agreed to be important members. If things did not work out, Hitler declared that he had bullets in his pistol for his collaborators and himself.

Things definitely did not work out. Lossow, Seisser, and Kahr, tepid revolutionaries from the outset, left the hall and proceeded to inform state authorities that they repudiated the putsch.[23]

Meanwhile, Ernst Röhm led another group of Hitler loyalists in the Löwenbräukeller across town. Röhm managed to capture the Bavarian War Ministry but erred by not taking over the telephone switchboard. Lossow was thus able to bring loyalist forces to Munich from nearby towns. Army troops and state police were soon besieging Röhm and his followers.

The next morning, a bitterly cold one, with the putsch rapidly crumbling, Hitler and Ludendorff decided on a demonstration march to Röhm's rescue through the city. Hitler believed that a march would engender overwhelming support. Ludendorff thought that the army would never fire at him, a revered military leader, and that if he were in the front ranks, the soldiers would back down.

The march began at noon. A cordon of men carrying banners preceded Hitler, Ludendorff, Göring, and Max Erwin von Scheubner-Richter, another party leader. At the Ludwigsbrücke the putschists confronted and overwhelmed a small group of policemen. Throngs of shouting, waving supporters greeted the marchers on Zweibrückenstrasse.

From the Marienplatz the marchers turned right into Weinstrasse, right again to Perusastrase, left into Residenzstrasse, and in a few minutes arrived at the Feldherrnhalle. Here the police had established a line blocking Residenzstrasse, and there were more police on the Odeonsplatz. A putschist fired a shot; the police hesitated, then fired back; more shooting occurred, and the putschists and the crowd of onlookers scattered in all directions.

Fourteen putschists and four policemen died. Hitler was wrenched to the ground and suffered a dislocated shoulder. A bullet killed Scheubner-Richter. Göring was shot in the leg.

Ludendorff, who had an iron nerve under fire, emerged unscathed. Oblivious to the bullets whizzing past his head, he marched straight into the arms of waiting police and was immediately taken into custody.

The trial of the putschists was held February 26, 1924, in the lecture hall of a school building at Blutenbergstrasse 3. During the trial Hitler was incarcerated a few doors away at Blutenbergstrasse 18. Hitler and Ludendorff were tried along with six others. One journalist attending described the process as a "political carnival." Hitler appeared in a suit, rather than in prison garb, wearing his Iron Cross, First Class. Ludendorff, who had not even been imprisoned, arrived in a limousine. "What a tremendous chap, this Hitler," one of the judges remarked. Judge Georg Neithardt, the president of the court, allowed Hitler to speak for four hours.

"The man who is born to be a dictator is not compelled; he wills; he is driven forward; he drives himself forward; there is nothing immodest about this," said Hitler in his closing statement. "The man who feels called upon to govern a people has no right to say, if you want me or summon me I will cooperate. No, it is his duty to step forward."

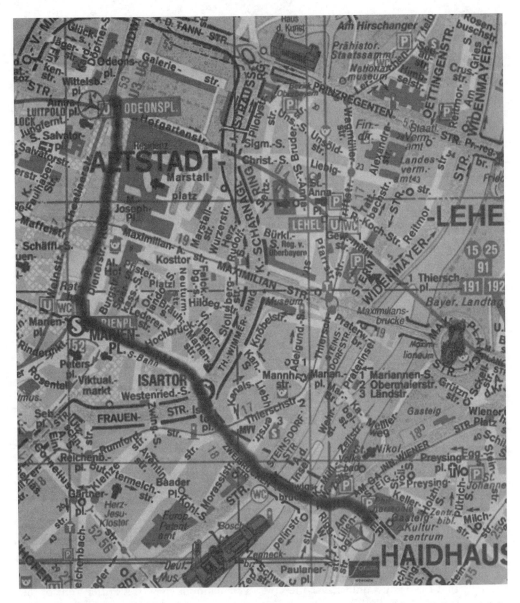

Route of putschists' march. The marchers began at the Bürgerbräukeller Beer Hall (lower right), proceeded across the Ludwigsbrücke, and met police gunfire at the Feldherrnhalle in the Odeonsplatz (map ©Falk Verlag, Ostfildern).

On April 1, 1924, Ludendorff was acquitted, which he took as an insult. Hitler and three others were found guilty and sentenced to five years in Landsberg prison for high treason.

When he came to power, Hitler built a Temple of Honor, with iron sarcophagi for the "blood-witnesses" of the November 1923 putsch. He told Albert Speer that he wanted his own sarcophagus here. The temple was dynamited in 1947, the sarcophagi destroyed, the putschists' corpses discarded. But pedestals still remain. Sometimes Nazi veterans gather around them. Historic preservation officials want to save them as "thought-stones of history."

Deming, Brian, and Ted Iliff. *Hitler and Munich: A Historical Guide to the Sights and Addresses of Munich Important to Adolf Hitler, His Followers, and His Victims.* Verlag A. Plenk KG. Berchtesgaden, Germany ca. 1986.

Friedrich, Otto. *Before the Deluge.* Harper and Row. New York 1972.

Kershaw, Ian. *Hitler. 1889–1936: Hubris.* Norton. New York 1998.

Speer, Albert. *Spandau. The Secret Diaries.* Translated by Richard and Clara Winston. Pocket Books. New York 1977.

Tuchman, Barbara. *The Guns of August.* Macmillan. New York 1962.

LANDSBERG AM LECH

Located 40 miles west of Munich, Landsberg am Lech is a charming walled town from medieval times, which is the site of a prison. Hitler was incarcerated here after the abortive 1923 Beer Hall Putsch.

When he arrived just after his arrest, Hitler was depressed but calm, dressed in a white nightgown, his left arm in a sling. Graf Anton von Arco-Valley, a young aristocrat, who had murdered Bavarian premier Kurt Eisner in 1919, was ejected from his spacious cell no. 7 to make room for the famous new prisoner.

Hitler's months in Landsberg Prison were more akin to a hotel sojourn than a penitentiary sentence. The windows of his large, comfortably furnished cell on the first floor gave him a fine view of the countryside. Attired in lederhosen, he spent part of his day reading newspapers in a wicker chair, his back to a laurel wreath sent by admirers. His large desk was piled with letters of praise and support, which poured in along

Top: **Temple of Honor, Munich (razed 1947), designed by Paul Ludwig Troost, housing sarcophagi of Hitler confederates who died in the 1923 Beer Hall Putsch. *Bottom:* Landsberg prison, built during the rule of the kaisers, where Hitler was incarcerated after the failed Beer Hall Putsch.**

with gifts and flowers. His jailers treated him with great deference, occasionally greeting him with "Heil Hitler!" While detained he dictated Mein Kampf to Rudolf

Top: Landsberg am Lech. The Bayertor, built in 1425, was the main entrance to Landsberg through the medieval fortress wall surrounding the town. The Bayertor's central tower is 36 meters tall. *Bottom:* Hitler poses before the Bayertor, just after his release from prison, December 1924 (Bayerische Staatsbibliothek).

could observe the miserable procession of prisoners to their work. When the 101st Airborne Division entered the camps, April 27–28, 1945, 14,000 inmates had died. American soldiers became so sick when they saw the heaps of corpses, they could not eat. They dumped their food into a large waste container; starving inmates quickly devoured the slop.

After the war Landsberg became the site of one of the biggest displaced persons camps in Germany. The Allies used Landsberg prison to hold war criminals; 300 were hanged here.

Anton Posset, a teacher who settled in Landsberg in 1975, has braved the considerable hostility of Landsberg's citizens to document the town's dark past. "I only want that we should say that we committed a great crime, that they recognize that right here, in Landsberg, thousands of Jews were exterminated." To Serge Schmemann, a *New York Times* reporter, Posset showed photos of troops of the 101st Airborne among fields of skeletal corpses in the liberated concentration camps.

Hess. When he was released, December 19, 1924, corrections officials did not allow him to be photographed in front of the prison, so he posed in front of the Bayertor, one of the medieval city gates.

In 1944 the Nazis set up eleven concentration camps around Landsberg to supply slave labor for local weapons manufacture. At least 30,000 Jews and others were imprisoned in the camps. From the western edge of the city, the citizens of Landsberg

In the summer of 1987 throngs of prostitutes appeared in Landsberg. Mayor Hanns Hamberger had announced that the town had grown to 20,000 inhabitants, the level at which prostitution becomes legal in a town. The ladies looked forward to a lucrative trade with the nearby German Army base. But when the results of the 1988 census were published, Landsberg turned out to have only 19,500 citizens. The police hustled the women out of town, and they won't be coming back soon. Bavarian law now requires 30,000 townsfolk before prostitution is legal.

Kershaw, Ian. *Hitler. 1889–1936: Hubris.* Norton. New York 1998.

Schmemann, Serge. Landsberg Journal. The prostitutes leave, but Nazi ghosts linger. *New York Times.* July 1, 1989, p. 4.

BERLIN

Hitler did not like the Berliners, who returned the compliment. In 1932, the year of the last free election, scarcely 24 percent of them voted for the Nazis, whereas 38 percent voted for the communists.[24] Understandably, Hitler contrived to spend as little time in the capital as possible. But with Albert Speer, his architect and later defense minister, he developed megalomaniacal plans to turn the city into "Germania," a colossal monument to his military victories. Because of the downward course of the war, these plans were never completed. Yet until the end of 1944, as Berlin burned and crumbled, Speer and his staff continued to work in a rural monastery, Kloster Corvey, on the blueprints for Germania. Ultimately, allied bombing raids flattened most of Berlin.

Ritzmann, Kai. Erstmals gezeigt: Wie die Nazis Berlin wiederaufbauen wollten. *Berliner Morgenpost.* April 20, 1997.

Russian War Memorial (in the Tiergarten)

The Russian War Memorial has a bronze figure of a Red Army soldier with fixed bayonet. Flanking the figure are two Soviet tanks, said to be the first to reach Berlin in 1945. In 1945–46 the Russians obtained the marble for their war memorial from the ruins of Hitler's New Reich Chancellery, on the corner of Wilhelmstrasse and Vossstrasse, which Albert Speer designed and finished in 1939.

Hitler had airily told Speer that the Old Reich Chancellery was "fit for a soap company." Located at Wilhelmstrasse 77, the old chancellery had been built 1736–39 as a palace for Count von Schulenburg. Otto von Bismarck remodeled the building as his chancellery.

Hitler decreed that the enormous New Reich Chancellery should impress every visitor with its monumentality. "On the long corridor from the entrance to the reception hall, they'll learn something about the grandeur of the German Reich," said the Führer. The long corridor was 300 meters, with a court of honor, a forecourt, a mosaic hall, a round hall, and a marble

Hitler receives the diplomatic corps in Bismarck's Old Reich Chancellery, Wilhelmstrasse 77, January 1, 1934. Hitler thought this building was "fit for a soap company."

gallery along the way. At 146 meters, the reception hall was twice as long as the hall of mirrors at Versailles. Hitler's own office was 400 meters square. From the exterior the Reich Chancellery had a stern, authoritarian appearance. The interior had an ascetic, cool splendor. Only German wood and marble were used in the building. Many of the couches were so heavy that four men were required to lift them. The East Germans began demolishing the bombed out chancellery in 1949 and didn't finish until 1956.

Chancellery marble was also incorporated into the Mohrenstrasse subway station. Authorities are divided over whether the red marble in the foyer of Humboldt University came from the Chancellery.

Kniess, Oliver. Geheimnis um roten Marmor wird gelüftet. Neue Belege: Edler Stein in der Humboldt-Unit stammt wohl doch aus der Reichskanzlei. *Berliner Morgenpost.* March 2, 1998.
Leser-Frage: Wo war die Reichskanzlei in der Wilhelmstrasse? *Berliner Morgenpost.* May 8, 1999.

Reichsbank (Middle, Werderstrasse, U-Bahn Station Hausvogteiplatz-Auswärtiges Amt)

In February 1933, a month after Hitler came to power, the Reichsbank held a contest for the design of a new building. Among the architects who submitted plans were Walter Gropius and Mies van der Rohe, two founders of the Bauhaus School. The judges excluded another eminent German architect, Erich Mendelsohn, because he was Jewish. Realizing that his career was finished in his homeland, Mendelsohn immigrated to America, where he built reproductions of Berlin buildings that the U.S. Army used to test bombing strategies during World War II.

Hitler rejected all the submissions and chose a plan by the bank's own architect, Heinrich Wolff, who had not even entered the competition. Wolff had designed a five-story structure with a stone facade, a low-pitched roof, and columns that evoke ancient Rome, a favorite motif during the

Top right: Ornate brass doors in New Reich Chancellery. *Bottom:* Room in New Reich Chancellery (Raimund Reichenberger).

Third Reich. In the basement a three-story vault could be flooded with water during a break-in. Gold seized from Jews and smelted into ingots was stored in this vault.

More than 5,000 people attended the 1934 ceremony to lay the cornerstone. Hitler saluted in front of huge swastika banners and torches. Dr. Hjalmar Schacht, president of the Reichsbank, made a speech. SA Brownshirt storm troops helped with the construction.

The Reichsbank was finished in 1940, as the war was underway. Albert Speer describes a 1943 visit to the offices of Walther Funk, who in 1939 succeeded Schacht as Reichsbank president:

With their gilded armchairs, heavy carpets, and marvelous Gobelins, these rooms reflected the wealth of the great promoters of the 1870s. From here, Funk directed his Reich Ministry of Economy with seeming looseness…. We withdrew to an adjoining salon, the walls of which were adorned with hand-stamped leather; valuable old carpets covered the floor. The furniture was hand-carved in a baroque manner; the woodwork of the heavy upholstered easy chairs was gilded. All these objects came from the days of Kaiser Wilhelm, when the German Reich Bank played a part in the financial politics of the world.

After 1945 the building became the Communist Party headquarters. Now it houses the foreign ministry.

Davis, Mike. Angriff auf "German Village." *Der Spiegel.* 41:238–43, 1999.

Speer, Albert. *Infiltration. How Heinrich Himmler Schemed to Build an SS Industrial Empire.* Translated from the German by Joachim Neugroschel. Macmillan. New York 1981.

Steinmetz, Greg. Some ghosts vanish as Germany relocates from Bonn to Berlin. Storied Reichsbank is typical of Nazi buildings getting an exorcising makeover. *Wall Street Journal.* January 22, 1999, p. 1.

Westphal, Dirk. Das Auswärtige Amt ist enthüllt.

Reichsbank exterior (Ullstein Bilderdienst).

Reichsbank interior, main hall and tellers' windows (Ullstein Bilderdienst).

Anbau für 150 Millionen Mark stellt früheres DDR-Staatsratsgebäude in den Schatten. *Berliner Morgenpost.* August 10, 1999.

Wilhelmplatz 8–9. Ordenspalais (destroyed) and Extensions (still standing). Propaganda Ministry.

In 1736 the architect Jean de Bodt built this palace for the Johanniterorden. In 1828 Karl Friedrich Schinkel rebuilt the palace in classical style. Because the Ordenspalais was too small for Joseph Goebbels's ministry, architect Karl Reichle expanded it twice, before 1940. On March 13, 1945, the Ordenspalais was blown to bits, as Goebbels described in his diary:

This evening's Mosquito raid was particularly disastrous for me because our Ministry was hit. The whole lovely building was totally destroyed by a bomb. The throne-room, the Blue Gallery and my newly rebuilt theater hall are nothing but a heap of ruins. I drove straight to the Ministry to see the devastation for myself. One's heart aches to see so unique a product of the architect's art, such as this building was, totally flattened in a second. What trouble we have taken to reconstruct the theater hall, the throne-room and the Blue Gallery in the old style! With what care have we chosen every fresco on the walls and every piece of furniture! And now it has all been given over to destruction. In addition, fire has broken out in the ruins, bringing with it an even greater risk, since 500 bazooka missiles are stored underneath the burning wreckage. I do my utmost to get the fire brigade to the scene as quickly and in as great strength as possible, so at least to prevent the bazooka missiles from exploding.... All my staff are on the spot ... and all of them make the greatest efforts to save whatever can be saved. But from the finest part of the building there is nothing to be saved.... We had all taken the Ministry so much to our hearts. Now it belongs to the past. I am firmly determined, however, that when this war is over, not only shall I construct a new monumental ministry — as the Führer says — but restore this Ministry in all its old glory.

An elementary school now occupies the site of the Ordenspalais. Reichle's additions were only lightly damaged. In 1947 the Soviet "Kommandatura" used them for their headquarters.

Goebbels, Joseph. Final Entries 1945. *The Diaries of Joseph Goebbels.* Avon Books. New York 1979.
Schubert. Peter. Umzug ins "Haus der Lügen." Die Last der Altbauten: Vom schwierigen Umgang mit der NS-Architektur. *Berliner Morgenpost.* June 3, 1997.

Mauerstrasse 45–53. Propaganda Ministry

Karl Reichle designed this four-story structure, built 1936–40, as a "functional neo-classical building." From 1940 to 1945 it housed part of Joseph Goebbels's organization. Goebbels's shuttled between Mauerstrasse and his offices on the Wilhelmplatz. After the war the Nazi insignias were removed from the 102-meter-long facade. During the Communist era the building was the media ministry, also called "the house of lies." On June 11, 1961, East German boss Walter Ulbricht gave a press conference here and solemnly announced that no one had any intention of building a Berlin Wall; two months later the wall appeared. The Mauerstrasse 53 section of the ministry building is called Kleisthaus because the dramatist Heinrich von Kleist (1777–1811) lived in a building on this spot. The Mohrenstrasse 49 side of the ministry building, with its three arched portals, is to accommodate the entrance of the Federal Labor Ministry.

Bahr, Christian. Licht Kunst gegen die Finsternis des Hauses. Arbeitsressort zieht in frühere NS-Zentrale. *Berliner Morgenpost.* June 18, 1998.
Schubert. Peter. Umzug ins "Haus der Lügen." Die Last der Altbauten: Vom schwierigen Umgang mit der NS-Architektur. *Berliner Morgenpost.* June 3, 1997.

Opera House (Deutsche Staatsoper) and Opernplatz (Bebelplatz)[25]

On May 10, 1933, in front of the opera house, Joseph Goebbels presided at the notorious book burning.

Georg Wenzeslas von Knobelsdorf built the opera house in neoclassical style, the first theater in Germany not part of a palace. In August 1843 the building burned to the ground. A year later Carl Ferdinand Langhans rebuilt it. In the 1920s it was modernized but burned down in 1941; it was rebuilt and destroyed in 1945. Under the first East German president, Wilhelm Pieck, the opera was rebuilt 1951–55 and inaugurated with a performance of Wagner's *Meistersinger.* In 1986 the old inscription "Fridericus Rex Apollini et Musis" was carved on the pediment. To the west of the opera house is Bebelplatz (formerly Opernplatz), where the books were burned.

In 1933 the Hitler regime drew up lists of scholars and writers unacceptable to the New Order. Among them were Albert Einstein, Sigmund Freud, Alfred Döblin, Erich Maria Remarque, Carl von Ossietzky, Kurt Tucholsky, Hugo von Hofmannsthal, Erich Kästner, and Carl Zuckmayer. These authors were deemed to have created works that were decadent, materialistic, representative of "moral decline" or "cultural Bolshevism."

On May 10, 1933, the books of unacceptable authors were burned. As Joseph Goebbels called out the names of ostracized writers, 20,000 volumes were heaved into a huge bonfire. University faculties and senates uttered nary a peep, and many attended. The poet Heinrich Heine, whose books were among those incinerated, had written, "Where books are burnt, in the end people are also burnt."

But if Dr. Goebbels didn't ostentatiously burn your books, you were insulted.

Humiliated and belittled at being denied this incendiary public recognition, playwright Bertolt Brecht (*The Threepenny Opera, Mother Courage*) wrote an angry poem, "Die Bücherverbrennung" (The Book Burning), demanding that the regime burn him, since it had not burned his writings.

There is a plaque at the book-burning site explaining what happened there. In the middle of Bebelplatz a 1995 memorial to the burned books, a glass window, looks down into a white chamber with empty bookcases. And every German schoolchild now reads Brecht, whose pacifism and antimilitarism are very much in vogue.

Bernhard, Marianne, Madeleine Cabor, Rainer Eisenschmid. *Baedeker's Berlin*. 3rd ed. Macmillan. New York 1994.

Brecht, Bertolt. *Ausgewählte Werke in sechs Bänden. Dritter Band*. Gedichte I. Suhrkamp Verlag. Frankfurt am Main 1997.

Kershaw, Ian. *Hitler. 1889–1936: Hubris*. Norton. New York 1998.

Terrance, Marc. *Concentration Camps. A Traveler's Guide to World War II Sites*. Universal Publishers 1999.

St. Hedwig's Cathedral (Opernplatz/Bebelplatz)

An irony of Goebbels's selection of Opernplatz for his book-burning extravaganza was undoubtedly not lost on the little propaganda minister. He incinerated the books a few meters from St. Hedwig's Cathedral, for two centuries a symbol of tolerance.

Frederick the Great and his architect, Georg Wenzeslas von Knobelsdorf, began building St. Hedwig's in 1747, the first Catholic church constructed in Berlin since the Reformation. The church is named for the patron saint of Silesia.

Unlike many rulers of his time, Frederick did not insist that his subjects adopt his religion. "All religions must be tolerated," he wrote, "because everyone must be spiritual in his own way."[26] In fact, Frederick himself was an atheist, contemptuous of all churches and religions. On one occasion, when the pious General Hans Joachim von Zieten arrived late at court after a long supper, Frederick asked, "Now Zieten, did you digest well the body of your redeemer?"

The king conceived the massive dome of St. Hedwig's, which he wanted to resemble the Pantheon in Rome. But he immediately had a falling out with his Catholic soldiers because he insisted that the Catholic community pay for St. Hedwig's.

In 1930 St. Hedwig's was designated a cathedral. During the Third Reich it became a little island of resistance. Bernhard Lichtenberg, the priest in charge, openly prayed for victims of the regime's persecution. The Nazis arrested Lichtenberg in 1941, and he died in 1943 while being transported to Dachau. Also in 1943, St. Hedwig's was destroyed during an air raid and was rebuilt 1952–1963.

Nayhauss, Dirk von. Adressen einst und jetzt. Beten für die Verfolgten. *Berliner Illustrierte Zeitung*. September 17, 2000.

Wiegrefe, Klaus. Staat von Blut und Eisen. *Der Spiegel* 4: 70–84, 2001.

Reichstag Building

A 1933 fire in this building decisively strengthened Hitler's grip on the government and opened the road to dictatorship.

In the Hall of Mirrors at Versailles, on January 18, 1871, Otto von Bismarck and the German princes proclaimed Wilhelm I to be German emperor. Berlin became an imperial capital, and the Reichstag, the imperial Parliament, needed a new home, after years of temporary housing in the Royal Porcelain Manufactory in Leipziger Strasse.

The architect Paul Wallot designed the massive, elegantly proportioned neo-Renaissance Reichstag building. The old emperor Wilhelm I laid the cornerstone in 1884. Construction was completed in 1894 under Wilhelm II, who hated the imperial Parliament and referred to the building as the "Reich monkey house." The cost, 30 million marks, came from French war reparations.

In 1916 the inscription "to the German people" (Dem deutschen Volke) was placed on the Reichstag pediment. The letters were cast from two French cannon captured during the wars of liberation, 1813–15, which Wilhelm II donated. Wilhelm wanted the inscription to read "to German Unity" but gave in because of the steadily worsening German position in World War I.

Troops were quartered in the Reichstag in 1919, when the government put down the bloody Spartacus revolt. At night 2,000 soldiers curled up in carpets and Gobelin tapestries. Three months later, after the soldiers had left, caretakers of the building described it as "louse-infested, filthy, and damaged." The repair bill came to 408,148.21 marks.

On the evening of February 27, 1933, a fire broke out in the Reichstag building. Reichstag president Hermann Göring, propaganda chief Joseph Goebbels, Vice Chancellor Franz von Papen, and Hitler raced to the scene. The Nazi leaders were certain that the fire was the signal for a Communist uprising, a "last attempt," said Goebbels, "through fire and terror to sow confusion, and in the general panic, to grasp power for themselves" (Kershaw, 1998)

The police immediately apprehended Marinus van der Lubbe, a former member of the Communist Party youth organization in Holland. Van der Lubbe confessed to the crime and stated that he alone had set fire to the building. But Hitler, in a near hysterical state, believed a Communist conspiracy was responsible. A frenzied Göring demanded mass arrests of Communists and socialists. The Prussian ministry of the interior, at Hitler's behest, enacted a decree,

"For the Protection of People and State" (also called the Reichstag Fire Decree). The decree suspended indefinitely such personal liberties guaranteed by the Weimar Constitution as freedom of speech, freedom of the press, and privacy of postal and telephone communications. Also, the reich government overrode the autonomy of the German states to restore order; the Nazis used this new power to persecute their political opponents.

The resulting violence and repression were quite popular. The average German had been yearning for another authoritarian leader since the abdication of Kaiser Wilhelm II in November 1918 and warmly welcomed the emergency decree and the dictatorship that followed. After the parliamentary elections of March 5, 1933, there was no significant opposition to Hitler left.

Hitler never rebuilt the Reichstag building, although, as he told Albert Speer, he liked the design and refused to raze the burnt-out hulk: "In the old [Reichstag] building, we can set up reading rooms and lounges for deputies. For all I care the chamber can be turned into a library. With its five hundred and eighty seats it's much too small for us. We'll build a new one right beside it. Provide a chamber for twelve hundred deputies."

After 1933 Hitler convened the Reichstag in the nearby Kroll Opera House. Antiaircraft guns were mounted on the Reichstag's corner towers in 1941. In 1943 the Charité Hospital moved its obstetric ward into the Reichstag. On birth certificates, officials duly recorded, "born in the Reichstag." Bombing and looting in 1945 reduced the remains of the Reichstag building to a blackened, graffiti-covered wreck.[27]

Reconstruction of the Reichstag was completed in 1970. The old dome, removed in 1957 because of the danger of collapse, has been replaced. But there is still considerable debate over the fate of the graffiti.

In 1945, using charred wood or blue

chalk, Soviet soldiers scribbled so many Cyrillic characters on the walls that they looked like a palimpsest. "Death to the Germans" was a favorite curse.

Delegates to the new Berlin parliament will be spared the sight of this particular imprecation, as well as Slavic obscenities. But Conservatives and the Greens want to keep scrawls like the following: "The Russian saber is stuck in the German sheath." Other lawmakers question the preservation of such deathless sentiments as "Nadia was here" (Bornhöft, 1999).

Bernhard, Marianne, Madeleine Cabor, Rainer Eisenschmid. *Baedeker's Berlin.* 3rd ed. Macmillan. New York 1994.
Bornhöft, Petra. Schweinkram mit blauer Kreide. *Der Spiegel* 26:46–47, 1999.
Chronik Berlin. *Chronik Verlag.* Munich. 3rd updated edition 1997.
Kershaw, Ian. *Hitler. 1889–1936: Hubris.* Norton. New York 1998.
Nayhauss, Dirk von. Adressen einst und jetzt. *Berliner Illustrierte Zeitung.* December 5, 1999.
Speer, Albert. *Inside the Third Reich.* Translated by Richard and Clara Winston. Avon Books. New York 1971.

Altes Museum Lustgarten (Museum Island, central Berlin)

Karl Friedrich Schinkel built Berlin's first public museum, 1824–30. The colonnade is a neoclassical masterpiece, as are the frescoes decorating the cupola. In 1935 the architect Konrad Dammeier leveled and paved Schinkel's exquisitely landscaped lustgarten, adjacent to the museum, to create a parade ground for the 1936 Olympic Games. After the war the East German Communist regime continued to use the parade ground and expanded it by leveling the Stadtschloss, the city palace of the kaisers. The Communists called the whole area Marx-Engels Platz.

Schauplatz Berlin. Vergangenheit, die nicht vergeht. Zum Umgang mit dem Bauerbe der NS-Zeit. *Neue Zürcher Zeitung.* March 28, 1998.

Lustgarten, National Work Day, 1934. Hitler departing after a speech to German youth.

Victory Column (Siegessäule)

This first monument to the founding of the German Empire in 1871 was one of the structures Hitler had transformed as part of his grandiose effort to convert Berlin into the new Reich capital, "Germania."

The royal architect Heinrich Strack designed the Victory Column, commissioned in 1865. On September 2, 1873, the third anniversary of the German victory over the French at Sedan, the Victory Column was dedicated with great pomp. Emperor Wilhelm I and his generals attended the military parade. The column now commemorated Chancellor Otto von Bismarck's three victorious wars, of 1864 against Denmark, 1866 against Austria, and 1870–71 against France. The column originally stood

Top: Victory Column, which Hitler moved and enlarged in 1938. The Victory Column originally stood on the Königsplatz, in front of the Reichstag building. *Bottom:* Statue of Otto von Bismarck. Sculptor Reinhold Begas portrayed Bismarck as a general of cavalry, who wears the helmet of a cuirassier. Kaiser Wilhelm II, who cashiered Bismarck in 1890, bestowed this rank on him. Wilhelm also conferred the title "Count of Lauenberg," on Bismarck, who contemptuously rejected the honorific, saying he would only use it if he wanted to travel incognito. Like the Victory Column, the Bismarck monument has many Soviet bullet gouges left after the battle for Berlin.

on the Königsplatz, in front of the Reichstag building, along with statues of Bismarck, Field Marshal Helmuth von Moltke, and war minister Albrecht von Roon (sculptor Haro Magnussen, 1904).

Incorporated in the shaft of the Victory Column are cannon barrels captured from the enemy. The shaft stands on a massive granite plinth with bronze reliefs of scenes from the three wars. Court artist Anton von Werner's mosaic, symbolizing the achievement of German unity in 1871, adorns the base of the column, surrounded by an open colonnade.

Crowning the column is sculptor Friedrich Drake's 40-ton, 8.32-meter, gilded brass rendering of Victoria ("Goldelse"), the winged goddess of victory. In her raised right hand she holds a laurel wreath, in her left an Iron Cross, and on her head she wears the Prussian eagle helmet. Drake's daughter Margarete was the model for Goldelse. Berliners joke that Goldelse is the

Top: Statue of Field Marshal Helmuth von Moltke (sculptor Joseph Uphues, 1904). The architect of Bismarck's military victories, Moltke was also a considerable linguist, but so taciturn that he was described as being "silent in seven languages." *Left:* Statue of war minister Albrecht von Roon (sculptor Haro Magnussen, 1904).

heaviest woman in the city and also the cheapest (one mark per visit).

In 1938 Hitler and Albert Speer had the Victory Column moved to the center of a traffic circle, the Grosser Stern, which was to demarcate the fulcrum of Berlin's new east-west axis. A tunnel was dug so that a visitor could reach the column without braving the fast-moving cars. Lavatories were built near the tunnel entrance. The base of the column was enlarged. To the three drums of the shaft, symbolizing the three wars, Hitler added, ominously, a fourth. To the 239 steps to reach the top were added another 39. The statues of Bismarck, Moltke, and Roon were placed nearby in the Tiergarten.

The Victory Column survived Allied bombing, though bullet gouges in the stone panels remain from the battle for Berlin. After the war the French wanted the Victory Column demolished, along with all other reminders of militarism and the Nazi era. But since the column stood in the British sector, it was not touched. In 1984 Charles Hernu, the socialist French defense minister, returned the two bronze reliefs from the base of the column, which the French had confiscated as war booty. The third relief, depicting the 1864 war against Denmark, surfaced later and was presented by French president François Mitterand at the ceremony marking the 750th anniversary of Berlin, August 1987. The men's lavatory is now popular with Berlin's gay community.

The Speer-Laternen (Speer's lanterns) in central Berlin are the only reminders of the planned great east-west axis. There are 1700 of the gigantic two armed streetlights from Theodor-Heuss-Platz to Kaiserdamm, Bismarckstrasse and Strasse des 17. Juni to Charlottenburger Tor. By the year 2001, the city had renovated all the Speer-Laternen along this three kilometer stretch with new long life, rustproof lights.

Speer installed his one-meter-tall lanterns in 1937, the same year Hitler made him inspector general of buildings for Berlin. The lights were first illuminated May 1, in honor of a meeting between Hitler and Benito Mussolini. After the war some people wanted the Speer-Laternen removed because of their unpleasant connotations. But the majority saw beauty in them, and they still glow today.

Alings, Reinhard. *Die Berliner Siegessäule.* Bezirksamt Tiergarten von Berlin-Gartenbauamt. 2nd ed. Berlin 1991.
Bernhard, Marianne, Madeleine Cabor, Rainer Eisenschmid. *Baedeker's Berlin.* 3rd ed. Macmillan. New York 1994.

Goldelse, the winged goddess of victory, atop the victory column. The nickname Goldelse probably comes from the novel (published 1867) of the same name by Eugenie Marlitt (1825–87), which Berliners were still reading in September 1873, when Drake's statue was unveiled.

Leser-Frage: Wann stand Bismarck vor dem Reichstag? *Berliner Morgenpost.* May 21, 1999.
Leser-Frage: Woher kommt der Name Goldelse? *Berliner Morgenpost.* April 10, 1999.
Neues Licht für alte Laternen. *Berliner Morgenpost.* January 21, 2000.
Opitz, Eckhardt, and Reinhard Scheiblich. *Auf Otto von Bismarcks Spuren.* Ellert & Richter Verlag. Hamburg 1998.

Brandenburg Gate

(S1 or S2 subway trains to Unter den Linden.) The architect Carl Gotthard Langhans built this sandstone structure in 1788–

91 for King Friedrich Wilhelm II.[28] Langhans modeled it after the Propylaeum of the Acropolis in Athens. He intended the Brandenburg Gate to be the terminal feature of the boulevard Unter den Linden. Six Doric columns form five passages, and more Doric columns adorn the two buildings, originally toll stations, at each side of the gate. The crowning feature is Gottfried Schadow's Quadriga, the four-horse chariot carrying Victoria, goddess of victory. The French dragged the Quadriga off to Paris after Napoleon's victories at the battles of Jena and Auerstadt in 1806. After the defeat of the French in the Wars of Liberation, General Gebhart von Blücher restored the Quadriga to its platform atop the gate on August 14, 1814.

The Brandenburg Gate has always been a military focal point for triumphant Prussian troops. On January 30, 1933, brown-shirted storm troops held a massive torchlight parade through the gate to celebrate Hitler's appointment as reich chancellor. The artist Max Liebermann, who watched from his house nearby, said, "It makes me feel sick." Another gala parade passed through the gate April 20, 1939, Hitler's fiftieth birthday.

The Quadriga was destroyed during World War II. The only remaining piece, the hollow head of one of the horses, is in Berlin's Märkisches Museum. In 1958 a new Quadriga was placed atop the gate.

Bernhard, Marianne, Madeleine Cabor, Rainer Eisenschmid. *Baedeker's Berlin*. 3rd ed. Macmillan. New York 1994.

Nazi storm troops marching through the Brandenburg Gate.

Unter den Linden. Neue Wache (New Guardhouse)

Karl Friedrich Schinkel built this small building 1816–18 on the site of an earlier guardhouse. The Neue Wache, of heavy brick with a Doric portico, resembles a Greek temple. In 1931 Reich president Paul von Hindenburg chose it as a memorial to

did not make his usual appearance. He was on a brief visit to the eastern front, the last time he ever left the Reich Chancellery. Hermann Göring, wearing a uniform with no medals, attended on Hitler's behalf. Members of all the front-line regiments paraded past, about 120 men of all ranks, most sporting the Knight's Cross. There were also official representatives of the party and the city but no spectators.

The missing crowds imparted an eerie feeling, and the destruction of the surrounding buildings added to the effect, as Lieutenant General Helmuth Reymann, military commander of Berlin, wrote (Read and Fisher, 1992):

> On the one side was the palace, completely gutted and severely bombed; on the other

the soldiers who perished in World War I. The architect Heinrich Tessenow redesigned the interior. In the main hall, faced with limestone slabs, was a massive block of black granite, the tomb of the unknown warrior, illuminated by a skylight, on which lay a wreath of gold and silver oak leaves.

In March 1945, at the last annual ceremony for Heroes' Remembrance Day at the tomb of the unknown warrior, Reichsmarschall Hermann Göring and Grand Admiral Karl Dönitz showed up, but Hitler

Top: Neue Wache, 1933. Nazi storm troops march in front. *Bottom:* Neue Wache, March 1935. Hitler greets World War I field marshal August von Mackensen (1849–1945) on Heroes' Remembrance Day. Hitler invited the popular Mackensen to many Nazi festivities, where the old soldier habitually wore his snugly fitting uniform of the Death's Head Hussars.

was the ruined cathedral. Opposite the war memorial stood the craggy shell of the Berlin Opera; it had been hit again the night before. Shortly before the beginning of the ceremony, Göring appeared in his big car, got out and looked at this picture of desolation, shaking his head. Then he and several other officers, including me, went up to the memorial, which, strangely enough, was almost completely undamaged. Göring laid a wreath, saluted, and then left without saying a word. The strangeness of the situation probably struck all of us who took part. We remembered the dead who had laid down their lives for a cause that was now on the point of collapse. I was shaken when I returned to my command post.

In November 1993 the Neue Wache became the main German memorial to the victims of war and dictatorship. The centerpiece is now an enlarged version of Käthe Kollwitz's sculpture, "Mother with dead son."

Bernhard, Marianne, Madeleine Cabor, Rainer Eisenschmid. *Baedeker's Berlin.* 3rd ed. Macmillan. New York 1994.
Read, Anthony, and David Fisher. *The Fall of Berlin.* Norton. New York 1992.

Unter den Linden. Cannon Monument (Kanonendenkmal)

This monument, which no longer exists, was built adjacent to the Neue Wache in 1820, a part of the planned *Via Triumphalis* following the wars of liberation from Napoleon. Originally the Cannon Monument was composed of two cannon, "Lazy Grete" and "Fat Bertha." In 1871 another cannon, "La Belle Josephine," taken from the French as booty after the Franco-Prussian War, was incorporated. In 1919, after the German defeat in World War I, La Belle Josephine went back to Paris. When Hitler overran France in June 1940, La Belle Josephine returned to the *Kanonendenkmal* but in 1945 went back to France. The victorious allies also removed Lazy Grete and Fat Bertha, as well as the fence that surrounded them. Their whereabouts are unknown.

Leser-Frage. Was wurde aus dem "Kanonendenkmal"? *Berliner Morgenpost.* December 15, 1998.

Kaiser Wilhelm Memorial Church (Gedächtniskirche). (Breitscheidplatz, Charlottenburg)

The architect Franz Schwechten built this neo–Romanesque church (1891–95) in honor of Kaiser Wilhelm I. In the interior are marble reliefs commemorating the victories in Bismarck's wars against Denmark, Austria, and France. An air attack destroyed the building on November 23, 1943. The ruins have been repaired several times, and the church is now a war memorial. Berliners call it "the broken tooth" and say it was the only structure in town whose appearance was improved by the bombing.

Bernhard, Marianne, Madeleine Cabor, Rainer Eisenschmid. *Baedeker's Berlin.* 3rd ed. Macmillan. New York 1994.

Alexanderplatz. Statue (die Berolina) Berolina

Berolina was a copper figure of a stately lady, almost eight meters tall, sculpted by Emil Hundrieser in 1895. Originally she stood on a pedestal in Alexanderplatz and was regarded as a sort of Berlin trademark. She was moved in 1927 during the building of the U-Bahn and repositioned in 1933. But like countless other Germans, Berolina did not survive Hitler. In 1944 the Nazis melted her down for war material. Many Berliners still remember her fondly.

Leser-Frage: Was wurde aus der Berolina? *Berliner Morgenpost.* November 18, 1998.

Egyptian Museum

(Schlossstrasse 70, U7 train to Richard Wagner Platz or U1 train to Sophie-Charlotte Platz). Dr. James Simon (1851–1932), a Jewish Berlin merchant, financed a Deutsche Orient-Gesellschaft expedition to Amarna, where in December 1912 Ludwig Borchardt unearthed the limestone bust of Queen Nefertiti (ca. 1350 B.C.), wife of the Egyptian pharaoh Akhnaton (Amenhotep IV). Simon initially kept the bust in his home and then lent it to the Königliche Preussische Kunstsammlung in 1913.[29] On July 11, 1920, he donated Nefertiti to the Prussian State.

In 1933 the Egyptian government demanded the return of the Nefertiti bust, which was on display in the Kaiser Friedrich Museum. Hermann Göring suggested to Egyptian King Fuᶜad I that the German government might not object. But Hitler had other plans.

Through the ambassador to Egypt, Eberhard von Stohrer, Hitler informed the Egyptian government that he was an ardent fan of Nefertiti (Ritzmann, 1997): "I know this famous bust. I have viewed it and marveled at it many times. Nefertiti continually delights me. The bust is a unique masterpiece, an ornament, a true treasure…! Do you know what I'm going to do one day? I'm going to build a new Egyptian museum in Berlin. I dream of it. Inside I will build a chamber, crowned by a large dome. In the middle, this wonder, Nefertiti, will be enthroned. I will never relinquish the head of the Queen." In the plans for the museum there was to be an even larger hall of honor with a bust of Hitler.

Hitler's message to Egypt alarmed Göring, who spoke of an "exceptionally precarious situation." But Nefertiti has remained in Berlin, despite many subsequent Egyptian demands. In solitary grandeur she is enshrined in her own room, illuminated by a spotlight. James Simon's descendants who escaped the Holocaust live in Beverly Hills, California.

Höhling, Cornelia. Mit der Schaufel den Weltwundern auf der Spur. Seit 100 Jahren ermöglicht die Deutsche Orient-Gesellschaft Grabungen in Ruinenfeldern. *Berliner Morgenpost.* January 24, 1998.
Ritzmann, Kai. Entscheidung vor 50 Jahren: Nofretete is Berlinerin. Als die Amerikaner den Rückgabestreit um die ägyptische Skulptur beendeten. *Berliner Morgenpost.* January 29, 1997.
Wilderotter, Hans, and Klaus D. Pohl. Der Letzte Kaiser. Wilhelm II. im Exil. Bertelsmann Lexikon Verlag/Deutsches Historisches Museum. Berlin 1991.

112 Strasse des 17. Juni. Ernst Reuter Haus. (Charlottenburg)

The cornerstone for this building was laid in 1938. Originally the building was to be "representative of new government buildings." Deutscher Städtetag, the self-chosen representatives of communities in Germany, founded 1905, which became "Deutscher Gemeindetag," was to be housed here. But the first tenant to move into the half-finished building, in 1942, was Inspector General of Buildings Albert Speer. The building was lightly damaged during the war, the middle section having never been finished. When completed in 1956, the building was named Ernst Reuter Haus, after a deceased mayor of Berlin.

Loos, Andreas. Umzug mit 60 Jahren Verspätung. *Berliner Morgenpost.* August 10, 1999.

Saatwinkler Damm (Charlottenburg). "Speerplatte" (razed)

Hitler named Albert Speer inspector general of buildings in Berlin, responsible for constructing the gigantic structures that would transform the city into "Germania," the new Reich capital. To accomplish this task, Speer had to organize a system for storage and transport of vast quantities of building materials and formed the *Transportstandarte Speer* to cart these materials. The hundred heavy trucks of the *Transportstandarte* were parked on a nine-hectare concrete slab, the "Speerplatte," built in 1942. The slab was razed in 1992.

Leser-Frage: Woher kommt der Name "Speerplatte"? *Berliner Morgenpost.* August 6, 1999.

Potsdamerstrasse/corner Pallasstrasse (Schöneberg). Sportpalast (razed)

The *Sportpalast* was the site of two historic speeches. In 1938 Hitler spoke on the Czech crisis. In 1943 the second and most famous speech was Joseph Goebbels's call for total war.

On September 26, 1938, Hitler had given the Czechs an ultimatum: by 2 P.M.

Hitler addresses a crowd in the *Sportpalast.* Directly behind him sits Joseph Goebbels (Ullstein Bilderdienst).

September 28 they had to accept German occupation of the Sudetenland (see Führerbau). The evening of the ultimatum, Hitler harangued a tense audience of 15,000 in the *Sportpalast,* among them diplomats and journalists.

The American journalist William Shirer, sitting in the balcony directly above the German chancellor, thought Hitler "in the worst state of excitement I've ever seen him in" (Kershaw, 2000). But Hitler's speech was "a psychological masterpiece" according to Goebbels. Indeed, Hitler was in his element as he heaped scorn on the Czechoslovakian state and its president, Eduard Beneš (whom Winston Churchill called "Beans").

Beneš was determined, Hitler shouted, slowly to exterminate Germany. Referring to the memorandum he had presented to British prime minister Neville Chamberlain, and the offer he had made to the Czechs, Hitler indicated that his tolerance of Beneš was now at an end. Cynically, Hitler praised Chamberlain for his peace efforts. He assured Chamberlain that he had no further territorial demands in Europe once the Sudeten problem was solved. He also guaranteed that he had no further interest in the Czech state. "We don't want any Czechs at all," he declared. The decision for peace rested with Beneš: "He will either accept this offer and finally give freedom to the Germans, or we will take this freedom ourselves!" Hitler promised to lead a united people as first soldier. "We are determined. Herr Beneš may now choose," Hitler concluded. The mob in the hall, which had interrupted almost every sentence with fanatical applause, shouted, cheered, and chanted: "Führer, command, we will follow!"

Hitler had worked himself into an almost orgasmic climax by the end of his speech. Goebbels, closing the meeting, pledged the loyalty of the German people to their Führer and declared, "a November 1918 will never be repeated." Hitler, according to Shirer, "looked up to him, a wild, eager expression in his eyes ... leaped to his feet and with a fanatical fire in his eyes ... brought his right hand, after a grand sweep, pounding down on the table and yelled.... 'Ja.' Then he slumped into his chair exhausted" (Kershaw, 2000).

But five years later, when Goebbels delivered his total war speech, the loyalty of the German people was fraying. Goebbels arrived at the Sportpalast at noon, February 18, 1943, in his bulletproof Mercedes, more tense than usual. He knew that he had to make the patently impossible sound possible.

The German Sixth Army had just suffered a catastrophic defeat at Stalingrad. For the first time Germans were losing faith in their Führer en masse.

All 15,000 seats in the Sportpalast were filled, mainly with party members and functionaries. As Goebbels mounted the podium, his dark eyes glowed with the fanaticism of the born demagogue.

Goebbels called the Stalingrad debacle the "great alarm call of destiny" and a symbol of the heroic struggle against the "storm from the Steppes," that "horrific historic danger" that relegated "all former dangers facing the West to the shadows." Behind the onrushing Soviet divisions, Goebbels saw "the Jewish liquidation commandos," whom international Jewry were using to plunge the world into chaos.

Joseph Goebbels harangues the party faithful in the *Sportpalast*, February 18, 1943 (Ullstein Bilderdienst).

Again and again during this diatribe, thunderous applause broke out. But Goebbels was just getting warmed up.

Terror must be fought with terror, Goebbels cried. There could be no more bourgeois prudishness.

Goebbels asked his now hysterical audience whether they believed in their Führer and the total victory of German arms. An ear-splitting Ja! was the reply.

"Do you want total war? Do you want it, if necessary, more total and more radical than we could even imagine today?" he screamed, whereupon pandemonium broke out in the Sportpalast.

"Now, Volk," Goebbels screeched, "arise and storm; go to it!"

The Sportpalast had turned into a raving madhouse, and German radio transmitted the mass hysteria throughout the country. Goebbels rightly ranked the speech as the rhetorical masterpiece of his life. Cynical as always, he wrote in his diary, "This hour of idiocy! If I had said to the people, jump out the fourth floor of *Columbushaus*, they would have done that too" (Fetscher, 1998).

Hitler's Czech crisis speech and Goebbels's total war speech were undoubtedly the most famous events in the history of the *Sportpalast*, but others were noteworthy: the boxing matches of Max Schmeling, as well as the concerts of Herbert von Karajan, rock group Deep Purple, and sex-machine James Brown. Indeed, the Sportpalast had been a venue for political and entertainment spectacles from the day it was built.

Construction of the *Sportpalast* began November 17, 1910, and was completed thirteen months later. The first show was an ice-skating revue. During the Weimar Republic all of the political parties, including the Nazis, held rallies in the *Sportpalast*.

On January 30, 1944, Allied bombs blasted and burned the Sportpalast to its foundations. In the early 1950s it was re-built, albeit less elaborately. But it could not withstand the competition of the *Deutschlandhalle*, and in 1973 it was razed. The sarcastically nicknamed *Sozialpalast*, a concrete block with 514 apartments and 2,000 tenants, replaced the *Sportpalast*. Once hailed as the most beautiful housing project in Berlin, the Sozialpalast acquired a dicey reputation as building defects, neglect, vandalism, and criminality reduced it to an eyesore.

Fetscher, Irving. *Joseph Goebbels im Berliner Sportpalast 1943*. Europäische Verlagsanstalt. Hamburg 1998.

Kershaw, Ian. *Hitler. 1936–1945: Nemesis*. Norton. New York 2000.

Schönrock, Dirk. "Diese Stunde der Idiotie." Augenzeugenbericht und Analyse: Irving Fetschers Buch "Joseph Goebbels im Berliner Sportpalast 1943." *Berliner Morgenpost*. May 10, 1998.

von Nayhauss, Dirk. Brot und Spiele — zwischen Sport und Propaganda. *Berliner Morgenpost*. September 19, 1999.

"Wollt Ihr den totalen Krieg?" *Berliner Morgenpost*. December 31, 1998.

Zum Schluss noch eine Party: Der Sportpalast hat ausgedient. *Berliner Morgenpost*. August 26, 1998.

Berlin Messegelände, Jafféstrasse (Charlottenburg). Deutschlandhalle

Hitler himself was the focal point of a mammoth rally inaugurating the Deutschlandhalle, November 29, 1935. Before 20,000 fanatic followers, he shouted that the German people would always stand by him.

The huge Deutschlandhalle had been completed in record time, nine months, at a cost of 3.9 million reichsmarks. The entire installation covered 60,000 square meters. The main interior arena had a surface area of 35,000 square meters and was 25 meters high, 160 meters wide, and 120 meters deep. The cantilevered roof, supported by a steel skeleton, allowed every spectator an unim-

peded view in all directions. In 1938 Hanna Reitsch made headlines by flying a helicopter within the auditorium.

British firebombs destroyed the Deutschlandhalle in 1943. Rebuilding began in November 1956, and the hall was reopened October 19, 1957. The last exhibition in the Deutschlandhalle took place in 1998. The building might be made into an ice hockey arena, or it could be razed.

Umbau zur Eisarena. *Berliner Morgenpost.* September 17, 2000.
Wehmut am Ende einer Berlin Tradition. Nach 62 Jahren die letzte Vorstellung in der Deutschlandhalle. *Neue Zürcher Zeitung.* January 3, 1998.

Top: **Deutschlandhalle, opening of the Winter Relief Agency drive, October 6, 1936. This organization began during the crisis winter 1931–32 to provide unemployed, needy people with money, groceries, meals, clothing, and fuel (Ullstein Bilderdienst).** *Bottom:* **Deutschlandhalle, Hitler addresses the Winter Relief Agency opening, October 6, 1936 (Ullstein Bilderdienst).**

Fehrbelliner Platz

(U7 or U2 trains) This plaza in West Berlin (Wilmersdorf) was a Nazi administration center during the 1930s, complete with Nazi-era monumental-style buildings. Some of these buildings are still government offices.

In 1936 the Nazis renamed one of the nearby streets, Dunckerstrasse, as Seebergsteig, after an anti–Semitic Protestant theologian, Reinhold Seeberg (1859–1936).

Fehrbelliner Platz, Nazi administration buildings, October 1936. These buildings still house government offices (Ullstein Bilderdienst).

"Jewry is the deadly enemy of every true culture," opined Seeberg.

On November 7, 2000, a plaque in memory of the actor Joachim Gottschalk (1904–41) was placed on the sidewalk in front of the house at Seebergsteig 2. The current owner would not allow the plaque to be directly attached to the house.

Gottschalk, "the German Clark Gable," was one of the most popular German film stars of the 1930s. But the Nazis pestered Gottschalk to divorce his Jewish wife, the actress Meta Wolff. Gottschalk refused. Finally, Joseph Goebbels prevented Gottschalk from acting in films, after having banned Meta Wolff in 1933.

In 1941 the Nazis slated Meta Wolff and her son, Michael, for deportation to Theresienstadt. Gottschalk begged to be deported with his wife and child, to no avail.

Gottschalk was scheduled to appear live in a drama entitled Karl und Anna on the new medium, television. But he did not report for the performance. He had committed suicide with his wife and son in his home the night before, November 6, 1941.

After turning on the gas, all three took overdoses of sleeping pills. In 1999 the city of Berlin declared the Gottschalk plot in Stahnsdorf cemetery an honored grave. Prominent Gestapo officials are also interred in Stahnsdorf.

Brühl, Carolin. Gedenktafel für Joachim Gottschalk. *Berliner Morgenpost.* November 7, 2000.
DPA. Ehrengrab für Joachim Gottschalk. *Berliner Morgenpost.* August 6, 1999.
Karwelat, Jürgen. Antisemit, Kriegshetzer. TAZ. October 7, 1996.
Klein, Honza. Unwürdiger Namenstreit. *Berliner Morgenpost.* March 11, 1998.
Schauplatz Berlin. Vergangenheit, die nicht vergeht. Zum Umgang mit dem Bauerbe der NS-Zeit. *Neue Zürcher Zeitung.* March 28, 1998.

Krausenhof (between Krausenstrasse and Schützstrasse)

This building stands in the traditional newspaper quarter of Berlin. With the postwar Axel Springer Verlag skyscraper and the

Mosse House, designed in 1923 by the architect Erich Mendelsohn, the Krausenhof forms a triangle.

The architect Hermann Dernberg designed the Krausenhof, which was built in 1911. In 1933 Scherl Verlag, the giant publisher, owned the Krausenhof. German nationalist media baron Alfred Hugenberg (1865–1951) controlled Scherl, as well as Universum Film AG (Ufa). The Ufa management offices were in the Krausenhof.

In 1937 the Nazis nationalized Ufa and other German film studios. Until 1945 the Krausenhof, situated near Joseph Goebbels's propaganda ministry on Wilhelmplatz, was the propaganda center of Hitler's Third Reich.

There is little to see today in the interior of the Krausenhof because in 1952 the East Germans remodeled it and installed their agricultural academy.

Schubert, Peter. Umzug in ein Haus voll deutscher Geschichte(n). Denkmalschützer jetzt im "Krausenhof." *Berliner Morgenpost.* April 30, 1998.

Urania 17. Kleistsaal. Lecture hall center

Joseph Goebbels used these rooms for his Reich Film Chamber. After the war the building became the Amerikahaus. It has now reverted to its former function, a movie theater and lecture center.

Leser-Frage: Wo befindet sich der Kleistsaal? *Berliner Morgenpost.* April 4, 2000.

Puchanstrasse 12. Köpenick

Memorial to Köpenick blood week (Gedenkstätte Köpenicker Blutwoche). A jail stood on this site in 1933. On the night of June 21, in this building, Köpenick SA Brownshirts were ordered to round up opponents of Hitler's regime. Until June 27 a Nazi militia, "Sturmbann 15," assisted by parts of the notorious "Maikowski-Sturmes," arrested hundreds of people in the Köpenick district of Berlin. Among the captives were social democrats, communists, unionists, Jews, Christians, and members of the Deutschnationale Volkspartei. The storm troops tortured and mutilated their victims. The former jail is now a memorial.

Spar, Jan. Gedenken an die Opfer der Köpenicker Blutwoche. *Berliner Morgenpost.* June 21, 1999.

Stauffenbergstrasse 13–14. Bendlerblock

(Formerly Bendlerstrasse, U1 train to Kurfürstenstrasse) Built 1911–14 and named after the master mason Johann Christoph Bendler, the Bendlerblock was one of the last classical buildings constructed in imperial Germany and was part of the Kriegsmarine headquarters (see Reichpietschufer 74–76, below). During the Third Reich, this building housed the supreme headquarters of the German Army. Five officers were shot here for their role in the July 20, 1944, attempt on Hitler's life.

Army officers had already tried and failed to kill the dictator on six occasions, because of Hitler's last-minute changes of plans. Now a bigger group was determined to finish him off once and for all and to arrest the leading figures of his government.

The head of the conspiracy, 37-year-old Count Claus Schenk von Stauffenberg, had been maimed in the African campaign. Having lost an eye, one hand, and part of the other, he had been reassigned to Berlin. Initially he was chief of staff to General Friedrich Olbricht, commander of the General Army Office. Then Stauffenberg became chief of staff to General Friedrich Fromm, head of the replacement army. Stauffenberg's office was in the army's Bendlerstrasse headquarters.

Obverse view

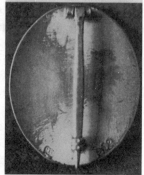

Reverse view

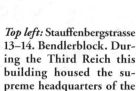

Top left: Stauffenbergstrasse 13–14. Bendlerblock. During the Third Reich this building housed the supreme headquarters of the German Army. Five officers were shot here for their role in the July 20, 1944, attempt on Hitler's life. *Middle left:* Bendlerblock courtyard. On the evening of July 20, 1944, after Joseph Goebbels had reestablished control in Berlin, Colonel Claus von Stauffenberg, General Ludwig Beck, General Friedrich Olbricht, Colonel Albrecht von Quirheim, and First Lieutenant Werner von Haeften were shot in the Bendlerblock courtyard. Hundreds of others were subsequently executed. The courtyard was made a memorial in 1953. *Top right:* July 20, 1944, wound badge. Stauffenberg's bomb wounded Vice Admiral Jesko von Puttkamer (bottom right photo), Hitler's adjutant to the Kriegsmarine. Hitler awarded this silver badge to Puttkamer and others injured in the attack. (Courtesy Charles E. Snyder) *Bottom left:* Bendlerblock memorial. At the center is Richard Scheibe's life-size statue of a naked man with arms manacled.

Stauffenberg and his co-conspirators had been strong supporters of Hitler initially. But they saw that a catastrophe was approaching, unless there was negotiation with the West. Hitler would never countenance negotiation, and the democracies were unlikely to want to talk unless Hitler was dead. After the unsuccessful assassination attempts by Major General Henning von Tresckow and the lawyer Fabian von Schlabrendorff, Stauffenberg determined to kill Hitler himself.

Initially, he planned to carry a bomb into a situation report at Rastenburg (Kętrzyn), Hitler's military headquarters in the East Prussian marshes. But the meeting was called off at the last minute.

Stauffenberg now turned to General Olbricht, and the two men hatched a more extensive plan. After Hitler was blown to smithereens, General Fromm's replacement army would take over Berlin and other important sites to intercept the SS. As part of an existing plot called "Valkyrie," Field Marshal Erwin Rommel and General Karl Heinrich von Stülpnagel would take control of the occupied territories. Field Marshal Erwin von Witzleben and General Ludwig Beck, who had been opposed to Hitler since the invasion of Czechoslovakia, were titular heads of the conspiracy. Carl Goerdeler, former mayor of Leipzig, would form an interim government with civilian and military members.

Stauffenberg planned to attend Hitler's situation report and carry a time bomb with which to kill Hitler, Göring, and Himmler. He would then call Olbricht in Berlin so that Valkyrie could be activated. Stauffenberg would fly back to Berlin and take command.

Four times Stauffenberg tried but failed. Twice at the Berghof, Hitler's Berchtesgaden retreat, he aborted his attempt because either Göring or Himmler was not in attendance.

On July 14, 1944, Hitler flew back to Rastenburg (Kętrzyn). Stauffenberg followed a day later with a bomb in his briefcase. As he telephoned his confederates in Bendlerstrasse to say he was about to kill Hitler, the dictator left the conference.

The situation became urgent when the plotters found out that the Gestapo was preparing to arrest Goerdeler, who went into hiding. For Stauffenberg, it was now or never. Abandoning his idea of killing three birds with one bomb, he decided to settle for Hitler alone. On July 20 he arrived at Rastenburg (Kętrzyn), where a situation conference was scheduled for noon. The bomb was again in his briefcase.

John von Freyend, Field Marshal Wilhelm Keitel's adjutant, graciously lent his room to Stauffenberg so that he might freshen up. Freyend also insisted on carrying Stauffenberg's briefcase into the conference, which had already begun; he stashed the briefcase under the map table, across from Hitler. Hitler greeted Stauffenberg, who pushed the briefcase with his foot to within six feet of the dictator.

The bomb was set to explode in five minutes. Stauffenberg made an excuse to leave the room. When he was out of range, a huge explosion convinced him that Hitler was no more. Stauffenberg was able to get past the guards and immediately flew back to Berlin.

In fact, Hitler had survived the blast. General Helmuth Stieff, a member of the conspiracy, was not aware that Stauffenberg had decided to strike. Stieff tried to lean across the table to look at the map, found the briefcase in his way, and moved it behind a heavy table support. By doing so Stieff had put a shield between the bomb and the twenty-four people at the conference. Many suffered burns and concussions but there were only two deaths, Colonel Heinz Brandt and General Rudolf Schmundt. Hitler sustained a ruptured eardrum and burned trousers.[30]

When news of the bomb attack reached

Berlin, Ernst Otto Remer, the Wehrmacht officer in charge of a Berlin guard battalion, was ordered to arrest Joseph Goebbels, the most senior Nazi official in Berlin that day. Believing Hitler was dead, Remer took 20 men with him and, brandishing a pistol, entered Goebbels's office to collar the propaganda boss. But Goebbels told Remer that he had just spoken to Hitler by phone. Goebbels made another call to Hitler's headquarters and handed Remer the receiver. Hitler asked Remer if he recognized his voice, instantly promoted him to colonel, and ordered him to crush the rebellion. Remer jumped to attention and did what he was told, leading an assault on the rebel officers.[31]

On the evening of July 20, after Goebbels had reestablished control in Berlin, five of the plotters were shot in the Bendlerblock courtyard: Stauffenberg, Beck, Olbricht, Colonel Albrecht von Quirheim, and First Lieutenant Werner von Haeften. Hundreds of others were subsequently executed.

The courtyard was made a memorial in 1953. At the center is Richard Scheibe's life-size statue of a naked man with arms manacled. When Berlin was a divided city, the Bendlerblock housed social welfare offices. The government has invested 107 million marks in the building to convert it to offices for the army and the defense ministry.

Bahr, Christian. Keine Scheu vor der Geschichte. Verteidigungsministerium folgt auf Reichswehr und Wehrmacht. *Berliner Morgenpost.* June 20, 1998.

Bernhard, Marianne, Madeleine Cabor, Rainer Eisenschmid. *Baedeker's Berlin.* 3rd ed. Macmillan. New York 1994.

Holden, Constance. Teeth of Evidence. *Science* 286:1473, 1999.

Sandvoss, Hans-Rainer. *Stätten des Widerstandes in Berlin 1933–1945.* Gedenkstätte Deutscher Widerstand. Berlin (undated).

Schubert, Peter. Baustart im künftigen Zweisitz von Minister Rühe. Bendlerblock wird jetzt saniert. *Berliner Morgenpost.* December 2, 1997.

Sereny, Gitta. *Albert Speer: His Battle with Truth.* Alfred A. Knopf. New York 1995.

Traynor, Ian. Hitler's saviour dies unrepentant. *The Guardian.* Manchester. October 7, 1997, p. 1.

Reichpietschufer 74–76

Former Kriegsmarine (navy) headquarters. The architects Heinrich Reinhardt and Georg Süssenguth designed this building, with its limestone Wilhelmine facade, which was built 1911–14 for the Reichsmarineamt. The column-lined sun court, adjacent to the entrance portal, is a striking feature. Grand Admiral Alfred von Tirpitz (1849–1930), navy chief during World War I, was the first tenant. During the Weimar Republic the *Reichswehrministerium* (defense ministry) moved in. The Nazis expanded the building around the corner into Bendlerstrasse (now Stauffenbergstrasse) by building the Bendlerblock, which became the name of the entire complex.

Many members of the B-Dienst, the *Kriegsmarine* code breakers, worked in this building. In 1935 Wilhelm Tranow, who had cracked British Royal Navy messages in World War I, solved the Royal Navy's most widely used code, the five digit Naval Code. In June 1941 the British introduced Naval Cipher No. 3, a more complex code, which Tranow solved in 1942. Using Tranow's B Dienst intercepts, Grand Admiral Karl Dönitz's U-boats decimated Allied convoys until June 1943, when the British replaced Naval Cipher No. 3. Thereafter, the B Dienst was unable to read most Allied radio messages. At the same time, British and American code breakers solved the German naval enigma, which was more complex than the Wehrmacht and Luftwaffe codes. This solution helped the Allies to crush the U-boat fleet and win the battle of the Atlantic.

In 1998 four massive wooden doors from the *Kriegsmarine* building, which had been stored for decades in the Spandau Citadel, were restored to their original places. Each door is three meters high, one and a half meters wide, and weighs 400 kilograms. Carved into the door panels are maritime motifs: buoys, anchors, and a diver's helmet. "Exactly when the doors arrived in the Spandau Fortress is unclear," Spandau cultural counselor Gerhard Hanke told *Berliner Morgenpost* reporter Michael Uhde. "One presumes that during the confusion of the last days of World War II, the doors were brought to Spandau for safety."

Reichpietschufer, on the northern border of the Landwehr canal in the Tiergarten, was named Grabenstrasse, 1831–67, then Königin-Augusta Strasse, 1867–33. From 1933–47 it was called Tirpitzufer. Max Reichpietsch (1894–1917) organized the 1917 sailors' revolt against the kaiser's fleet and was sentenced to death with another revolutionary, Albin Köbis, after the navy had put down the rebellion.

Bahr, Christian. Keine Scheu vor der Geschichte. Verteidigungsministerium folgt auf Reichswehr und Wehrmacht. *Berliner Morgenpost*. June 20, 1998.

Kahn, David. *Seizing the Enigma. The Race to Break the German U-Boat Codes.* Houghton Mifflin. Boston 1991.

Leser-Frage: Woher kommt der Name für das Reichpietschufer? *Berliner Morgenpost*. March 22, 1999.

Uhde, Michael. Historische Türen kommen zurück in den Bendlerblock. *Berliner Morgenpost*. July 6, 1998.

Plötzensee Prison

(Hüttig-Pfad, Buses 105, 123, 126) In a brick warehouse on the prison grounds 2,500 people were killed for thear opposition to Hitler between 1933 and 1945. Among the victims were men and women, Germans, Czechs, Poles, French, Austrians, Dutch, and Belgians. The execution chamber, now a memorial, is in northwest Berlin, on the border of the districts Charlottenburg and Wedding. Plötzensee is close to Brandenburg Prison, which was the largest penitentiary in northern Germany. In Hitler's time a high wall surrounded Plötzensee.

The executioner plied his murderous task with diabolic diligence. For example, on the night of September 7–8, 1943, between 7:30 P.M. and 8:30 A.M., 186 persons were dispatched, hanged in groups of eight. As the reich justice minister, Dr. Otto Thierack,[32] wrote in his official account (Zipfel, Aleff, Schennthal, Göbbel, 1972):

"Report of executions at Plötzensee (8 September 1943, 1 P.M.): 186 condemned were executed. 117 are still imprisoned. More sentences will be carried out today after 6 P.M. Another 17 executions are to be done. The State Secretary's report on these will be forthcoming." The judicial process for some of the victims of these mass hangings had not even been completed. No matter. In the next two days there were more hurried executions. Afterward, 300 corpses were heaped up to be used as anatomical specimens for medical students. But

Plötzensee Prison. In this brick warehouse on the prison grounds 2,500 people were killed for their opposition to Hitler between 1933 and 1945.

according to the testimony at Nuremberg of the prison priest, Harald Poelchau, it was impossible to transport this large number of bodies to the medical school anatomy department quickly enough. And by government decree, the bodies could not be turned over to the families.

The condemned were sent to the so-called death house, not very far from the courtroom. After they had been notified of their fate, they were held manacled on the first floor, in little, cold, poorly illuminated cells, until they went to the death chamber. Just before execution, the victims' hands were chained behind their backs, and the women's hair was shaved. The condemned wore wooden clogs. For each execution, guards received a special ration of eight cigarettes.

The report of a former prisoner, Victor von Gostomski, describes the cynicism of prison officials. One guard forced sick prisoners to crouch on the cold stone floor, and refused entreaties for help, saying, "Don't worry, your noodle will soon be hacked off!"

The execution chamber was a low brick building. In the back of the chamber, on the right, stood the guillotine, which was employed before Hitler came to power. On the left wall of the chamber was a washbasin.

As of March 29, 1933, hanging was also used, first sparingly, but soon more frequently. One witness described a typical execution (Zipfel, Aleff, Schennthal, Göbbel, 1972):

Air attacks severely damaged the building, but it was hastily rebuilt. The chamber was four meters wide by eight meters long. A black curtain divided the room in two. Only two narrow windows admitted daylight. Between the windows were eight hooks suspended from the ceiling, from which the condemned were to be hanged.... The first victim was former General..., led through the curtain by two hangmen. The state's attorney read the death sentence: "Condemned, the people's court has sentenced you to hang. Executioner, carry out your task."

The executioners hustled the condemned man, head held high, to the back of the room. There he had to turn sharply, and the noose was placed around his neck. The hangmen raised him up while attaching a loop in the rope to a hook. Then the victim fell heavily, and the noose squeezed his neck tightly. It looked to me as though he died very quickly.

After the sentence had been carried out, a narrow black curtain was pulled in front of the suspended corpse, so that the next victim would not see it. Quickly General ... was brought in. He knew he was taking his final walk. After each hanging, another curtain was used, so that the next victim could not see the previous ones. The hangings proceeded rapidly, and the condemned went to their deaths in a manly fashion, without a word of complaint.

On the right side of the execution chamber stood a table. Seated around it were witnesses, the official responsible for carrying out the executions, and other prison officials. In some cases attorneys for the condemned received an invitation card for the execution. The card helpfully suggested the wearing of a dark suit.

Married couples were executed, 14 in 1943 and 15 in 1944. The plea of husband and wife to be allowed to see each other one last time was routinely denied.

Some of the most gruesome executions were of men who had plotted but failed to murder Hitler on July 20, 1944. Hitler ordered that they be hung with piano wire so that they would slowly choke to death, and that all the hangings be filmed. After the first one the cameraman refused to stay for any others.

An SS officer invited Albert Speer, as Hitler's armaments minister, to a showing of the film. Speer declined the invitation. "The very thought made me sick," he told journalist Gitta Sereny three decades later.

There is some question whether Hitler ever watched this film. Hitler biographer John Toland quoted (from a 1971 *Playboy*

Execution chamber, Plötzensee Prison. The hooks used for the hangings are still in place.

interview) Speer's saying that "Hitler and his guests attended a screening" and that "Hitler loved the film and had it shown over and over again: it became one of his favorite entertainments."

"I didn't say that," Speer told Sereny. "As far as I knew Hitler never saw the film, and I have always said so. It was not his nature to want to see a thing like that. I doubt, too, that he looked at the photographs any more than I did." He added mildly, "I think a number of misquotes were probably due to linguistic misunderstandings, no doubt my fault; my English was not that good." He shrugged. "It happens often."

During the closing days of the war the executioner was still hard at work. On April 25, 1945, Soviet troops captured Plötzensee. SS men on this day had already shot many prisoners.

In 1952 the Berlin Senate erected a public monument to the victims of the Hitler dictatorship on the site. The execution chamber has been preserved, hooks and all. The guillotine disappeared at the end of the war. The former penitentiary now houses a youth reformatory.

Sereny, Gitta. *Albert Speer: His Battle with Truth.* Alfred A. Knopf. New York 1995.

Zentner, Christian, and Friedemann Bedürftig, eds. *The Encyclopedia of the Third Reich.* English translation edited by Amy Hackett. Macmillan. New York 1991.

Zipfel, Friedrich, Eberhard Aleff, Hans Ludwig Schoenthal, Wolfgang Göbbel. *Gedenkstätte Plötzensee.* Gedenkstätte Deutscher Widerstand Berlin. 1972.

Theodor Heuss Platz

Before 1933 this Berlin square was called Reichkanzlerplatz. The composer Richard Strauss lived here 1913–17, Joseph Goebbels until 1933. In the same year, the square was renamed Adolf Hitler Platz. Hitler planned to build a giant Mussolini monument for the square, which the Führer had personally sketched. Two ten-meter-tall, half-cross-shaped arcades would border the square. In the center a naked hero brandishing a sword would crown a 45-meter column. Work on the monument had hardly begun in 1940 when the war brought it to a stop. The square is now named after Theodor Heuss (1884–1963), first president of the Federal Republic of Germany.

Nayhauss, Dirk von. Adressen einst und jetzt. Ein nackter Held für Mussolini. *Berliner Illustrierte Zeitung*. February 13, 2000.

Tempelhof Airport

The discussion of the building project took place in the office of Major Rudolf Böttger, director of Tempelhof Airport. Present were representatives from the military, a district leader, and, of course, the man who commissioned the project, Adolf Hitler. The date was October 29, 1934.

Hitler had decided that Tempelhof was to be a Nazi monument, and he described his vision for the airport. After fifty minutes the other men endorsed Hitler's decision: Tempelhof Airport must be the "biggest and most beautiful" civilian airport in the world.

Tempelhof Airport had opened on October 8, 1923. The first commercial flight, a Junker plane, took off for Munich at 10:45 A.M. Five minutes later, an Aero Lloyd plane took off for Königsberg. By year's end 150 passengers had come and gone.

The first impetus to enlarge Tempelhof came in 1929. Nine thousand passengers passed through the airport that year, and the number was expected to increase to 200,000 by 1936.

Hitler emphasized to architect Ernst Sagebiel that the airport design should first and foremost promote the development of air traffic. The renovated airport must accommodate not 200,000 but 600,000 passengers yearly.

Hitler also insisted that Sagebiel build a Reich monument, not simply a big airport. "I am eager for German ideas to become unique in all the world," the dictator told his architect. When a foreigner arrived at Tempelhof, the building's monumentality and beauty should mute any criticism the traveler might level against Germany.

Sagebiel took less than a year to complete the new plans. In 1935 he presented a gigantic scale model to an astounded German public. Among Sagebiel's innovations were multiple-level passenger concourses, as well as accommodations for visitors, baggage, airmail, and freight. Runways would be parallel so that planes would not cross each other's paths. The symmetrical main building would have broad, open boarding areas, without columns or pillars. The passenger concourse, 40 meters wide and 12 meters high, would open directly on to the boarding areas. The arched front of the building facing the runways would be 1200 meters long. The entrance hall was to be 24 meters high (the hall is not as high today, because of a false ceiling).

In fact, Sagebiel may have cribbed some of his design from American airports built 1928–29, which incorporated many of the same features. Designating Tempelhof as a Nazi building cannot withstand critical scrutiny, according to Bernhard Liscutin, of the Interessengemeinschaft City-Airport Tempelhof. Moreover, it is hard to pigeon-hole Sagebiel's style because the architect mixed Nazi-aesthetic "neoclassicism" with what today might be called "technocracy." Sagebiel combined volume, material, and form to create a somewhat threatening ambience, reflecting the power of Hitler's Reich and his airport at the same time. Even today, Tempelhof still boasts the fourth largest enclosed airport space.

On completion, 1942–43, Sagebiel's new airport accommodated only warplanes. The last wartime flight, a Lufthansa Ju 52, departed April 21, 1945. By April 28 Soviet troops occupied Tempelhof. American troops

Top: Hitler arrives at Tempelhof Airport from Vienna, March 16, 1938, just after he annexed Austria to the reich. To the right is Hermann Göring, who holds his field marshal's baton in his right hand; behind them is General Wilhelm Keitel, head of the Wehrmacht Supreme Command, and Julius Schaub, Hitler's personal SS adjutant (Ullstein Bilderdienst). *Bottom:* Tempelhof Airport, 1953, with Berlin Airlift monument in front. Note the huge Nazi eagle still on the roof of the main building (Ullstein Bilderdienst).

succeeded the Russians on July 4 and named the airport "the clothes hanger" for the main building's resemblance to this object.

On June 26, 1948, the Berlin Airlift began, in order to combat the highway blockade that Josef Stalin had ordered to cut off all provisions to the city. On May 12, 1949, when Stalin gave up and lifted his blockade, 1344 "raisin bombers," mostly American, had flown in 9,993 tons of food and medicine to beleaguered Berliners. In gratitude, Berlin mayor Ernst Reuter christened the area in front of Tempelhof "Berlin Airlift Place." During the following 41 years this space was restricted to Allied airlines. Today Tempelhof is the world's oldest airport in continuous use.

Almstedt, Jan. Innovativer Monumentalbau. Flugplatz Tempelhof: Nazi Prestigeobject für dreissigfache Passagierzahlen geplant. *Berliner Morgenpost*. September 26, 2000.

_____. Mutterede für Bauern, barras, Bomber. *Berliner Morgenpost*. September 19, 2000.

Der "Kleiderbügel"-eine Chronik. *Berliner Illustrierte Zeitung*. October 4, 1998.

Spandau Prison (Wilhelmstrasse 21–24, Spandau, Razed)

The Spandau district of Berlin, once known as Wilhelmstadt, was a military garrison. There are still old barracks buildings made of red brick. Until 1916, the Schmidt-Knobelsdorf-Kaserne (barracks) stood on the street of the same name. The gymnasium of the Seeckt-Kaserne, built in 1936, is located between Seeburgerstrasse and Seecktstrasse.

In 1878 the fortress prison on Wilhelmstrasse was converted to a penitentiary. In 1947 it became world famous, especially its heavily guarded entrance. As the prison for war criminals it was governed by the four Allied Powers (United States, Britain, France, and the Soviet Union).

On July 18, 1947, seven prisoners were moved from Nuremberg to Spandau: Baldur von Schirach, Grand Admiral Karl Dönitz, Constantin Freiherr von Neurath, Grand Admiral Erich Raeder, Albert Speer, Walther Funk, and Rudolf Hess. Von Schirach, the Hitler youth leader, got 20 years, Dönitz 10, diplomat von Neurath 15, Speer 20, Reichsbank president Funk life, and Hess life. Von Neurath was released after 8 years in 1954, Raeder after 9 years on account of age and weak health in 1955, Dönitz after 10 years in 1956, Funk after 11 years in 1957, Speer and von Schirach after 20 years in 1966.

The last prisoner in Spandau, Rudolf Hess, committed suicide August 17, 1987, aged 93 (see also Wunsiedel). In May 1941 Hess had piloted a Messerschmitt 110 plane to Scotland, intending to arrange a peace accord between England and Germany.

Winston Churchill called Hess's flight an act of "lunatic benevolence."

After Hess's incarceration in England, "he knew only the world of high prison walls for 46 years," wrote the *Berliner Morgenpost* in his obituary. The governments of the United States, Britain, and France repeatedly urged his release, but the Russians said nyet. From the Russian viewpoint, a life sentence for Hess meant just that.

Immediately after Hess's death the Allies razed Spandau Prison and buried the fragments around Gatow Airport to prevent their falling into the hands of souvenir hunters.[33] The British then built a store for their personnel on the prison site. They renamed the nearby Train-Kaserne-Militär-Areal as the Smuts Barracks, which they occupied until 1994. After their departure the barracks buildings remained empty or were rented out. The Seeckt-Kaserne became a school, the Gottfried-Kinkel-Realschule. German government officials moved into some of the other buildings. The former British store is now a shopping center. But business has not been especially good. The merchants have been forced to cut their prices to attract customers.

Uhde, Michael. In den Kasernen büffeln jetzt Schüler. Deutschlands Hauptstadt: Die Spandauer Wilhelmstadt und ihre militärische Vergangenheit. *Berliner Morgenpost*. October 1, 1998.

Spandau. Evangelisches Wandkrankenhaus

The orthopedic section of this hospital is housed in a building once part of a complex for slave laborers. Inspector General of Buildings Albert Speer erected the nine-building complex in 1939, of which three buildings remain. Eight thousand workers were here, of the 100,000 needed to create "Germania," Hitler's redesigned Berlin. The Spandau laborers were to construct a gigantic domed hall that would dwarf St. Peter's in Rome. An exhibition on the history of the site, with photos, blue-prints, letters from the slave workers, and other documents, may be seen in the Kul-turhaus at Mauerstrasse 6.

Baecker, Brigitte. Zwangsarbeit: Die dunkle Seite der Geschichte eines Krankenhauses. *Berliner Morgenpost.* January 9, 1998.

Lichterfelde Barracks

(Finckensteinallee 63) Site of first Hitler purge in 1934, called the "Night of the Long Knives." Hitler's principal target was Ernst Röhm, a captain in World War I, who was chief of the Sturm Abteilung (SA), Hitler's Brownshirt army. Röhm had marched with Hitler in the 1923 Beer Hall Putsch and had been sentenced to 15 months probation. But Röhm's storm troopers had grown too powerful, and Hitler became convinced that his old com-rade was plotting against him. On June 30, 1934, Hitler and his entourage routed Röhm out of his bed in Wiessee, a lakeside resort not far from Munich. As Albert Speer recalled:

Hitler was extremely excited and, as I believe to this day, inwardly convinced that he had come through a great danger. Again and again he de-scribed how he had forced his way into the Hotel Hanselmayer in Wiessee-not forgetting, in the telling, to make a show of his courage: "We were unarmed, imagine, and didn't know whether or not those swine might have armed guards to use against us." The homosexual atmosphere had disgusted him: "In one room we found two naked boys!" Evidently he believed that his per-sonal action had averted a disaster at the last minute: "I alone was able to solve this problem. No one else!"

The next day, two SS men handed Röhm a pistol and left him alone in his cell in Munich's Stadelheim prison to commit suicide. "If I am to be killed," Röhm told them, "let Adolf Hitler do it himself." The two SS men then shot him point blank.

In Berlin Göring and Goebbels de-cided to liquidate others. Plainclothes SS men drove to General Kurt von Schleicher's villa in Wannsee and mowed down both Schleicher and his wife. Schleicher had been a professional army officer and last chan-cellor of the Weimar Republic. Other SS men arrested Gregor Strasser, leader of the social-revolutionary North German wing of the Nazi Party and Hitler's most dangerous rival. They brought Strasser to Gestapo headquarters on Prinz Albrechtstrasse. A police officer shot Strasser through the bars of his cell, wounding him, and the hulking Strasser lay for hours in a pool of his own blood before he died. More assailants went to the office of Franz von Papen, who had been reich chancellor in 1932 and Hitler's deputy chancellor during the first two years of Nazi rule. They shot two of his assistants, smashed all the furniture, and arrested Papen, who survived because of Göring's intervention. Another 150 "enemies of state" were rounded up and dispatched by firing squad at the Lichterfelde barracks, a cadet school since 1717.[34]

Hitler's guard regiment, SS-Leibstan-darte Adolf Hitler, was billeted in the Lichterfelde barracks. In 1936 architect Al-bert Speer built the largest enclosed swim-ming pool in southwest Berlin for this guard regiment, 50 meters long by 25 meters wide. The government is now try-ing to raise money to restore the decaying swimming pool and the brick building that houses it. The Bundesarchiv uses the other Lichterfelde buildings. There is a plaque at the entrance describing their his-tory.

Eversloh, Saskia. In Bundesarchiv diente einst Hitlers Leibwache. *Berliner Morgenpost.* August 13, 1999.

Friedrich, Otto. *Before the Deluge.* Harper and Row. New York 1972.

Gorf, Martina. Flickwerk am Bad Finckensteinallee. Grundsanierung der maroden Schwimmhalle gefordert. *Berliner Morgenpost*. January 26, 2000.

_____. Wie geht es weiter mit dem Finckenstein-Bad? *Berliner Morgenpost*. January 26, 2000.

Knopf, Volker, and Stefan Martens. *Göring's Reich. Selbstinszenierungen in Carinhall*. Ch. Links Verlag. Berlin 1999.

Speer, Albert. *Inside the Third Reich*. Translated by Richard and Clara Winston. Avon Books. New York 1971.

Former Berlin Document Center

Wasserkäfersteig 1, Zehlendorf (parts of complex have been razed). On October 18, 1994, amid some protest, the U.S. government turned over this archive of 25 million Nazi documents, opened in 1946, to Germany. The largest collection in the archive was the entire Nazi Party membership record, more than 11 million cards. In the last days of World War II Nazi clerks tied the cards into tight bundles and sent them from the basement of the Nazi Party administration building in Munich, Meiserstrasse 10, to a paper mill for mulching. But local farmers showed American soldiers the location of the cache, and all the cards were saved, including cards of people barred from party membership. One card of party rejects, drawn at random, contains information about a man accused of masturbating at age fourteen. Another gives the name of a man who was treated by a Jewish doctor.

A second collection in the archive contained records of Nazi agencies that controlled culture and education. These records chronicled the party membership of thousands of artists, writers, performers, musicians, and university professors.

"For me, the culture archive is one of the real jewels here," David Marwell, the last American director of the center, told *New York Times* reporter Stephen Kinzer in 1994. "It gives a real sense of how systematically the Nazis tried to control what people were allowed to read, see, and hear."

A chilling part of the collection was the SS section. An SS member who wanted to marry had to submit his family genealogy and that of his prospective bride, dating to 1800, or 1750 for officers. The Nazi hierarchy wanted to exclude anyone with hereditary disease, Slavic, Jewish, or other blood that would make his or her offspring unsuitable for membership in a "pure" Germanic tribe.[35]

Ethnic Germans born outside of Germany who wanted to join the SS or to apply for German citizenship had to submit to examination by trained specialists. The applicant's facial characteristics were broken into 21 categories and assessed with a complex grading scale. The successful applicant could not have a big nose or big ears, irregularly spaced eyes, a swarthy complexion, or any feature unbefitting an Aryan.

The Berlin Document Center was located in buildings and an underground complex that once housed Hermann Göring's surveillance center. Göring's multilingual staff monitored telephone calls and spied on persons considered dangerous to the Reich. When Gerald Posner, a New Yorker writer, visited in 1994, the place still had the appearance of a secret Nazi installation, that is, entirely unremarkable.

The above-ground buildings, a row of whitewashed houses and an alpine-style home, formed a cul-de-sac. An SS unit once lived in the houses. The center's documents were kept in mazes of subterranean corridors with the air of a military installation, complete with escape hatches and heavy safes.

The most important records were two stories below ground, in caverns behind a massive steel door. Walls of concrete, several feet thick, enclosed a huge central hall with small passages branching off. Here resided Göring's own dossier, as well as SS chief Heinrich Himmler's and Josef Mengele's. Mengele, the evil doctor of Auschwitz, is notorious for his gruesome human experiments on children, especially twins.

During his visit to the document center, Posner examined the half-inch-thick file of Amon Göth, the sadistic camp commandant of *Schindler's List*. Göth was a Viennese who joined a Nazi youth group at age 17 and the outlawed Austrian Nazi Party a few years later. He was party member no. 510,964 and SS member no. 43,673. His file contains a photo of Göth in profile, the brooding face of a "low level hood," with greased-back dark hair. Dressed like a Teutonic Damon Runyon character, the six-foot-four-inch Göth wears a black shirt and bright checked tie.

Göth's neatly handwritten file indicates he abandoned the teachings of Catholicism, risked jail to become a Nazi, and was chased by Austrian authorities for "crimes involving explosives." His commitment to National Socialism was "paramount," Göth wrote, and his superiors lavished praise upon him: "He has the right attitude and shows a completely agreeable disposition and nature."

But Göth's racial classification was not superior (he had "Eastern" features). Also he and his wife did not get the Nazi Party commendations ordinarily awarded to couples that had produced a large family. Their only child, a son, born in 1939, died a year later of unrecorded causes.[36]

Göth was transferred to the SS police services in 1942 and was a model noncommissioned officer. In August 1942 he was sent, as part of the Aktion Reinhard, to murder more than two million Polish Jews in Lublin. Afterward, he was promoted to commandant of the forced labor camp at Plazów, in southern Poland. In *Schindler's List* he stands bare chested on the balcony of his house, blithely using the prisoners below for target practice. (Many Plazów survivors testified that Göth actually did this.) After the war the Poles executed Göth.

When the document center was opened, many people thought that its records could be used to identify former Nazis, like Göth, and keep them out of important jobs in business, industry, government, and jour-

nalism. But the hoped-for de-Nazification of Germany never occurred. This idealistic notion was overwhelmed by events, mainly the cold war. The United States, especially, wanted West Germany as an anti–Communist bastion. The goal of keeping old Nazis out of every big job fell by the wayside.[37] Nevertheless the document center's records were extensively used in the Nuremberg trials of 1945–49.

They occasionally caused a stir. A London researcher got hold of the Nazi and SS file of Baron Günther von Reibnitz, father of Princess Michael of Kent, and the British tabloids had a field day. *Spy* magazine caused a bigger sensation when it published a copy of the Nazi Party card of Arnold Schwarzenegger's father.

In the hunt for old Nazi criminals the records of the Berlin Document Center are still vital, as Posner learned from Elliot Welles, of the Anti-Defamation League in New York. Welles was pursuing several miscreants with the help of document center files. One, a man living in Europe, had chosen Welles's mother for execution in the Riga ghetto. "I was fourteen when they killed her," Welles said. "I lost every family member I had in the war."

Although microfilms of the entire contents of the Berlin Document Center are now in Washington, Welles and others are dismayed. "We should have kept the B.D.C," said Welles. "We should have insisted that it be open always, for anyone who wanted to go there."

German archivists are fanatic about privacy and permit fewer people to see original documents than American archivists did. As Klaus Oldenhage, a senior Bundesarchiv official, told Posner, "If *Der Spiegel* wants to do a good general war crimes article, then it can have all the documents it wants. If it wants to do an article about a particular action that took place in a single village during the war, then it can get the information, but no names. And if all it wants to do is go out and expose someone as having a Nazi past or a Nazi parent, then the answer is, 'I'm so sorry, but no.'"

Attitudes like Oldenhage's leave many people fuming. "The hunt for Nazi criminals is biologically finishing," said Simon Wiesenthal, the world's most famous Nazi hunter. "The survivors are dying. There are only a few years left for justice here, and why is it now that the center is returned? Germany feels strong and wants it back? That's not enough. The document center is very important because if you are looking up whether somebody is a Nazi, you can see the whole development of that man, what he says in his own words in his autobiography — those papers simply don't allow people to lie in later years. Those documents are a holy matter."

The original documents are no longer in Göring's subterranean Berlin redoubt. In 1988 thousands were stolen from the center. After the United States relinquished the rest in 1994, they went to the Bundesarchiv.[38] The Bundespost, the German postal service, sold the Wasserkäfersteig property to Hochtief, the same giant construction firm that built the Führerbunker. Hochtief demolished all the buildings, except for a few under landmark protection, and plans to build 40 houses on the site. The builders are converting the caverns into a parking garage.

Diering, Frank. Document Center abgerissen. Nur die denkmalgeschützten Gebäude bleiben stehen. *Berliner Morgenpost*. January 29, 1999.

Kinzer, Stephen. Torch is passed, and the past is in German hands. *New York Times*. April 1, 1994, p. A4.

Posner, Gerald. Secrets of the files. *New Yorker*. March 14, 1994, pp. 39–47.

Tucek, J., and U. Thiede. Brisantes Erbe: Fast 90 Prozent des Archivs der Waffen-SS lagert in Prag. *Berliner Morgenpost*. October 31, 1997.

Eichborndamm 179 (Reinickendorf)

Wehrmachtsauskunftstelle (WASt) (Wehrmacht Information Office). Did a burning tank destroy your Wehrmacht relative in a fire? Did a grenade blow him to bits? Did he starve to death or die of disease in a prisoner of war camp? Was he reported missing in action? Many Germans haven't a clue. More than 1.2 million Wehrmacht soldiers are classified as lost, and their fate may never be known.

But the destinies of 3.1 million of Hitler's warriors are on file in the archive for military personnel information in the Wehrmacht Information Office (officially *Deutsche Dienststelle für die Benachrichtigung der nächsten Angehörigen von Gefallenen der ehemaligen deutschen Wehrmacht*).[39] This gargantuan collection of 18 million alphabetically indexed yellowing cards was begun in 1939, at the onset of the war. It holds all official personnel reports of German soldiers. Five hundred clerks tend the files housed in this bland brick building, located next door to the state archive (Landesarchiv).

Widows, children, grandchildren, former Kameraden and others are entitled to information from this archive. Laws awarding compensation to victims and prisoner of war reparations necessitate the maintenance of these records for the German public. Old soldiers use the information to demonstrate that their current illnesses are service related. Former laborers in the *Reichsarbeitdienst*[40] or members of the Waffen-SS obtain evidence of service to collect pensions.

Archivists take about four months to research an individual case. "We often get grandchildren of Wehrmacht soldiers," says archive director Peter Gerhardt. "After they find out where their grandfather was killed, they travel there, to bring the past into the present." After 40 years in the archive, Gerhardt reports favorable experiences; for example, there was the female singer in the Swedish pop group Abba. In the 1970s she found the record of her lost German father, who was still alive.

But information in the archive is not

always accurate. "As a matter of interest," archivist Gerd-Michael Dürre showed *Berliner Morgenpost* reporter Iwan Zinn the card of his father, Gerhard Dürre. Though the elder Dürre had returned to Germany from Russian captivity in 1949, he was registered as missing. According to Herr Dürre, "There were cases where survivors stood before their own graves."

The German Red Cross Search Service (DRK Suchdienst, Sandwerder 3, Wannsee) also has information on missing German soldiers and civilians, including 123,000 who ended up in Soviet captivity. Of these, 43,000 died of starvation or disease, and

Reinhard Heydrich's grave in Section A of the Invalidenfriedhof. In 1942 Heydrich was buried with full military honors next to General of the Infantry Count Tauentzien von Wittenberg, who fought against Napoleon in the wars of liberation (1813–15). Heydrich was to have had a monumental tomb, designed by the architect Wilhelm Kreis and the sculptor Arno Breker. Because of the downhill course of the war, the tomb was never built. Heydrich's grave marker (shown above) disappeared in 1945 (Bildarchiv Preussischer Kulturbesitz).

756 more were executed. The Russians snatched many of these people off the streets after the war because someone might have denounced them as Nazi collaborators. Family members frequently had no inkling of what had happened to them.

DRK erhält Geheimdaten über die NKWD-Lager. *Berliner Morgenpost.* May 5, 1999.
Zinn, Iwan. Soldatenschicksale auf vergilbten Karteikarten. Auskunftstelle am Eichborndamm verwaltet das grösste Wehrmacht-Personalarchiv. *Berliner Morgenpost.* September 26, 1999.

Invalidenfriedhof. Scharnhorststrasse 33

(S-3 train, Lehrter Stadtbahnhof) The Invalidenfriedhof (cemetery for war disabled) was laid out alongside the Berlin-Spandau ship canal in 1748 and holds the remains of famous Prussian and German officers.[41] Frederick the Great, who commissioned the Invalidenfriedhof, is said to have come here to sit under a tree and converse with his dead soldiers. With Hitler in attendance, Reinhard Heydrich was buried in Section A, adjacent to the front entrance, with great pomp, after his assassination in 1942.

Demps, Lawrence. *Zwischen Mars und Minerva. Wegweiser Invalidenfriedhof.* Verlag für Bauen und Bauweisen. Berlin 1998.
Stengel, Mathias. Grabfelder im Schatten der Mauer. Vor 250 Jahren liess Friedrich II. den Invalidenfriedhof anlegen. 1961 mussten viele Ruhestätten dem Todesstreifen weichen. *Berliner Morgenpost.* November 10, 1998.

Corner General-Papestrasse/ Löwenhardtdamm. Tempelhof.[42]

Large load body (Grossbelastungskörper) The large load body, 14 meters high, 21 meters wide, 12,360 tons, sits near the center of Berlin. In 1941 the regime paid the firm Dyckerhoff and Widmann 400,000 reichsmarks to build this huge concrete hulk. French prisoners of war did the work. A mysterious edifice, now gray, cracking, and surrounded by weeds, the large load body serves no purpose but would be difficult to remove.

Aficionados of Nazi architecture know that the large load body is one of the key structures Hitler left behind. Architect Albert Speer wanted to test the load bearing capacity of the sandy Berlin subsoil for "building T." By 1950 at the latest, as a monument to victory, Hitler wanted to crown his capital, renamed Germania, with a gigantic triumphal arch. If the subsoil could support the large load body, it would support the arch.

The large load body covers a surface area of 100 square meters and compresses the earth to a depth of 18 meters with a force of 12.5 kilograms per square centimeter. Within the concrete are three measurement rooms; one is 10 meters deep, at groundwater level. Using a so-called tube-balance system and a level, Speer's engineers found a 19-centimeter settling of the large load body and declared that the subsoil could support the triumphal arch.

Hitler had first sketched his arch in 1925. It was to be 140 meters high, 170 meters wide, 119 meters long, and demarcate one end of the new north-south axis for Berlin, a boulevard 120 meters wide by 5.5 kilometers long. Within a wreath on the arch masons would chisel the names of all soldiers who had fallen in World War I. Hitler dreamed that the street under his arch would remind every visitor to Berlin that he was in the domain of the "masters of the world" and would "take his breath away."

Albert Speer presented Hitler with a model of the arch on April 20, 1939, during the Führer's 50th-birthday dinner party:

Berlin. Large load body. As a monument to victory Hitler wanted to crown his capital, renamed Germania, with a gigantic triumphal arch. The large load body was built to test the weight-bearing capacity of the sandy Berlin subsoil. If the subsoil could support the large load body, it would support the arch (Hans Peter Stiebing).

Hitler and Albert Speer inspect an architectural model (Süddeutscher Verlag Bilderdienst).

At midnight the diners offered Hitler the proper congratulations. But when I told him that to celebrate the day I had set up a thirteen foot model of his triumphal arch in one of the salons, he immediately left the party and hurried to the room. For a long time he stood contemplating with visible emotion the dream of his younger years, realized in this model. Overwhelmed, he gave me his hand without a word, and then, in a euphoric mood, lectured his birthday guests on the importance of this structure for the future history of the Reich. That night he returned to look at the model several times.

In September 1941 the German government contracted for shipments of Swedish granite for the arch. But because of reverses on the battlefields, the arch was never built, and only the large load body remains.

Until the 1990s the German Research Society for Terrestrial Mechanics used the large load body for many investigations and published its findings in international journals. But in the past few years the civil engineers have abandoned the structure, which Berliners call "the mushroom." When home-less people moved into the rooms within the large load body, they were evicted and work-men sealed off the entrance.

The large load body has been under landmark protection since 1995. But no one knows quite what to do with it.

Hyngar, Michael. 12,360 Tonnen Beton: Investor verzweifelt gesucht. Hinterlassenschaft Albert Speers steht unter Denkmalschutz-Wie der "Grossbelastungskörper" künftig genutzt wird, ist unklar. *Berliner Morgenpost.* January 5, 2000.
Krüger, Karl Heinz. Die entnazifizierung der Steine. *Der Spiegel* 4:64–81, 1989.
Leser-Frage: Wer war General von Pape? *Berliner Morgenpost.* November 14, 1999.
Leser-Frage: Wo liegt der Betonklotz für Messungen der Nazis? *Berliner Morgenpost.* July 3, 1999.
Speer, Albert. *Inside the Third Reich.* Translated by Richard and Clara Winston. Avon Books. New York 1971.

Köpenickerstrasse 24, Kreuzberg

Victoria-Speicher I (destroyed warehouse, memorial plaque). From 1937 to

1939 the Nazis used a building on this site to store "degenerate art." The Aktion Entartete Kunst had confiscated this art: 16,558 expressionist, abstract, and socially critical works, as well as the works of Jewish artists. A plaque commemorates the closing of the warehouse on March 20, 1939. The building itself was destroyed during the war.

In summer 1937 Joseph Goebbels's degenerate art commission canvassed Germany, searching public and private collections. Propaganda office officials seized the works of Otto Dix, Oskar Kokoschka, Erich Nolde, Ernst Ludwig Kirchner, Max Pechstein, and Käthe Kollwitz, among others. Especially hard hit was the modern art division of the Berlin National Gallery, which lost 136 paintings, 28 sculptures, and 324 drawings.

Goebbels first visited the warehouse on November 4, 1937. The painter Adolf Ziegler, president of the Reich Chamber of Artists, and architect Albert Speer accompanied him. In his diary Goebbels wrote, "Very few borderline cases. The rest is such dreck that a three hour visit makes one sick."

In order to convince Hitler to legalize the confiscations that had already taken place, Goebbels gave him a tour of the warehouse on January 13, 1938. "No picture was acceptable," wrote Goebbels in his diary. "Führer also wants no compensation paid to the owners. We will exchange a few of the works outside of Germany for real masterpieces."

On May 31, 1938, the seizure without compensation of degenerate art was legalized ex post facto. At the same time, avantgarde artists living in Germany were forbidden to paint. To obtain foreign currency, four German art dealers were appointed to find foreign customers for some of the degenerate art. Most of the remainder was sent to a gallery in Lucerne for international sale. Before shipment the works were displayed

Degenerate Art Exhibit catalogue cover, 1937 (above). The Hitler regime also deprecated modern music as degenerate (below).

in the rooms of a castle, Schloss Nieder-schönhausen.

Franz Hofmann, the director of fine art and art critic of the *Völkischer Beobachter*, recommended that "the worthless, unsalable remainder be dumped in a trash heap and symbolically burned," Goebbels wrote. "I should also deliver a peppery eulogy."

But Goebbels reserved many works for an "instructional" and propaganda exhibit, "Degenerate Art," which traveled to large German and Austrian cities. From February 26 to May 8, 1938, the works were on display in Berlin, at the "Haus der Kunst," Königsplatz 4.

The exhibit catalogue is a rarity today. It disparaged the antiwar pictures of Otto Dix as "defense-sabotage." A painting by a schizophrenic in a mental hospital "looks more human than any concoction of Paul Klee." A painting by Kurt Schwitters was "the height of stupidity or impudence — or both." But one German commented, "The Nazis, in spite of themselves, gave us the chance to become acquainted with the crème of modern art, all in one place."

Goebbels continued to sift through his art hoard until 1939. Then he burned 1,004 paintings, 3,825 watercolors, and assorted drawings in the courtyard of Berlin's main firehouse.

Merten, Jola. Der Ort, an dem die Nazis Kunst lagerten. Gedenktafel erinnert an Depot der Goebbels-Aktion. *Berliner Morgenpost*. March 22, 1999.

Olympic Stadium

(Charlottenburg, take the U1 train to Olympiastadion). The architect Werner March designed this brobdingnagian arena, one of the most costly that had ever been built (1934–36). In 1936 the summer Olympics were held here, in spite of boycott efforts by liberals in the United States, Britain, and France.

The Olympic Stadium replaced the German Stadium on the same site, which had been built in 1913 by Otto March, father of Werner March. The Olympic Stadium is the center of the Reich Sport Field, a group of athletic facilities, including the Harbig Sports Hall, the Sports Forum (built 1926–28), the House of German Sport (1932), the 7,600 seat swimming stadium, a hockey stadium, and a riding track. The stadium is a prime example of the monumental architecture of which Hitler was so fond.

The stadium itself is only 54 feet high, because architect March took advantage of the terrain to place the interior field 40 feet below ground level. The main entrance is the eastern Olympic Gate. A second entrance, the western one, is called the Marathon Gate.

Since its construction, there has been a persistent rumor that a tunnel network extends from the stadium. This rumor may have grown from the presence of a small underground entrance below the Marathon Gate, built so that supplies could be brought in. Alternately, the rumor may stem from the windowless dressing rooms and training rooms, which are sometimes described as catacombs. But there is, in fact, no tunnel network.

To the west of the stadium is the bell tower, 253 feet high. Its clock bears the inscription, "I call upon the youth of the world." The old cracked bell is next to the southern gate of the Olympic Stadium. To the north of the bell tower is the Woodland Theater, which Werner March also designed. The theater has an open-air stage with 20,000 seats. The Nazis intended the theater for plays with German mythical themes, of which Hitler was fond. The May Field, a huge expanse of turf, some 130,000 square yards, with low tiers of seats on both sides, was to provide the setting for Nazi Party rallies. The entire stadium complex was but one German achievement Hitler wanted to trumpet.

To turn the Berlin summer games into a showcase for other German achievements, Hitler made efforts to play down his regime's notorious anti–Semitism. He allowed a few token Jews to represent the Reich, among them the fencer Helene Meyer and the hockey star Rudi Ball. Another Jew, Wolfgang Fürstner, built and organized the Olympic Village. Anti–Semitic posters along the highways, and notices barring Jews from resorts, were taken down. Julius Streicher's rabidly anti–Semitic newspaper, *Der Stürmer*, vanished from Berlin newsstands. These gestures received international publicity, and foreigners flocked to Berlin, where they were enthusiastically received.

On August 1, under a clear blue sky, Hitler led the parade into his new Olympic Stadium, the world's largest, along the Via Triumphalis. Richard Strauss conducted the orchestra in a brassy 30-trumpet fanfare, then *Deutschland über Alles* accompanied by a chorus of 3,000, then the *Horst Wessel Lied*, and finally the Olympic Hymn, which Strauss had written specially for the occasion. The crowd of 11,000 cheered wildly as Hitler took his seat in the official stand.

The next day Hitler congratulated Hans Wölke, a German, for breaking the Olympic record for the shot put. He also congratulated three Finns for winning the 10,000-meter run and two German women who placed first and second in the javelin throw. But he was not present to shake the hands of three American winners, among them two blacks. As a result, the president of the International Olympic Committee informed the Führer that, as guest of honor, he should congratulate all the victors or none at all.

Hitler chose the latter option, and turned his back on Jesse Owens, the magnificent black American athlete who won four gold medals. As Albert Speer recalled: "People whose antecedents came from the jungle were primitive, Hitler said with a shrug; their physiques were stronger than those of civilized whites. They represented unfair competition and hence must be excluded from future games." Strangely, Owens later claimed that Hitler did pay him a tribute: "When I passed the Chancellor, he arose, waved his hand at me, and I waved back at him. I think the writers showed bad taste in criticizing the man of the hour in Germany."

Hitler attended almost every track and field event. Face contorted, he watched the German athletes with puerile enthusiasm. When the games ended on August 16, Hitler was present for the closing ceremonies, although he had no official role. There were a few isolated cries of Sieg Heil! Others took up the cry, and in a moment the entire Olympic Stadium reverberated with the chant, "Sieg Heil! Unser Führer, Adolf Hitler, Sieg Heil!"

Olympic Games 1936. Nazi propaganda poster.

Olympic Stadium. Hitler and the international and national Olympic committees have passed through the marathon gate and are descending the marathon steps into the stadium, as the games open, August 1936 (Süddeutscher Verlag Bilderdienst).

The games were almost an unqualified Nazi propaganda triumph. The Germans had won the most gold medals, 33, and many visitors left Berlin impressed by the Reich and flattered by their hosts' cordiality. Leni Riefenstahl's famous film of the event is considered a documentary classic and is available on video today.

There was a melancholy aftermath. Because of his Jewishness Wolfgang Fürstner was replaced at the last minute as commandant of the Olympic Village. After he attended the banquet for his successor, he shot himself.

In March 1945 the defenders of Berlin fortified the Olympic Stadium. The members of the people's army took their oaths here before they marched off to be slaughtered. Carl Diem, the German sports organizer, delivered a fiery oration, invoking Sparta, praising sacrifice, and adjuring the Great Germany division of the Hitler Youth to fight a victorious final battle. A month later, after combat-hardened Red Army troops had finished with them, more than 2,000 Hitler Youth lay dead on the Reich Sport Field, all between the ages of 13 and 14.

On the wall of the Marathon Gate is a portrait plaque of Carl Diem, who died in bed, age 80, in 1962. Nothing in the stadium commemorates the massacre of the Hitler Youth. Germans call this phenomenon "selective remembering."

Today, at a distance, the Olympic Stadium presents the same hallmarks it did in the old photographs: the colonnades; the long, imposing driveway; and the mammoth May Field, large enough to hold 250,000 troops marching in formation. A stone tablet stands at the western entrance, inscribed with the names of Jesse Owens and other gold medal winners from the 1936 games. The stadium design has an eerie, harsh, symmetrical quality, typical of Hitler's buildings, which look as forbidding as the ideology they were meant to reflect.

But on closer inspection the deterioration of Hitler's Olympic Stadium is overwhelming. Saplings grow out of the top of the clock tower. Stalactites protrude from the ceiling joints where water has seeped through the mortar. Above the bleachers workers have removed 100 limestone panels from the facade, fearing that they might come crashing down on the heads of spectators. Nets have been stretched under the masonry to catch any falling debris. Parts of the structure are propped up with steel I-beams. The ceiling of the anteroom to the marathon gate, where Olympic athletes made their triumphal entrances, is reinforced with steel braces.

Although the decrepit stadium is still in use, recently for a Rolling Stones concert, building officials are becoming increasingly worried. "Maybe it will collapse one day," said Ulrich Stange, head of above-ground construction for the Berlin government. Before each event where a crowd of 50,000 or more is expected, Stange thoroughly inspects the tottering structure. The stadium was designed to hold 92,000 for Hitler's propaganda spectaculars, but anxious officials have reduced this number to 75,000. In anticipation of the Rolling Stones concert Stange's technicians used low frequency sound waves to simulate the rocking of fans to the music. "If the vibrations of the music and the people dancing happened to match the natural frequency of the building, then these plates could fall down," said Stange, pointing to the remaining limestone panels anchored to the facade with rusty steel wires (Krüger, 1989).

Berlin's wet winter weather has aggravated the building's problems. Rain has seeped into cracks in the cement, freezing and expanding, enlarging the cracks and allowing even more water to enter.

The Bonn government, which owned the stadium until 1994, grievously neglected it, although Robert Efren, the finance minister, says that the government did put in $30 million over the past 20 years. The stadium has been transferred to the Berlin government, but the damage has been done.

"As the owner, the federal government had the responsibility for maintaining it in a proper way," said Frank Bielka, state secretary for housing and construction in the Berlin government. Bonn "shirked its responsibilities in a criminal manner," he said, and estimated that the cost of bringing the stadium up to modern standards would be at least $225 million.

Stange and Bielka think the cheapest solution to the problem would be to raze the stadium and build a new one. But historic preservation laws forbid demolition or alteration. "The Eiffel tower doesn't look very pretty either, but would you tear it down?" asks Bielka. "Both buildings are symbols. You have to keep them because of their historical dimension" (Krüger, 1989).

Bernhard, Marianne, Madeleine Cabor, Rainer Eisenschmid. *Baedeker's Berlin*. 3rd ed. Macmillan. New York 1994.

Krüger, Karl Heinz. Die Entnazifizierung der Steine. *Der Spiegel* 4:64–81, 1989.

Leser-Frage. Stimmt es, dass vom Olympiastadion ein Tunnelsystem ausgeht? *Berliner Morgenpost*. March 6, 1999.

Read, Anthony, and David Fisher. *The Fall of Berlin*. Norton. New York 1992.

Toland, John. *Adolf Hitler*. Doubleday. Garden City, N.Y. 1976.

Walsh, Mary Williams. Berlin considers future of Hitler's field of dreams. *Los Angeles Times* August 25, 1995, p. 5.

Rosenstrasse-Middle

Memorial to mass wives' protest against deportation of Jewish husbands. Mixed marriages were a thorny problem for the Nazis. When the final roundup of Berlin Jews began on Saturday, February 27, 1943, some 10,000 Jewish men who were partners in mixed marriages were segregated from the other

Jews. The men were taken to the Jewish Sozialverwaltung building, Rosenstrasse 2, and the Jewish old age home in Grosse Hamburgerstrasse. Sunday morning, the non–Jewish wives banded together and went out to find their Jewish husbands. They converged on Rosenstrasse 2. There they stood, refusing to leave, shouting and screaming for their men, hour after hour, throughout the day and the night and into the next day.

Worried SS leaders assembled in their nearby Burgstrasse headquarters, not knowing what to do. They had never been faced with such a situation. Would they have to machine-gun thousands of German women? All night the arguments raged, until at noon on Monday a decision was reached: all men married to a non–Jewish wife could return home. "Privileged persons," the official announcement said, "are to be incorporated in the national community." The Jewish men remained in an uneasy state of limbo until the end of the war (Read and Fisher, 1994).

A monument on Rosenstrasse commemorating the wives' protest was dedicated in 1995. Ingeborg Hunzinger, a Jewish sculptress who fled Berlin in 1939, created the memorial from porphyry. But Frau Hunzinger complained that she had been underpaid for her work. The Berlin Senate finally made a supplementary payment to the 82-year-old sculptress in 1997.

Fischer, Vera. Senat lenkt ein: zusätzliches Honorar für Bildhauerin. *Berliner Morgenpost.* December 19, 1997.
Read, Anthony, and David Fisher. *Berlin Rising.* Norton. New York 1994.
Merten, Jola. Gedenken an zivilen Protest gegen Fabrikaktion 1943. *Berliner Morgenpost.* March 1, 1999.

Wedding. Humboldthain Park, U-Bahn Station Gesundbrunnen

Ruins of flak tower and intact bunker. Albert Speer's office designed three huge flak towers in the style of medieval fortresses. Hitler wanted them to be the first buildings for his rebuilt Berlin (Germania). One was in the Zoological Gardens, another in the Humboldthain Park, and a third in Friedrichshain Park.

The flak towers were bomb-proof and shell-proof, with walls of reinforced concrete more than eight feet thick. Solid steel shutters could close off deeply cut window slits.

The towers, 120 feet or more in height, were built above bunkers, some as many as six levels below ground. The towers had their own water and electricity and their own hospitals, and they held enough food and ammunition to withstand a 12-month siege.

Eight 12.8 mm guns sat atop each tower in pairs — "double-barreled," Hitler called them, "the most beautiful weapons yet fashioned" (Read and Fisher, 1992). Twenty-one gunners, commanded by a noncommissioned officer, manned each pair of guns, which could fire a salvo of eight shells every 90 seconds. Set to explode simultaneously at a given height and in a planned pattern, the shells created a killing area, called a "window," 260 yards across. Any plane in the window was quickly destroyed.

Four more gun positions, just below the roof, accommodated twelve multi-barreled 20 mm quick-firing "pompoms" and 37 mm cannon, capable of annihilating low-flying aircraft. "When the guns start firing, the earth trembles, and even in our flat the noise is ear-splitting," wrote one Berlin resident in her diary.

The Zoo tower was the largest of the three. It was 132 feet tall, the equivalent of a 13-story building. It had five levels above ground. The top level, immediately beneath the gun platforms, was a barracks for the gun crews. On the fourth level was a 95-bed hospital, fully staffed and equipped, complete with two operating rooms. The third level was a secure warehouse, containing the treasures from Berlin's art galleries and museums. The two lower levels served as an air-raid shelter for 15,000 members of the public, as well as kitchens, storerooms, and emergency quarters for the staff of the *Deutschlandsender* radio station. Below ground were the power generators, air-conditioning units, and other service equipment. Also in the basement were the magazines for ammunition, which was carried to the guns by elevators.

Alongside the flak towers were slightly smaller communications and radar control towers, with radar dishes on their roofs. Cannon, too, defended these towers. Adjacent to the radar dishes was an observation turret, large enough to accommodate at least a dozen people, usually Nazi officials, who could watch the progress of a raid. From the Zoo communications tower Luftwaffe controllers directed the air defense of the city, issuing orders to all Berlin's flak and searchlight units.

"From the flak tower, the raids on Berlin were an unforgettable sight," wrote Albert Speer, "and I had constantly to remind myself of the cruel reality in order not to be completely entranced by the scene: the illuminations of the parachute flares, which the Berliners called 'Christmas trees,' followed by flashes of explosions which were caught by the clouds of smoke, the innumerable probing searchlights, the excitement when a plane was caught and tried to escape the cone of light, the brief flaming torch when it was hit. No doubt about it, this apocalypse provided a magnificent spectacle."

The Humboldthain tower, though slightly smaller than the Zoo tower, could provide shelter for 20,000 Berliners because its lower floors were connected to one of the deepest stations in the U-Bahn system, *Gesundbrunnen*. A modest door in the station leads into this large bunker, which was "awakened from its Cinderella sleep" in

March 1998, and is now under monument protection. The bunker encompasses 1,000 square meters on four levels and has 40 mostly empty rooms. Phosphorescent signs marking corridors and stairways glow weakly in the darkness. The infirmary is painted with glowing stripes from top to bottom. Pneumatic tubes once carried messages in cartridges to the Berlin post office, part of a 254-kilometer system with 27 lines. Air pressure moved the cartridges along at a speed of 10 meters per second. A *Torfklo* (peat toilet) is in one of the rooms.

On September 1, 1999, 60 years to the day after the onset of World War II, an exhibit opened in the *Gesundbrunnen* bunker entitled "The nights after the day." The exhibit tells the stories of six Russian and six German soldiers killed in the war and later exhumed by chance.

The remains of missing soldiers are frequently discovered around Berlin. The soldiers in the exhibit had been hastily buried in furrows or shallow graves on the street. Among the artifacts on display are a rusted pocket watch with a blue dial and gold numerals. The watch stopped at 8:55, the moment of death, and is seared by the heat of an explosion. The owner, an unknown Russian infantryman, was discovered in May 1999, during excavation to extend the Halbe-Teupitz Autobahn. The workmen also found tin bowls torn by grenade fragments, a burned tobacco can, and the so-called frozen flesh order, a simple medal awarded to soldiers who had fought in the winter battle for Leningrad, 1941–42.

Merten, Jola. Als die Uhr stehen blieb. Ausstellung zum 60. Jahrestag des Beginns des II. Weltkriegs. *Berliner Morgenpost.* September 2, 1999.

Merten, Jola. Erfolg der "Bunkerküsser." Die Schaustelle führt erstmals in die Unterwelt. *Berliner Morgenpost.* June 6, 1999.

Read, Anthony, and David Fisher. *The Fall of Berlin.* Norton. New York 1992.

Speer, Albert. *Inside the Third Reich.* Translated by Richard and Clara Winston. Avon Books. New York 1971.

Bundesstrasse 96. Waldstadt Wünsdorf

Zeppelin Bunkers (Bunkeranlage Zeppelin). This suburb, 25 miles south of Berlin, became a military enclave in 1907. The army installed a troop training ground (Truppenlager Zossen), a military exercise field, and an infantry school. By 1914 the site was the largest military installation in Europe. Soldiers received their basic training here before being sent to the front to fight for the kaiser. After World War I, Freikorps troops occupied the barracks.

In the course of war preparations the Nazis did not ignore Wünsdorf. In 1937–40 they built the Zeppelin Lager, site of an elaborate communications center for the army high command. The post office (Reichspost) designed and managed the complicated electronic information network, code named Exchange 500.[43]

From 1939 to 1945 Hitler's orders to his troops in the field passed through Exchange 500. When the war began, part of the Wehrmacht high command had their headquarters in the complex, where they planned the invasion of the Soviet Union, Operation Barbarossa.

The huge Zeppelin Lager installation was carefully camouflaged. It looked like a country village, with red-brick cottages, well-trimmed lawns, and a red-brick church, located on the outskirts of a dense pinewood. Pigeons nested in the eaves. But the place was *deutschsauber* (German-clean), a bit too neat and tidy.

Grouped in clearings in the woods, linked by sandy tracks, were 24 concrete buildings, all heavily disguised. The Wehrmacht had hung netting across the concrete footpaths so that they would not be visible from the air.

The buildings were grouped into two main centers, for the army high command and the supreme commander of the armed forces. Code-named Maybach I and II, they were sealed off from each other by barbed-wire fences. The most important parts of the centers, including the operations rooms, were buried deep underground. Between them, interred even more deeply, about 70 feet below the surface, was Exchange 500, the all-important communications center, the central nervous system of a vast telephone, teleprinter, and radio network that stretched from the Arctic to the Black Sea, and from the Atlantic coast of France in the west to the Caucasus Mountains deep in the Soviet Union. The center was completely self-contained, with its own power generators, water supplies, and air-conditioning filtered against poison gas.

Despite the importance of the Zeppelin bunkers, the Allies did not know of their existence. In March 1945 American planes bombed barracks but not the bunkers.

The first Soviet troops to arrive in April 1945 were astounded at the extent and complexity of the underground installations. Hans Beltow, the engineer in charge, stayed behind after his cohorts had fled and took the Russians on a tour. The elevators were not working, so the men had to descend by a spiral staircase, winding downward to vast corridors lined with numbered doors. Behind them were offices, storerooms, bedrooms, floors strewn with documents, maps, and reference books — all the detritus of a military headquarters. In the bedroom of General Hans Krebs, the army chief of staff, a dressing gown lay flung over a writing desk, and a pair of carpet slippers lay on the floor. The bed in the adjoining room was unmade. On a small table stood a bottle of wine, a couple of half-full glasses, and a dish of apples. Underwear and family photographs were in an open suitcase.[44]

In Exchange 500 telephones and teleprinters were still working, spewing out messages from Berlin. A German clerk had left large handwritten notices in Russian on the teleprinter consoles, warning: "Do not damage this equipment. It will be valuable to the Red Army."

A Soviet soldier answered one of the phones. A voice demanded to speak with a German general. The Russian replied: "Ivan is here. You can go —!"[45]

The sole defenders of Wünsdorf were four portly, inebriated German soldiers, three of whom immediately surrendered; the fourth was too intoxicated to do anything and had to be carried away on a stretcher.

After 1945 the Soviets moved their German supreme command into the Wünsdorf complex, which Berliners called the "forbidden city." From Wünsdorf, Russian commanders were prepared to direct a nuclear war against the West. Between 30,000 and 70,000 Soviet soldiers and their families lived in the military enclave, which they did not vacate until September 1994.

Today the 1916 officers' headquarters building, imperial stables, and bunkers are protected monuments. Each week several hundred tourists descend into the frosty 107,000-square-foot Zeppelin bunker, whose reinforced walls were too thick for the Russians to demolish.

The government of Brandenburg now presides over the building of a whole new city in Wünsdorf, where no one had ever lived without a uniform. Planners have proposed turning the old troop exercise grounds into an artists' colony. The empty imperial stables might become a military museum, art gallery, printing plant, or space for publishers. The elegant old Prussian officers' headquarters complex, with its austere Lenin statue in front, still awaits the right investor.

Die zwei Gesichter der Militär-Geschichte in Wünsdorf. *Berliner Morgenpost.* March 30, 1997.
Fischer, Jan Otakar. Beating swords into suburbs in East Germany's bunker capital. *New York Times.* March 16, 2000, F1.
Hammes, Katharina. Wie ein Ort des Krieges zur Friedenstadt wird. Waldstadt Wünsdorf-von Hauptquartier der sowetischen Truppen zum beliebten Wohn-und-Arbeitsort. *Berliner Morgenpost.* January 17, 2000.
Huber, Andrea. Einblicke in eine einst "verbotene Stadt." *Berliner Morgenpost.* October 13, 1997.
Huber, Andrea, and Katrin Schoelkopf. Leben in lachsrosa Kasernen. Was aus dem Plan geworden ist, Wünsdorf in eine Waldstadt zu verwandeln. *Berliner Morgenpost.* December 20, 1997.
Jäckel, Hartmut. *Menschen in Berlin. Das letzte Telefonbuch der alten Reichhauptstadt 1941.* Deutsche Verlags-Anstalt. Stuttgart München 2000.
Read, Anthony, and David Fisher. *The Fall of Berlin.* W.W. Norton. New York 1992.
Schoelkopf, Katrin. Der Fall Barbarossa und der Mauerbau … oder weshalb die Telefonkabel vom Wünsdorfer Zeppelin-Bunker zur Post in Zossen führen. *Berliner Morgenpost.* April 8, 1998.

Wannsee and Schwanenwerder

Wannsee House. Haus der Wannsee Konferenz. Am grossen Wannsee 56–58. On a wintry Tuesday, January 20, 1942, in this elegant suburban Berlin villa, now a Holocaust memorial, Reinhard Heydrich, chief of the Reich Security Service, announced Hitler's decision to murder the Jews of Europe. Fourteen other high Nazi officials, among them Adolf Eichmann, were in attendance.

Schwanenwerder. A bridge connects this little island to the popular Wannsee beaches. In 1936 Joseph Goebbels bought the villa on Inselstrasse 8–10, which had belonged to Oscar Schlitter, a director of the Deutsche Bank. In 1938 a neighbor, the Jewish banker Samuel Goldschmidt, was forced to sell his property to Goebbels for a pittance. On March 27, 1945, Goebbels sent his wife to the villa. He wrote in his diary: "Magda has gone to Schwanenwerder to make preparations for the move of our children there. But she has again somewhat overdone it and is now ill in bed. That is the last straw."

Goebbels had wanted his wife and six

Wannsee Villa, where Reinhard Heydrich announced Hitler's decision to murder the Jews of Europe.

children to escape Berlin by boat, from the dock at Schwanenwerder up a tributary of the Elbe. "But Frau Goebbels said no," recalled Annemarie Kempf, Albert Speer's secretary. "One knew she would, one knew her closeness to Hitler. Many people thought she had always been in love with him," Kempf told journalist Gitta Sereny.

Magda Goebbels and her children moved into Hitler's bunker alongside her husband.[46] On May 1, 1945, Joseph and Magda Goebbels poisoned their children and then committed suicide in the bunker courtyard. "That way, you won't have to carry us up the stairs," said Goebbels to Hitler's telephone operator, Rochus Misch.

During the Third Reich, Schwanenwerder was also home to the Reich Bride School, Inselstrasse 38, where young women learned "true motherhood in family and career."

Lehrer, Steven. *Wannsee House and the Holocaust.* McFarland. Jefferson, N.C., 2000.
Merten, Jola. Wannsee-Idyll und Nazi Terror.

Schau in der Gedenkstätte informiert über die wechselhafte Geschichte der vornehmen Villenkolonie. *Berliner Morgenpost.* June 21, 2000.

Berlin's Prince Albert District (Prinz-Albrecht-Gelände)

The former Prinz Albrechtstrasse (now Niederkirchner Strasse), Wilhelmstrasse, Anhalter Strasse, and the former Saarlandstrasse (now Stresemannstrasse) border this area east of the Martin Gropius Building.

During the Third Reich the Prinz Albrecht District was home to Hitler's most feared organs of terror: the Gestapo, the Reichsführer SS, the Sicherheitsdienst (SD, security service) of the SS, and after 1939 the Reich Security Main Office. This was an unprecedented concentration of power in a neighborhood that had a rural character two centuries earlier. There is a temporary exhibit, Topography of Terror, at Stresemannstrasse 110.

Terrance, Marc. *Concentration Camps. A Traveler's Guide to World War II Sites.* Universal Publishers 1999.

The District, 1688–1880. In the seventeenth century the Prinz Albrecht District was a quiet area southwest of Berlin. In 1688 the district was part of a separate city, Friedrichstadt, but in 1710 was included in the new royal residence city of Berlin.

In 1732 the "soldier king," Friedrich Wilhelm I, and his chief architect, Philipp Gerlach, extended Friedrichstadt to the south. The extension led to development of three north-south main boulevards, Wilhelmstrasse, Friedrichstrasse, and Lindenstrasse, which opened into a circle called the Rondell (later Belle-Alliance-Platz, today Mehringplatz).

At the same time, in the northern section of Friedrichstadt, the nobility were building impressive palaces. After the founding of the German Empire in January 1871, these buildings were gradually renovated to serve as government buildings and embassies. Protestant Germans, emigrating from Bohemia, were settling in the neighborhood. Another immigrant was Baron Mathieu Vernezobre de Laurieux, who built a magnificent palace on the Wilhelmstrasse.

The southern portion of Friedrichstadt became the site of two major rail terminals, the Potsdamer Bahnhof in 1838 and the Anhalter Bahnhof in 1841. Yet this part of Friedrichstadt retained its suburban character for decades. According to the Baedeker Guide (1878); "the southern half of Friedrichstadt is tranquil and more uniform than the northern half, which offers little peace and quiet." But the Museum of Applied Arts and the huge new Anhalter Bahnhof were under construction. The character of Friedrichstadt and the Prinz Albrecht District was undergoing a sea change.

Rürup, Reinhard et al. *Topographie des Terrors.* Verlag Willmuth Arenhövel. Berlin 1987, p. 16.

The District, 1880–1918. Berlin, the capital of the new German Empire, grew exponentially. The railroad stations, inadequate for the traffic load, were enlarged and rebuilt. In 1872 the Potsdamer Bahnhof got a bigger entrance hall. The rebuilt Anhalter Bahnhof, finished 1880, was a masterpiece of railway station construction. The vast platform hall was 170 meters long, 60 meters wide, and had an iron roof spanning an area of 10,200 square meters. The reception hall was brick adorned with terra cotta and stone. The streets surrounding the stations, especially Königgrätzerstrasse, became a center of visitor traffic, catered to by dozens of hotels, large and small.

The "breakthrough of the modern" in the Prinz Albrecht District became official in April 1877, when the cornerstone was laid for the Applied Art Museum, designed by Martin Gropius and Heino Schmieden. The museum, with its magnificent exhibit halls, libraries, and lecture halls, was finished in 1881. In the same year, the Anthropology Museum was dedicated. Both museums were reactions to the pressure for modernization, which Wilhelmine Germany perceived competing European powers to be exerting. Industrialists, merchants, high officials, and artists had been demanding an applied art museum for a decade in order to help raise the world's opinion, and thus the competitiveness, of German products. The Anthropology Museum was a showplace for the influx of goods from the first German colonies. On the ground floor was the pièce de résistance of its collection, King Priam's treasure, which Heinrich Schliemann had excavated from the ruins of Troy, Homer's *Iliad* in one hand and a spade in the other.[47]

Just after the two museums were completed, the growing rail traffic led to a hotel construction boom. One of the largest new hostelries in the district was the Hotel Vier Jahreszeiten, renamed the Hotel Prinz Albrecht at the turn of the century. In the meantime all around the Prinz Albrecht Palais one new building after another was going up, and access to them was becoming difficult. Some could be reached only by means of little paths. In 1898, when the Prussian House of Delegates was finished, across from the Applied Art Museum, city authorities wanted to enlarge and lengthen nearby Zimmerstrasse. But the War Ministry, a neighbor, blocked this proposed change.

In 1900 a new building went up on the vacant lot between the Applied Art Museum and the Hotel Prinz Albrecht. Because the Museum was short of space, it put its lecture halls and library in the new building and in 1905 named it the Applied Art School Building.

Thus in a few decades the entire character of the Prinz Albrecht District was transformed. It was now an integral part of the government quarter, as well as the main business district, since the new Wertheim's Department Store was on the adjacent Leipzigerstrasse. The Prinz Albrecht District was also very close to the giant newspaper and book publishers Mosse, Ullstein, and Scherl, between Zimmerstrasse and Kochstrasse.

Berlin 1856–1896. *Photographien von F. Albert Schwartz mit Bilderläuterungen von Hans-Werner Klünner und einer Einführung von Laurenz Demps.* Nicolaische Verlagsbuchhandlung. Berlin 1991.
Rürup, Reinhard, et al. *Topographie des Terrors.* Verlag Willmuth Arenhövel. Berlin 1987, pp. 23–24.

The District, 1918–1933. With the German defeat in World War I came social conflict and drastic change. The upheaval after the fall of the Hohenzollern Monarchy occurred not only in the government buildings but also in the streets of Berlin. Revolutionaries placed machine gun nests at street corners and in front of the Stadtschloss, the former city palace of the kaisers. Speeches, huge demonstrations, and sporadic gunfire were everyday occurrences.

The Prinz Albrecht District was in the center of the melee. When bloody battles took place between government troops and revolutionaries in the publishing quarter, the troops were quartered in the Prinz Albrecht Palais. Peace finally came when the new parliamentary democracy fell into the hands of conservative forces. But all this commotion had not affected Hohenzollern ownership of property in the district.

During the 1920s there was a change in the composition of the Prinz Albrecht District. The Applied Art Museum moved into the vacant Stadtschloss, and the prehistoric collection of the Anthropology Museum was transferred to the former Art Museum. The Applied Art School merged with the College of Fine Arts and relocated to Charlottenburg. Only the State Art Library remained in a side wing of the museum building, and studios in the attic, under the Mansard roof, were rented to artists. A private concern leased most of the building. The lease expired on March 31, 1933.

In 1932 the government took over the Hotel Prinz Albrecht. Hitler and Goebbels, as well as representatives of the Prussian State Legislature, used the building for lectures and assemblies.

Rürup, Reinhard, et al. *Topographie des Terrors.* Verlag Willmuth Arenhövel. Berlin 1987, p30.

The District during the Third Reich. Even before Hitler came to power in 1933, Nazi leaders had been eyeing the Prinz Albrecht District for their headquarters because it was so near the main government buildings in the Wilhelmstrasse. In October 1932 the editorial offices of *Der Angriff*, the newspaper Joseph Goebbels began in 1927, moved to Wilhelmstrasse 106. The building was christened *Angriff Haus*. In April 1934 *Der Angriff* moved again to nearby Zimmerstrasse. The leaders of the SA Brownshirts took over Wilhelmstrasse 106 until 1937, when the SS moved in.

In 1934 the Hotel Prinz Albrecht became the offices of the *Reichsführung SS* and its boss, Heinrich Himmler. Hitler enjoined Himmler's organization with perpetuating, in Winston Churchill's words, a "monstrous tyranny never surpassed in the dark, lamentable catalogue of human crime":

• Spying on, pursuing, and eliminating all opposition to the Nazi State

• Preserving and propagating the Aryan race, and creating a racially pure Germany by the persecution, expulsion, and murder of the Jews

• Conquering more living space and spreading the "New Order" throughout Europe

Because of the vast scope of this wickedness, the SS expanded to many parts of Berlin. The SS inspector of concentration camps was in the suburb of Oranienburg. Adolf Eichmann's Jewish Affairs Bureau, originally in the Prinz Albrecht Palais, moved to Kurfürstenstrasse 115–16.

Still, the Prinz Albrecht District remained the center. The infamous *Einsatzgruppen,* murderers who butchered millions in Eastern Europe, were organized here. The mass murders of German and European Jews were planned here, as well as the deportations and the Wannsee Conference. The order to massacre millions of Soviet war prisoners came from here. The opponents of the regime were spied on from here. The occupied territories were governed from here.

Some of the men in the Prinz Albrecht District who gave the slaughter orders stayed far away from the sites of their crimes. But others had been murder commandos in *Einsatzgruppen* in Poland and the Soviet Union.

As the need for more surveillance men and secret police grew, the buildings in Prinz Albrechtstrasse and Wilhelmstrasse no longer could accommodate the burgeoning organization. By 1943 the Reich Security Main Office alone filled 30 buildings strung out between Wannsee and Weissensee. And the Reich Security Main Office was only one of twelve divisions of the SS.

But until the end of the war, Prinz Albrechtstrasse and Wilhelmstrasse remained the "government quarter of the SS state." In these offices were the desks of Himmler, Gestapo chief Heinrich Müller, Heydrich, and Heydrich's successor Ernst Kaltenbrunner.[48]

Rürup, Reinhard, et al. *Topographie des Terrors.* Verlag Willmuth Arenhövel. Berlin 1987, p. 30.

Wartime Destruction of the Buildings in the District. In November 1943 the Americans and the British began heavily bombing the center of Berlin. In April and May 1944 the Prinz Albrecht District and the Government Quarter suffered devastating destruction. The Prinz Albrecht Palais was gutted. On September 15, 1944, the journalist Ursula von Kardorff, whom the Gestapo was interrogating, described the buildings on Prinz Albrechtstrasse as being "half burned out," with gaping holes in the exterior walls and blown out windows. SS officials set concentration camp inmates to work cleaning up the rubble. Shortly before noon on May 7, 1944, twenty inmates of the Sachsenhausen camp were killed during a bombing raid as they sought shelter in a bomb crater.

During another raid, February 3, 1945, the Gestapo headquarters was hit many times. In the last days of the war, artillery and antitank gunners were killed by the score around Prinz Albrecht Strasse. After April 26 Soviet troops penetrated deeply into Berlin, and there was fierce fighting in the Government Quarter until the commandant of Berlin, General Helmuth Weidling, capitulated on May 2, 1945.

The extent of destruction in the Prinz Albrecht District varied from building to building. The Hotel Prinz Albrecht and most of the other buildings in the Wilhelmstrasse were flattened. The Prinz Albrecht Palais sustained devastating damage. But other buildings had not been completely ruined. The Gestapo main office (Prinz Albrechtstrasse 8) and the neighboring Gropius Building were burned out, but their frameworks and facades remained intact. In fact, the Gestapo "house prison" was in use until just before the capitulation, though the air raid of February 3, 1945, had cut off power and running water. In the night of April 21–22 the Gestapo marched most of the prisoners, prominent political figures, to a nearby ruin and shot them. (See Dorotheenstädtischer Friedhof, Berlin.) When Prinz Albrechtstrasse 8 was liberated, six prisoners were still alive.

By this time, almost all high SS, Gestapo, and Security Service officials had fled Berlin. Himmler, General Otto Ohlendorf, and General Walter Schellenberg had taken refuge in Schleswig-Holstein. Ernst Kaltenbrunner had moved his headquarters to Alt-Aussee in Steiermark, followed by Adolf Eichmann.

Rürup, Reinhard, et al. *Topographie des Terrors.* Verlag Willmuth Arenhövel. Berlin 1987, pp. 178–79.

The District from the End of the War to the Building of the Berlin Wall (1945–1961). At the end of 1948 the government of Berlin was split, and the city itself was divided into eastern and western halves. The southerly Friedrichstadt and the Prinz Albrecht District had sustained so much damage that they were unrecognizable. The former government quarter had become a wasteland, an unnaturally quiet district in the middle of the bustling city. In both East and West Berlin new centers were arising.

Prinz Albrechtstrasse was in the eastern sector. The former Reich Security Main Office lay on the border between east and west. Of the Wilhelmstrasse buildings, which had belonged to the Gestapo and the Security Service (SD), practically nothing remained by 1950. Because of "structural weakness" the Communist government razed and dynamited whatever survived the bombing.

The leveling of the remains of Hitler's new Reich Chancellery received considerable notice. But no one paid much attention to the East Germans when they dynamited the ruins of the Prinz Albrecht Palais, April 27–28, 1949. This neglect is surprising because the building was one of the last and most elegant works of Karl Friedrich Schinkel, one of the greatest German architects, who designed many other Berlin buildings, as well as the Iron Cross.

The razing of the former Gestapo headquarters, Prinz Albrechtstrasse 8, 1953–59, and the relatively undamaged Anthropology Museum, 1962–63, followed the destruction of the Prinz Albrecht Palais. The East Germans renamed Prinz Albrechtstrasse, Niederkirchnerstrasse, in honor of a Communist resistance fighter who had been executed by the SS.[49] The honor was somewhat hollow, as the street ran through an architectural desert, one vacant lot and patch of weeds after another.

City planners had many ideas about what to do with the large, empty Prinz Albrecht District. In the 1950s the East Germans considered constructing a helicopter-landing pad in the center. Another cherished idea was the building of a highway through the district, an extension of the Kochstrasse, which would run diagonally to the Landwehr Canal. In 1957 the West German government held a competition for the best plan to rebuild the district along with the entire center of Berlin. Nothing came of this.

When the Berlin Wall went up in August 1961, the fate of the district was sealed. The wall ran through the south of Friedrichstadt along Niederkirchnerstrasse, and turned the area into a no-man's land. The empty ruin of the Gropius Building deteriorated from year to year. The former center of Nazi terror languished, virtually forgotten.

Rürup, Reinhard, et al. *Topographie des Terrors.* Verlag Willmuth Arenhövel. Berlin 1987, pp. 195–96.

Rediscovery of the District's Repressed Past. In the years after the Berlin Wall was built the realization gradually sank in that Berlin might never be unified politically. The building plans for Friedrichstadt were put aside, and the area languished.

In the 1970s the architectural historian Dieter Hoffmann Axthelm reawakened interest in the history of the Prinz Albrecht District. His "Berlin International Building Exhibition" (1979) made reference to the original character of the district.

By 1980 various groups were recommending a memorial to the Nazi victims in the Prinz Albrecht District. Public officials took notice of the recommendation when they began using the partially restored Gropius Building for commercial exhibitions. In 1981 an exhibit entitled "Prussia: The Search for a Balance" was set up near the Gropius Building, on the site of Prinz Albrechtstrasse 8, the former Gestapo headquarters. Evil deeds that many people had tried to forget were once again thrust into the public consciousness. Many young people, born after the end of the war, were becoming interested in the dark history of the Hitler era.

In 1986, to document the topography of the Prinz Albrecht District, German researchers excavated the area. They found parts of foundations, cellars, and a section of the Gestapo house prison floor, along with cell walls that had been built in 1933. In March 1987 the researchers uncovered an unknown cellar of a building built for the Gestapo during the war. A roof now protects the entire site from the elements. An exhibition hall, the Topography of Terror, has been built on the site, augmented by the cellar rooms. The situation of the vanished buildings can be seen on information boards. The most notorious addresses and persons associated with the one-time center of Nazi terror include the following.

Prinz Albrechtstrasse No. 8

The building of the former School of Applied Art was the Gestapo headquarters from 1934 onward. Men and women were incarcerated in its cells for weeks, months, sometimes years.

Prinz Albrechtstrasse 8 was the most dreaded address in Berlin. Cold-blooded brutality and murder were meted out here to opponents of the regime: Communists, social democrats, and officers who tried to kill Hitler. So brazen were the Gestapo murderers that instead of trying to hide their deeds, they sent their victims' bodies to the Berlin morgue, where records of the autopsies still exist. Gestapo chief Heinrich Müller presided over this bureaucracy of torture and death.

Müller was born in Munich on April 28, 1901, of Catholic parents. During World War I he served as a flight leader on the eastern front and was awarded the Iron Cross, First Class. After the war the enterprising Müller began his career in the Bavarian police, specializing in the surveillance of Communist Party functionaries and making a special study of Soviet Russian police methods. Partly because of Müller's expertise in this field, Reinhard Heydrich picked him to be his closest associate and second-in-command of the Gestapo.

From 1935 the short, stocky Müller, with his square peasant's head and hard, dry, expressionless face, was virtual head of the Gestapo. The man Adolf Eichmann described as a "sphinx" was cold, dispassionate, and a bureaucratic fanatic.

Müller was politically suspect to influential members of the party, who resented his past record in the Munich State

Police, which opposed the Nazis. Not until the end of 1938 was he officially admitted to the party, as member number 4,583,189. Yet the obdurate, bigoted Müller was highly regarded by both Himmler and Heydrich, who admired his professional competence, blind obedience, and willingness to execute "delicate missions," spying on colleagues, and unscrupulously disposing of political adversaries. Müller combined excessive zeal in his duties with docility toward his masters. Germans call such a person a *Radfahrer*, a bicycle rider, because his head is always bowed while his feet are pounding the pedals below.

Heydrich rapidly promoted Müller to SS Standartenführer (colonel) in 1937, SS Oberführer (brigadier general) on April 20, 1939; SS Brigadeführer (major general) on December 14, 1940; SS Gruppenführer (lieutenant-general) and police chief on November 9, 1941.

As head of *Amt IV* (Gestapo) in the Reich Security Main Office from 1939 to 1945, Müller was more directly involved in murdering Jews than even his superiors, Heydrich and Himmler. No doubt this qualification was responsible for his presence at the Wannsee Conference (see Wannsee Villa). His cruelty and callousness toward the fate of the Jews are demonstrated in a letter he sent February 28, 1942, to Under State Secretary Martin Luther of the Foreign Office (Pätzold and Schwarz, 1992):

I am writing with regard to the anonymous letter sent to the Foreign Office about the solution of the Jewish question in the Warthegau [German occupied western Poland]. You included this letter in your communication of February 6, 1942, and I have referred it for investigation. The results should be available soon.

Such protests are unavoidable. We must let the chips fall where they may. The opponent will always try to use any and all measures to arouse pity and engender hope. Since we began working to crush him, the Jew tries to escape his fate by sending anonymous letters everywhere in the Reich.

Müller subsequently signed an order requiring the immediate delivery to Auschwitz by January 31, 1943, of 45,000 Jews for liquidation. He approved many similar mandates. In the summer of 1943 he was sent to Rome to pressure the Italians, who were proving singularly inefficient and unenthusiastic in arresting Jews. Until the end of the war Müller continued his remorseless prodding of subordinates to greater efforts in sending Jews to Auschwitz. In his hands mass murder was just another administrative procedure. Müller ordered the murder of Russian prisoners of war and gave the order to shoot British officers who had escaped from detention, near Breslau, at the end of March 1944.

Müller's whereabouts at the end of the war are still a mystery. He was last seen in the *Führerbunker* on April 28, 1945, after which he disappeared. Though his burial was recorded on May 17, 1945, when the body was later exhumed it could not be identified. There were persistent rumors that he had defected to the East (he had established contact with Soviet agents), either to Moscow, Albania, or to East Germany. Other uncorroborated reports placed him in Latin America.

Pätzold, Kurt, and Erika Schwarz. *Tagesordnung: Judenmord. Die Wannsee-Konferenz am 20. January 1942.* Metropol Verlag. Berlin 1992.
Wistrich, Robert S. *Who's Who in Nazi Germany.* Routledge. London 1982.

Prinz Albrechtstrasse No. 9

In 1934, when Heinrich Himmler moved in, the Hotel Prinz Albrecht became known as the SS-Haus. The second most powerful man in the Third Reich, Himmler controlled the police and, toward the end of World War II, even parts of the army.

Heinrich Himmler was born October 7, 1900, in Munich. The son of a Catholic secondary schoolmaster, Himmler received a diploma in agriculture after World War I and soon joined militant rightist organizations. As a member of one of these, the Reichskriegsflagge, he participated in Hitler's abortive Munich (Beer Hall) Putsch in November 1923. Himmler joined the Nazi Party in 1925 and rose steadily in the party hierarchy, but the foundations of his future importance were laid with his appointment as *Reichsführer* of the SS, Adolf Hitler's elite bodyguard nominally under the control of the Sturmabteilung (SA). After Hitler's accession to power (January 30, 1933), Himmler became head of the Munich police. He established the Third Reich's first concentration camp at Dachau and soon began to organize the political police all over Germany. In April 1934 he was appointed assistant chief of the Gestapo (secret police) in Prussia, and from this position he extended his control of police forces over the whole Reich, assuming full command of them in 1936. In the June 30, 1934, purge, Himmler's SS eliminated the SA as a power factor, thus strengthening Hitler's control over his own party and the German Army, which had viewed the SA as a serious rival. Himmler then began to build the SS into the most powerful armed body in Germany next to the armed forces. Until World War II its tasks ranged from the security service of party and state, known as the Sicherheitsdienst (SD), to studies and campaigns designed to protect the purity of the "Aryan race." After the mass murder of European Jewry began in 1941, Himmler organized the extermination camps in eastern Europe that were to wipe out all but a fraction of Europe's Jewish population by the end of the war.

The small, diffident Himmler looked more like a humble bank clerk than Germany's police dictator. His pedantic demeanor and "exquisite courtesy" fooled one English observer into stating that "nobody I met in Germany is more normal" (Snyder, 1978). He was a curious mixture of bizarre,

romantic fantasy and cold, depraved efficiency. Described as "a man of quiet unemotional gestures, a man without nerves," he suffered from psychosomatic illness, severe headaches, and intestinal spasms. He almost fainted at the sight of a hundred eastern Jews, including women, being executed for his benefit on the Russian front. After this experience Himmler ordered a more "humane" method of execution, the use of poison gas in specially constructed chambers disguised as shower rooms.

On July 21, 1944, a day after a failed assassination attempt, Hitler made Himmler head of the People's Army. In early 1945, as the Russians were closing in on Berlin, Hitler named Himmler to defend the capital and also head the Werewolf Unit, which would make a last stand in the mountains of Bavaria and murder German collaborators in Allied-occupied territory.

By now a worried Himmler was looking out for Number One. In April 1945 he maladroitly approached the Swedish Count Folke Bernadotte, offering to free Jews from concentration camps. Himmler also suggested a capitulation. When Hitler, in his bunker, got this news, he furiously demanded Himmler's arrest.

On May 21, 1945, after Germany had surrendered, Himmler shaved his mustache, put a patch over one eye, and assumed the uniform and identity of a discharged Gestapo agent. British troops captured him near Bremen. His papers made them suspicious, and they quickly discovered his identity. While a British doctor was examining him at Lüneburg, he bit down on a cyanide phial concealed in his mouth and died almost instantly. He is buried in an unmarked grave on the Lüneburg Heath.

Bernhard, Marianne, Madeleine Cabor, Rainer Eisenschmid. *Baedeker's Berlin*. 3rd ed. Macmillan. New York 1994.
Snyder, Louis L. *Encyclopedia of the Third Reich*. McGraw-Hill. New York 1978.
Wistrich, Robert S. *Who's Who in Nazi Germany*. Routledge. London 1982.

Wilhelmstrasse No. 102

This building, the Prinz Albrecht Palais, changed hands many times before Reinhard Heydrich and the Security Service moved in. It was built in 1737 as a palace for Baron Mathieu Vernezobre de Laurieux and served the baron as a summer home, called the Palais Vernezobre. In 1760 the banker Werstler acquired it. In 1763–64 it housed Turkish diplomats to the Prussian court. In 1769 the Prussian minister Freiherr von Hagen bought it. In 1772 Princess Amalie, sister of Frederick the Great, acquired the palace as a summer home. The Margrave of Ansbach-Bayreuth bought the palace in 1790, and it became the *Ansbachisches Palais*. The Prussian royal family took it back in 1806, but in 1807 it fell into the hands of Napoleon's troops, who used it as a barracks. In 1810 a soup kitchen for the poor was installed in the basement, which functioned until the 1830s.

In 1812 the Prussian king, Friedrich Wilhelm III, allowed a religious order, the Luisenstift, to use the building, and Wilhelm von Humboldt briefly considered making it part of the newly founded University of Berlin. A few years later the king began moving in his art collection. By 1826 the palace became the restoration workshop for the royal collections. Twelve hundred paintings were stored in some of its rooms, and artists used other rooms as studios.

In 1830 the palace became the property of Prinz Albrecht of Prussia, son of King Friedrich Wilhelm III. The prince commissioned the court architect Karl Friedrich Schinkel to remodel it, and Schinkel added a magnificent, sweeping double stairway to the foyer, as well as an elegant ballroom. Peter Joseph Lenné expanded the park, and Adolph Lohse renovated some of the rooms. The palace was renamed the Prinz Albrecht Palais, and Albrecht lived in it until his death in 1872.

The building then became the property of his son and grandsons. In 1924 the family sold the west part of the park to developers, and in the late 1920s Schinkel's stable and other buildings were demolished, replaced by the eleven story Europahaus. The Weimar government leased the palace from the former Prussian royal family as a guesthouse, and among others, the king of Afghanistan, the king of Egypt, British prime minister Ramsay MacDonald, and British foreign minister Neville Henderson stayed there.

After Hitler came to power, the SS rented the palace, which became the Berlin headquarters of Reinhard Heydrich, who had moved to the capital from Munich in April 1934. Heydrich was head of the Sicherheitsdienst (SD, Security Service) of the SS, and from 1939 the Reichssicherheitshauptamt (Reich Security Main Office). Heinrich Himmler's chief lieutenant in the SS, Heydrich instituted mass executions in the occupied territories during the opening years of World War II. On January 20, 1942, Heydrich organized the Wannsee conference, where he announced the decision to destroy the Jews of Europe. The journalist Gitta Sereny described Heydrich as the darkest personality in the Nazi firmament, a talented man, whose ambition it was, without any doubt, one day to follow in the steps of or to supplant his boss, Himmler.

Reinhard Tristan Eugen Heydrich was born March 7, 1904, in Halle, Germany. He was the son of Bruno Heydrich, a composer and conservatory director in Halle. At the age of 14 young Reinhard joined a Free Corps gang, in which he became schooled in street fighting, terrorism, and looting. In 1922 he joined the navy, rising to the rank of first lieutenant, but was expelled in 1931 for a morals infraction, breach of promise, the lady in question being the daughter of a Kiel shipyard manager.

Heydrich joined the Nazi Party and, soon after Hitler became chancellor, was

Reinhard Heydrich in the uniform of an SS Obergruppenführer (general). Among his medals is an Iron Cross, First Class, which he was awarded for his Luftwaffe service at the beginning of the Russian campaign in 1941 (Ullstein Bilderdienst).

appointed chief of the political department of the Munich police force, with control over the notorious Dachau concentration camp. In 1934 he was appointed SS chief for Berlin and was later made deputy chief of the SS under Heinrich Himmler. Blond, handsome, vain, and fiercely ambitious, Heydrich was also a fine violinist, a champion skier and fencer, a fearless pilot, and an outstanding organizer. A virtually friendless loner, he was pitiless in dealing with "enemies of the state," so hated and feared by anti–Nazi elements throughout Europe that he was called "the Hangman."

Those who met Heydrich were impressed by his ambition, ruthlessness, and duplicity. Eugen Dollman, his interpreter on a trip to Italy in 1938, recalled, "Of all the great men with whom I came into contact, he was the only one I instinctively

feared." Even within the Nazi security police Heydrich was dreaded rather than loved. His own protégé, Walter Schellenberg, who later rose to head the German intelligence service, found his boss's very appearance sinister (MacDonald, 1998):

He was a tall, impressive figure with a broad, unusually high forehead, small restless eyes as crafty as an animal's and of uncanny power, and a wide full-lipped mouth. His hands were slender and rather too long; they made one think of the legs of a spider. The breadth of his hips, a disturbingly feminine effect that made him appear even more sinister, marred his splendid figure. His voice was much too high for so large a man and his speech was nervous and staccato.

Schellenberg described his chief as a born intriguer with "an incredibly acute perception of the moral, human, professional and political weaknesses of others.... His unusual intellect was matched by the ever watchful instincts of a predatory animal.... He was inordinately ambitious. It seemed as if, in a pack of ferocious wolves, he must always prove himself the strongest and assume the leadership." Wilhelm Hoettl, another member of the Nazi security service, remembered Heydrich as a man without a moral code: "Truth and goodness had no intrinsic meaning for him; they were instruments to be used for the gaining of more and more power.... Politics too were ... merely stepping stones for the seizing and holding of power. To debate whether any action was of itself right appeared so stupid to him that it was certainly a question he never asked himself." His was "a cruel, brave and cold intelligence" and his life "an unbroken chain of murders." According to Pierre Huss, an American journalist who knew him well, Heydrich "had a mind and mentality something like an adding machine, never forgetting or lapsing into the sentimental.... Nobody ever got a break or considerations of mercy." Heydrich disliked criticism and reacted badly to the inquiries of foreign pressmen: "A single evening of him on his best behavior was enough to convince every one of us that he was a bad one to deal with if you were on the wrong side of the fence" (MacDonald, 1998).

Though by all accounts he was devoted to his three children (a fourth was born after his death), his relationship with his wife was strained. A compulsive womanizer, Heydrich was a familiar figure in the red-light district of Berlin. He would compel his subordinates to accompany him on epic binges in the bars and brothels of the capital, occasions dreaded by his staff because he was dangerously unstable when drunk and displayed a strong sadistic streak. They came to fear the afternoon phone call from their chief, the leering voice and the request that they join him for dinner and then "go places." Lina Heydrich resented her husband's infidelity, and he in turn suspected her of affairs, including one with Walter Schellenberg, and had the security police watch her.

In 1941 Himmler, eager to put some distance between his ambitious subordinate and the center of power in Berlin, got Hitler to name Heydrich the reich protector of Bohemia-Moravia (Czechoslovakia), replacing the ineffectual diplomat Konstantin von Neurath (later, after his Nuremberg trial, the oldest prisoner at Spandau). Heydrich's brief governorship, during which he persuaded many Czechs to cooperate with him, was triumphantly successful. He highlighted his rising status by an act of homage to his father, a suspected Jew, who was never quite accepted by polite old–German society. On the evening of May 26, 1942, Reinhard Heydrich inaugurated the Prague music festival with a concert of Bruno Heydrich's chamber works, performed by a quartet of Bruno's former pupils from the Halle conservatory. Heydrich himself wrote the program notes. According to Lina Heydrich, this event was the fulfillment of an old dream. The musical establishment of

Prussia had disdained Bruno Heydrich's talent, but his son, a member of the new Nazi elite, had recognized it.

The following day, Heydrich was to depart Prague for a bigger job in Germany. But two young Czechs, Jan Kubiš and Josef Gabčík, sent from London to assassinate him, ambushed his open Mercedes as he drove the twenty kilometers from his residence, the castle of Jungfern-Breschan, to his Prague office in the Hradcin Palace. In *The Killing of Reinhard Heydrich*, Callum MacDonald describes what happened.

Gabčík raised his gun and pulled the trigger at point blank range, but the weapon failed to fire. Heydrich then made a fatal error. Instead of ordering his driver, Oberscharführer (technical sergeant) Klein, to speed away from the ambush, Heydrich stood up, drew his pistol, and ordered that the car be stopped. Neither Heydrich nor Klein had seen Kubiš and thought they were dealing with a lone assassin.

Kubiš stepped forward and tossed a bomb at the two men in the Mercedes. But his aim was poor, and instead of landing in the open car, the bomb exploded against the right rear wheel. Shrapnel flew back into Kubiš's face and shattered the windows of a trolley which had stopped on the other side of the road. Passengers screamed as they were hit by shards of flying glass and metal. The Mercedes lurched violently, coming to rest in the gutter, belching smoke. The blast hurled upward two SS jackets folded on the back seat of the car; they landed over the trolley power lines.

Heydrich and Klein jumped from the wrecked car, brandishing pistols, to fight it out with their assailants. The strapping six-foot Klein made for Kubiš, who was staggering away, half-blinded by blood. Klein tried to shoot Kubiš with his automatic, but inadvertently pressed the magazine release catch, jamming the gun. Kubiš grabbed a bicycle, fired his Colt pistol into the air to scatter the crowd of shocked passengers pouring out of the trolley, and pedaled away furiously.

Heydrich, meanwhile, lurched towards Gabčík, weaving like a drunk. Gabčík ducked behind a telephone pole, trading shots with Heydrich, who took cover behind the stalled tram. Suddenly Heydrich, wounded and in pain, doubled over and staggered to the side of the road. The bomb had broken one of his ribs and had driven fragments of horsehair and wire from the upholstery of the car into his spleen. Heydrich collapsed against a fence, supporting himself with one hand against the railing, as Gabčík sprinted away. As Klein returned from his unsuccessful pursuit of Kubiš, Heydrich, his face etched with pain, gestured with his free hand and gasped, "Get that bastard!" Klein dashed after Gabčík while Heydrich staggered along the pavement, finally falling against the hood of the wrecked Mercedes. Although the crowd of trolley passengers observed his desperate struggle, no one stepped forward to help the badly wounded man in SS uniform.

Finally, a young blond woman recognized Heydrich and shouted for a car to take him to a hospital. An off-duty Czech policeman, who had been a passenger in the trolley, hailed a passing baker's van. The driver, hesitant to get involved, argued heatedly with the policeman. Heydrich remained slumped against his car as a dark bloodstain spread across his uniform.

A small truck carrying a load of floor polish was finally commandeered, and the policeman helped shoehorn the wounded Heydrich into the cramped cab. The ride in the jolting truck quickly overwhelmed Heydrich, and he asked the driver to stop. He was moved into the back of the truck, where he flopped on his belly among the boxes of wax and floor polish, one hand across his face, the other pressed against his wound. At eleven o'clock, he arrived at Bulkova Hospital.

In the emergency room a young Czech physician, Vladimir Snajdr, cleaned Heydrich's wound. "I took forceps and a few swabs and tried to see whether the wound was deep…. He did not flinch although it must have hurt him." A Dr. Dieck, the German hospital director, ordered x-rays of what appeared to be only a superficial wound. The films showed the broken rib, a ruptured diaphragm, and metal fragments in the region of the spleen.

Dr. Dieck recommended immediate surgery, but Heydrich did not want to trust his life to a Prague surgeon and demanded someone from Berlin. After some arguing Heydrich agreed to an operation but only if the top Nazi surgeon in Prague, Dr. Hohlbaum of the German Clinic, was called in. Shortly after noon, Heydrich was wheeled into an operating room.

Himmler sent his friend, Dr. Karl Gebhardt, and Hitler's doctors, Dr. Karl Brandt and Dr. Theodor Morell, to Prague to look after Heydrich. At first, Gebhardt was optimistic and believed Dieck and Hohlbaum had done good work. But in a few days Heydrich's condition deteriorated. He developed peritonitis and septicemia, his temperature soared, and he was in great pain. Gebhardt refused to operate and remove Heydrich's infected spleen. Instead, he gave the patient large doses of morphine, blood transfusions, and an antibacterial sulfa drug to control infection.

On June 2, Himmler flew to Prague to visit the mortally ill Heydrich. During their conversation Heydrich quoted from his father's fourth opera, *Amen*: "The world is just a barrel organ which the Lord God turns himself. We all have to dance to the tune which is already on the drum." Heydrich slipped into a coma and died at 4:30 A.M., June 4, 1942.

The SS was ruthless in pursuing Heydrich's assassins. The Gestapo searched the home of Marie Moravec, who had helped the conspirators. Mrs. Moravec asked if she could go to the toilet. Once she had locked

Heinrich Himmler eulogizes the fallen Heydrich in the Mosaic Hall of the New Reich Chancellery, June 9, 1942 (Ullstein Bilderdienst).

herself in, she swallowed a cyanide capsule. The Gestapo took her son, Ata Moravec, to the cellars of the Pecek Palace, where he was tortured for half a day. Then he was stupefied with alcohol and presented with his mother's head floating in a fish tank. Finally breaking down, he told his interrogators that the assassins might be in the catacombs of the Karel Boromejsky Church.

To force Kubiš, Gabčík, and their accomplices from the church crypt, the Prague fire brigade pumped in water. The conspirators used their last bullets to kill themselves rather than be taken alive.

Nazi revenge against the Czechs followed swiftly. On June 9 the SS surrounded the village of Lidice on the pretext that it had provided refuge for the assassins and razed it; 199 adult males were shot; 191 women were sent to Ravensbrück concentration camp, where 50 of them were to die;

and the village's 98 children were deported to Germany, where only 25 survived.

But this atrocity was not Heydrich's most terrible legacy to the twentieth century. Heydrich is also credited with the concept of the extermination camps and in particular the creation of the Sonderkommandos, groups of strong young Jews who on arrival in the killing centers were temporarily kept alive to clean, sort the victims' possessions, burn the corpses, bury the ashes and efface the traces until, burnt out or at the Germans' whim, they too were gassed. Heydrich boasted that he had drawn the idea from his study of Egyptian history, where a similar need to preserve the secrets of the tombs of the Pharaohs found the same solution: the immediate death of all those who had built them. In June 1942, a few weeks after Heydrich's own death, Himmler named the organization in occupied Poland, which administered the four extermination camps in which two and a half million Jews were to be gassed over the next sixteen months, the *Aktion Reinhard* in his honor.

The British journalist Gitta Sereny interviewed Heydrich's nephew and godson Thomas, a well-known German cabaret artist who sings and recites, mostly from works by Jewish poets. Thomas Heydrich was eleven years old when his father's much-loved older brother was killed.

"I was very angry because at that time I was of course a passionate *Pimpf* [junior Hitler Youth]," he told Ms. Sereny, when she met him in 1990.

"He was a hero to us; we didn't know anything about politics, we only knew that he was a fantastic sportsman. And of course he was always in the papers, standing next to our idol, the Führer. I was sad because I knew my father would be very unhappy. My uncle was a very good, tender father," he said, thoughtfully. "It's almost a cliché now, isn't it, about these appalling men? But that doesn't make it any less true. One just doesn't like to think of it. Can you imagine? Tender?" He repeated the word bitterly.

Thomas Heydrich's family lived on the exclusive Prinzregentenstrasse in Berlin when he was small. The large house next door —"It had lovely big steps on which I played as a child"—belonged to Jews. "It was burned down during the Kristallnacht," he says. "I watched furniture being thrown out of a window, including a piano — imagine, a piano! I remember wondering why anybody would do this rather than calling the fire brigade. I mean, our family was musical, and I knew those neighbors were too. I asked, but was told to hush."

Thomas noticed placards on shops and park benches: *Juden Verboten* (Jews forbidden). Again he was rebuked when he asked questions. He despises the Nazi generation of Germans who insisted, to the end of their lives, that they knew nothing, saw nothing, and even suspected nothing reprehensible during the Nazi time.

"I saw all this, and everybody else did too. They are all liars," he said.

Thomas thinks his father, who was a journalist, began to have doubts in 1941. "He suddenly asked for a posting to the eastern front as a private in an army information unit," he said. "He was by nature a very happy, jolly sort of man. I adored him. Every time he came home on leave after this, he was more depressed. My mother often asked why he was so sad, and he would invariably answer, 'We'll talk about it after the war.'"

Thomas believes his father only found out the worst things his uncle had been responsible for after Reinhard Heydrich's assassination.

"There is a photograph of my father at my uncle's state funeral in June 1942, standing in his sergeant's uniform between Hitler and Göring. Later that day an officer came, bringing my father a thick letter from my uncle that had been found in his safe. He took it and went to his study. Hours later he came out, ashen-faced, with this sheaf of pages.

"He went into the kitchen, which still had an old wood stove, and burned them one by one, very slowly, almost like a ceremony. There must have been a hundred pages. We all stood there watching, and at the end, when he looked as if he was about to drop and my mother put her arms around him and asked him what was in the letter, he said, 'Don't ever ask. I can't talk about it, ever, not until it's all over.'"

Thomas feels sure that in the letter his uncle explained to his father everything he was planning and offered justification for everything he had done. Thomas's conviction stems from the fact that his father became as of then an active anti–Nazi, using the printing facilities available to him to produce passports and other papers to spirit people — most of them Jews — out of

Germany. In late 1944, believing himself discovered, he wrote a good-bye letter to his family and shot himself.

The family never learned about his father's anti–Nazi activities until after the war, when a man who had worked with him told them. "We never knew whether he'd really been discovered," Thomas said, "but a prosecutor had come that evening and they'd spent all night in his study, talking. Soon after the man left, he killed himself." A trade-off, Thomas thinks: the suicide and the family's safety, rather than a scandalous treason trial of Reinhard Heydrich's brother. A few weeks after the end of the war Thomas read what had been done and saw the photographs. As of that moment "and forever," he says, he carried his family's guilt. "I was, if you like, deputizing for all the others," he said, "my aunt, who, inconceivable as it is, felt proud of her husband; four children, who, incomprehensibly to me, claim to feel nothing; my mother, who, having always instinctively disliked my uncle, was able to hide comfortably behind that early rejection.

"My father, who would have helped me shoulder this guilt, was no longer there. Somebody had to feel guilt for the devilish things my uncle had done."

After Reinhard Heydrich's death, his office building, the Prinz Albrecht Palais, did not fare well. Heydrich had ordered extensive renovations of the building, but a bombing raid in May 1944 badly damaged it, and before the end of the war it sustained even more destruction. In April 1949 it was demolished, and in 1958 the land on which it stood was completely cleared of rubble. In 1961 the Berlin Senate became the owner of the land.

Heydrich, Lina. *Leben mit einem Kriegsverbrecher*. Verlag W. Ludwig. Pfaffenhofen, Germany 1976.
Sereny, Gitta. *Albert Speer: His Battle with Truth*. Alfred A. Knopf. New York 1995.
MacDonald, Callum. *The Killing of Reinhard Heydrich*. DaCapo Press. New York 1998.

Bernhard, Marianne, Madeleine Cabor, Rainer Eisenschmid. *Baedeker's Berlin*. 3rd ed. Macmillan. New York 1994.

Kurfürstenstrasse 115–116. "Jewish Brotherhood Building"

Built around the turn of the century, this building housed Bureau IV B 4 of the Reich Main Security Office after 1939. Adolf Eichmann, the "desk criminal," organized the Wannsee Conference (see Wannsee Villa) and the murder of the Jews of Europe from here. The building was demolished in 1961, when Eichmann was on trial in Jerusalem. "Sylter Hof," a hotel, replaced it. The city has placed two plaques commemorating the history of the site on a nearby bus stop shelter.

Among the men responsible for the Holocaust, Americans and Israelis are most familiar with Adolf Eichmann. While Eichmann was incarcerated in Jerusalem, he was the subject of meticulous interrogation and study. His name will forever be synonymous with the mass murder of European Jews.

Eichmann was born in Solingen on March 19, 1906, the son of a bookkeeper for the Solingen Light and Power Company. The family moved to the Austrian city of Linz, where Eichmann grew up. Eichmann attended a vocational secondary school where he studied engineering but never received a degree. From 1925 to 1933 he worked as a traveling salesman, his last employer being the Vacuum Oil Company (today the Mobil Oil Company).

On April 1, 1932, Eichmann joined the Austrian Nazi Party as member number 889,895 and the SS as member 45,326. When the Austrian government banned these organizations on June 19, 1933, Eichmann decamped to Germany, where with other Austrian SS members he received military training. He was assigned to the SS camps in Lechfeld and Dachau but soon found them dreary.

His prospects improved when on October 1, 1934, he was assigned to the SD (Security Service) in Berlin under Reinhard Heydrich. The SD was the original Nazi organization and was becoming more influential. Eichmann's job was keeping track of Jews and Jewish organizations, both inside and outside of Germany, and planning the expulsion of the Jews from the reich.

In 1937 Eichmann traveled with his superior, Herbert Hagen, to Alexandria and Cairo. Their mission was to evaluate the possibility of deporting German Jews to Palestine and to develop contacts with anti–Jewish Arab circles.

When Hitler annexed Austria in 1938, Eichmann became leader of the newly formed Central Office for Jewish Emigration in Vienna. His mission was to plunder Austria's Jews, rendering them destitute before forcibly expelling them. So effective were his tactics that Heydrich considered them a model to be used in other countries.

The 82-year-old Sigmund Freud received the attentions of Eichmann's office. On their first visit to his home, Gestapo officers looted 6,000 Austrian shillings from a safe, prompting Dr. Freud to observe that he had never taken so much for a first visit. Just before leaving Vienna for London on June 4, 1938, Freud remarked, "I can heartily recommend the Gestapo to anyone." Freud's four elderly sisters stayed behind and were murdered at Auschwitz.

In April 1939 Franz Walter Stahlecker, a former superior, summoned Eichmann to Prague. Eichmann's task was to oust Jews from Bohemia and Moravia. In the following months Eichmann shuttled between Prague and Berlin but left his family in Austria, where they remained until the end of the war.

After Hitler overran Poland in September 1939, he determined to Germanize the conquered territory, converting it into a district of the Greater German Reich. Eichmann was put in charge of organizing the effort to drive out Jews and Poles. His first plan, submitted February 5, 1940, entitled "Emigration and Evacuation," later became infamous under the designation "IV B 4." By March 1, 1941, the plan bore the title "Jews and Evacuation Issues." In the meantime the war had turned the trickle of emigrants into a torrent.

Eichmann's authority continued to broaden. He was responsible for depriving all forcibly evacuated German Jews of citizenship, which was immediately forfeited when they were deported. Their money went to the Reich treasury. Eichmann's large offices were now in the center of Berlin, on the Kurfürstenstrasse. He was the boss of five SS officers of varied ranks, as well as secretaries and assistants.

As the leader of IV B 4, in 1940 and early 1941, Eichmann worked together with German railway officials to arrange for the transport of huge numbers of people, to whose fate Eichmann was completely indifferent. Among these people were tens of thousands of Poles and Jews, forcibly evacuated to the east under deplorable conditions. Eichmann made official trips to the conquered territories and knew, by his own observation, the results of his work.

A decisive turn in Eichmann's duties occurred after Hitler invaded the Soviet Union, June 22, 1941. Eichmann learned of Hitler's decision to begin murdering Jews and received the "Incident Reports" describing the massacres. He knew also that the transports he was organizing served to deliver the victims to their killers.

Before the Wannsee Conference Heinrich Müller, Eichmann's boss, had sent him to inspect the murder sites. Eichmann witnessed shootings and, in Kulmhof, December 1941, the killing of Polish Jews from the Łódź ghetto in gas trucks.

"I saw the following," Eichmann testified in Jerusalem:

a room.... There were Jews in it. They had to undress, and then a sealed truck drove up. The doors were opened; it drove up to a kind of ramp. The naked Jews had to get in. Then the doors were closed and the truck drove off.... The whole time [the truck] was there, I didn't look inside. I couldn't. The screaming and ... I was much too shaken.... I drove after the truck ... and there I saw the most horrible sight I had seen in all my life. [The truck] drove up to a fairly long trench. The doors were opened and corpses were thrown out. The limbs were as supple as if they'd been alive. Just thrown in. I can still see a civilian with pliers pulling out the teeth.

Eichmann described more of what he saw in a memoir he wrote in his Jerusalem cell: "Corpses, corpses, corpses. Shot, gassed, decaying corpses. They seemed to pop out of the ground when a grave was opened. It was a delirium of blood. It was an inferno, a hell, and I felt I was going insane." He turned to the bottle, he wrote, for relief.

Back in Berlin Eichmann made a new determination of the number of Jews living in the Reich territory, to decide how many should be deported to the east or Theresienstadt. He hoped that by having an accurate census, he would be able to employ the available rail transport most efficiently. His success, in the case of victims not living in the Soviet Union, would depend on access to enough trains, careful preparation of timetables, and efficient Gestapo roundups. The killing in the death camps would also need to be accomplished with dispatch. Eichmann had no real desire to inspect the camps, but he had to understand the intricacies of the entire murder process. In 1944 he became more intimately involved, when he went to Budapest to oversee special commandos, in league with Hungarian fascists, who were deporting Hungarian Jews to Auschwitz.

During the first Nuremberg trials in 1946, Eichmann's name came up many times, but the prosecutors thought he had died at the end of the war. In reality, he had acquired the uniform of an SS officer and also a pilot's outfit. He moved from Austria to Bavaria to a detention camp, where some of his fellow inmates recognized him. Camp officials also knew he was an SS member because, like all SS men, he had his blood type tattooed in his armpit.[50] Nevertheless, he managed to escape to the Lüneburg Heath, near Hamburg, where he was a woodworker for the forest superintendent's office.

In 1950 Eichmann decided to leave Germany because he wanted to be reunited with his family, who were still living in Austria. He chose Argentina as his place of exile because many other Nazi criminals had hidden there. He traveled through Austria to Italy and sailed from Genoa to Buenos Aires with a passport identifying him as Ricardo Klement.[51] Two years later his wife and sons joined him.

Eichmann worked in a Mercedes-Benz factory in central Buenos Aires and lived quietly in a suburb, Villa San Fernando. A neighbor, Cecilio Guillermo, remembered him as "a polite German who bought lots of pastries but didn't like to talk much. When they told us that he was a Nazi who had killed all those people, we didn't believe them."

Israeli Mossad agents kidnapped Eichmann on May 11, 1960, a chilly, rainy night, as he walked home from his commuter bus stop. One agent, Peter Z. Malkin, approached Eichmann and said, "One minute, sir." Suddenly, Malkin spun his quarry around by the shoulders, pinning his arms behind his back. Eichmann screamed. The two men fell into a ditch, where other agents grabbed Eichmann, shoved him into a car, and sped away. Years later, Malkin commented, "All I was thinking was, don't let him get away, because then you'll be known as the guy who had his hands on Adolf Eichmann and let him slip away."

The Mossad agents hid Eichmann in a house, handcuffed to a bed. There Malkin interrogated his prisoner, as he recounted in his book, *Eichmann in My Hands*:

"I love children," [Eichmann] put it to me one night early on, smiling almost dreamily.

"You love children?" I shot back, unable to help myself. "You must mean some children."

"No, I love all children."

"Do you?" Once again I found myself struggling for self-control in his presence.

"Look," he replied evenly, daring to broach the subject himself, "perhaps to you it seems as if I hate Jews. I don't. I was never an anti–Semite. I was always repulsed by Streicher and the *Stürmer* crowd." The reference was to the most primitive racist ideologue at the top echelons of Nazism and his venomous magazine. In fact, he continued, "I have always been fond of Jews. I had Jewish friends. When I was touring Haifa, I made a point of finding Jewish taxi drivers. I always liked Jews better than the Arabs...."

I paused, almost unable to contain myself. "My sister's boy, my favorite playmate, he was just your son's age. Also blond and blue-eyed, just like your son. And you killed him."

Perplexed by the observation, he actually waited a moment to see if I would clarify it. "Yes," he said finally, "but he was Jewish, wasn't he?"

Eleven days after the abduction, the Israeli agents spirited Eichmann out of Argentina illegally in an El Al airplane. The Israeli action led the Argentine government to mount a vigorous protest in the United Nations Security Council, June 22, 1960. The lively debate engendered considerable controversy over old Nazis still living in West and East Germany.

In Jerusalem an Israeli captain, Avner Less, interrogated Eichmann and recorded the proceedings on tape (Lang and Sibyll, 1983). Born on Prager Strasse in Berlin in 1916, Less had been educated in German schools until he fled to Paris in 1933. He immigrated to Palestine with his Hamburg-born wife in 1938. His father was deported to the east in January 1943, in one of the last transports to leave Berlin.

Less was disappointed when he first saw Adolf Eichmann at 4:45 P.M., May 29, 1960. The prisoner was a thin, balding, utterly ordinary-looking man in a khaki shirt, trousers, and open sandals. Eichmann looked nothing like a Hollywood movie Nazi.

Moreover, he was a bundle of nerves. The left half of his face twitched. He hid his trembling hands under the table. Because Eichmann was a heavy smoker, Less made sure he had plenty of cigarettes. The jailers had taken away his glasses, and Less had to arrange for a new pair with plastic lenses.

After about a week Eichmann recovered his composure. But he did have one moment of panic a few days later, when he thought his last hour had arrived. The officer of the guard had stepped into the room and informed the prisoner that he had come to escort him to the judge. Terrified, Eichmann rose. As one of the guards blindfolded him, to prevent his getting an overall view of the prison compound, his knees buckled. "But Herr Hauptmann [captain]," he bleated, "I haven't told you everything yet." Less reassured the frightened man that he was only being taken to a justice of the peace for renewal of his order of detention, after which the interrogation would continue. Eichmann immediately recovered his soldierly demeanor and marched out of the room flanked by two guards.

Eichmann's German was atrocious. Although a native German speaker, Less had great difficulty understanding the jargon of the Nazi bureaucracy rendered in a mixed Berlin-Austrian accent, further garbled by Eichmann's fondness for endlessly complicated sentences, in which he himself occasionally became lost.

Even Eichmann's German attorney had difficulty understanding his client. Because no Israeli lawyer would defend Eichmann, the Parliament ordered that a foreigner be engaged. The eventual choice was a lawyer from Cologne, Dr. Robert Servatius. During the Nuremberg trials Servatius had defended Fritz Sauckel, who went to the gallows for his treatment of slave laborers.

After Servatius's first visit Eichmann told Less: "Herr Hauptmann, do you know what Dr. Servatius said? He objected to my German. He said, 'You'll have to relearn your language. Even the best translator won't be able to find his way through those convoluted sentences of yours.' Is my German actually that bad, Herr Hauptmann?" When Less agreed that it was, Eichmann was offended.

Less was struck by Eichmann's complete lack of humor. On the rare occasions when Eichmann's razor-thin lips broke into a smile, his eyes remained mirthless. His expression was sardonic, often aggressive.

Eichmann's cell, which measured ten by thirteen feet, was furnished with a cot, a table, and a chair. Every day the prisoner

Adolf Eichmann on trial in Jerusalem (Ullstein Bilderdienst).

cleaned the cell and the adjoining toilet and shower room with thoroughness and dedication.

Elaborate precautions were taken to prevent Eichmann from committing suicide. A guard sat in the cell with him day and night. Outside the cell door sat a second guard, who watched the first guard through a peephole and made sure there was no contact between the guard and Eichmann. A third guard, in a vestibule outside the door, constantly watched the second guard.

An electric light was left on all night. When the light disturbed his sleep, Eichmann would pull his woolen blanket over his head, whereupon the guard would pull it back, to be certain the prisoner was not trying to kill himself under the blanket.

None of the guards spoke either of Eichmann's two languages, German or Spanish, but their officers spoke at least one. To prevent any act of revenge, no one who had lost family members in the Holocaust was chosen for the guard unit. When Less interrogated Eichmann, the officer responsible for Eichmann's transfer from his cell to the interrogation room entered first, followed by two guards with Eichmann between them. Eichmann stood at attention behind his chair until Less asked him to be seated. Though Less had told Eichmann that there was no need to stand at attention, Eichmann went on doing so throughout his incarceration.

Eichmann's military formality did not stop there. When on January 1, 1961, Less mentioned that a new year had begun, Eichmann replied, "Herr Hauptmann, may I take the liberty of wishing you a happy New Year?" And he performed a sort of seated bow and clicked his heels under the table.

Eichmann was indicted on February 1, 1961. The chief prosecutor, Gideon Hausner, initially introduced 1,300 documents into evidence, to which 300 were later added.

Eichmann's prosecution in Jerusalem was the world's first televised trial. The rapt courtroom spectators, mostly Israelis, found it hard to listen to the gruesome details of their families' fates but were unable to turn away. Occasionally there was an outburst from an onlooker who couldn't bear any more. A prosecutor broke off his examination of a man who had just told of his last glimpse of his young daughter, a speck of red in a mass of women and children marked for extermination; the prosecutor was apparently silenced by thoughts of what it would be like to watch his own daughter vanish.

Seated in a bulletproof glass booth, Eichmann showed no reaction to the horrors he was hearing. Head tilted, lips tight, twisted mouth moving as though he were tasting something very disagreeable, he looked to the *New York Times*'s Walter Goodman like a silent movie actor playing a villain. Was this really the man in SS uniform witnesses remembered, hand on pistol, barking orders?

During the trial's climax, when Eichmann took the stand, his testimony was a grim travesty of what had happened. He "sought peaceful solutions acceptable to both parties," he said. He complimented himself on having paid a rabbi to teach him Hebrew rather than forcing the rabbi to give him free lessons.

After the Wannsee Conference, Eichmann testified, he sat "cozily around a fireplace" with Heydrich and Gestapo chief Heinrich Müller, drinking French cognac and chatting. "At that moment, I sensed a kind of Pontius Pilate feeling, for I was free of all guilt.... Who was I to judge? Who was I to have my own thoughts in this matter?" He, Heydrich, and Müller were only carrying out the law, decreed by the Führer.

Eichmann sought to portray himself as an uninfluential shipping clerk, who had no responsibility whatsoever for the fate of his human freight. In fact, he controlled the final solution from a desk in Berlin. But he insisted that the sight of blood upset him. "I was not the right man for these things." The exasperated prosecutor replied, "If you want to be a laughingstock, do so." Undeterred, Eichmann averred that he was "on the lowest rung," that his "position was too insignificant." His oft-repeated mantra was, "I had to obey." In his Jerusalem memoirs, Eichmann was more specific: "Obeying an order was the most important thing to me. It could be that is in the nature of the German."

"Humanity does not know how to punish people like this," remarked one Israeli (Goodman, 1997).

Convicted and sentenced to death by hanging, his plea for mercy rejected by the court, Eichmann was executed in Rameleh Prison, Tel Aviv, May 31, 1962. He was cremated and his ashes scattered in the sea. An Auschwitz survivor, watching the dispersal of the remains, remembered that the heaps of human ashes from the camp crematoria were spread over the icy paths so that the guards would not slip on patrol.

Hannah Arendt (1906–75), the German-born U.S. political philosopher, covered the trial for the *New Yorker* and later produced a book about it, *Eichmann in Jerusalem: A Report on the Banality of Evil.* In her epilogue, she wrote,

The trouble with Eichmann was precisely that so many were like him, and that the many were neither perverted nor sadistic, that they were, and still are, terribly and terrifyingly normal. From the viewpoint of our legal institutions and of our moral standards of judgment, this normality was much more terrifying than all the atrocities put together.

Arendt, Hannah. *Eichmann in Jerusalem. A Report on the Banality of Evil.* Viking Press. New York 1965.
Eichmann Interrogated. Transcripts from the Archives of the Israeli Police. Edited by Jochen von Lang in collaboration with Claus Sibyll. Translated from the German by Ralph Mannheim. Farrar, Straus, and Giroux. New York 1983.
Faure, Michel. Argentine. Sur le piste des der-

niers Nazis. *L'Express*. April 9, 1998, pp. 44–51.

Goodman, Walter. Crime and Punishment: The Trial of Eichmann. *New York Times*, Late Edition (East Coast), April 30, 1997, C14.

Grimes, William. Capturing the man who caught Eichmann. *New York Times*. November 10, 1996, sec. 2, p. 18.

Jones, Ernest. *The Life and Work of Sigmund Freud*. Edited and abridged in one volume by Lionel Trilling and Steven Marcus. Basic Books. New York 1961.

Malkin, Peter Z., and Harry Stein. *Eichmann in My Hands*. Warner Books, New York 1990.

Sims, Calvin. Film stirs Argentines' memories of a Nazi. *New York Times*. March 5, 1996, sec. C, p. 11.

Rürup, Reinhard, et al. *Topographie des Terrors*. Verlag Willmuth Arenhövel. Berlin 1987.

Lehrer, Steven. *Wannsee House and the Holocaust*. McFarland. Jefferson, North Carolina 2000.

Cohen, Roger. Why? New Eichmann notes try to explain. *New York Times*. August 13, 1999, p. 1.

Seewald, Stefan. Buswartehäuschen erinnert an berüchtigtes Judenreferat. *Berliner Morgenpost*. December 12, 1998.

Air Ministry. Wilhelmstrasse 81–85 (corner Leipziger Strasse)

The Air Ministry (1936) was the first large Nazi building in Berlin. Designed by Ernst Sagebiel, the structure was finished in 18 months. The enormous terra cotta front, 280 meters long and five stories high, dominated the entire neighborhood. The severe right angles of the 4,000 windows and the sharply cut, plain facade augment the impression of enormous mass.

The central corridor is 300 meters long. The 60-centimeter-thick concrete roof still has five antiaircraft gun pedestals. In 2,500 rooms Hermann Göring and his underlings managed all civilian and military aviation. Göring's own villa, Leipzigerplatz 11, was in the park behind the Air Ministry and had been the office of the Prussian commerce minister; Albert Speer renovated the villa for Göring, 1933–34.[52]

The Air Ministry, the first large Nazi building in Berlin.

A lobby exhibit of the Air Ministry's history has old photos, blueprints, and a time capsule from the cornerstone, which workmen turned up by accident while boring into the foundation. A decaying bunker is below the Leipzigerstrasse facade.

Knopf, Volker, and Stefan Martens. *Göring's Reich. Selbstinszenierungen in Carinhall*. Ch. Links Verlag. Berlin 1999.
Schubert, Peter. Das grösste Bürogebäude Berlins. Ex-Reichsluftfahrtministerium im Umbau zum Bundesfinanzministerium. *Berliner Morgenpost*. July 31, 1997.

BERLIN BUNKERS

Hitler Bunker (Führerbunker) (Near the Intersection of Wilhelmstrasse and Vossstrasse)

Under Hitler's New Reich Chancellery in Wilhelmstrasse, Albert Speer built an air raid shelter of almost 100 rooms. Wounded soldiers and passersby used this shelter. The Wehrmacht had a communication center here, with a shortwave radio connected to an antenna often damaged in air raids. SS Brigadeführer (major general) Wilhelm Mohnke, commander of a thousand-man guard regiment, used some of the vaulted rooms for his headquarters.

Beneath the chancellery garden, architect Carl Piepenburg and the construction firm Hochtief began building a Führerbunker in 1943.[53] The cost was 1,353,460.16 reichsmarks. The bunker came into use before it had even been completed in late

1944. The concrete was still wet. Cables and water pipes were everywhere. On January 16, 1945, Hitler moved in permanently and unobtrusively. A single soldier-valet lugged the dictator's personal belongings from the chancellor's luxury apartment in the old Reich Chancellery, 100 yards away.

The Führerbunker's foundation was twelve meters below the ground. The 4.5 meter thick concrete roof lay two meters below the earth surface. When Berlin was shelled, the structure trembled in the sandy soil.

A 60-kilowatt diesel generator provided uninterrupted power for heat and ventilation. Hitler was terrified of dying from Russian poison gas and regularly saw to the changing of the intake and exhaust filters. A pump and an underground well furnished water. A microphone hidden in an external ventilator brought in the sounds of the surrounding area.

The bunker entrance was located in the cellar of the chancellery. Past a little kitchen and troop canteen, stairs led through three steel doors that could automatically seal off the prebunker, six basement bedrooms, and conference rooms to the left and right of a central corridor, built in 1936. The corridor led to a circular stairway, which descended to the Führerbunker.

On the right of the Führerbunker passageway stood a generator room and a little telephone switchboard, near two cupboards with doors. Further down were a guardroom, secretary's desk, and four-room medical office. The medical office ultimately became home to the Reich minister for

Opposite: Diagram of Hitler's bunker with street map. (1) Hitler's bedroom; (2) conference room; (3) Hitler's living room, where Hitler and Eva Braun committed suicide; (4) Hitler's study; (5) Eva Braun's living room and bedroom; the room for Hitler's dogs is adjacent; (6) Goebbels's bedroom; (7) first aid station; (8) secretaries' room; (9) weapons room; (10) guardroom; (11) telephone switchboard. At bottom is the passageway to the prebunker, two meters above, with conference rooms and rooms for the Goebbels family. At top is the stairway and exit to the Reich Chancellery garden (*Der Spiegel*).

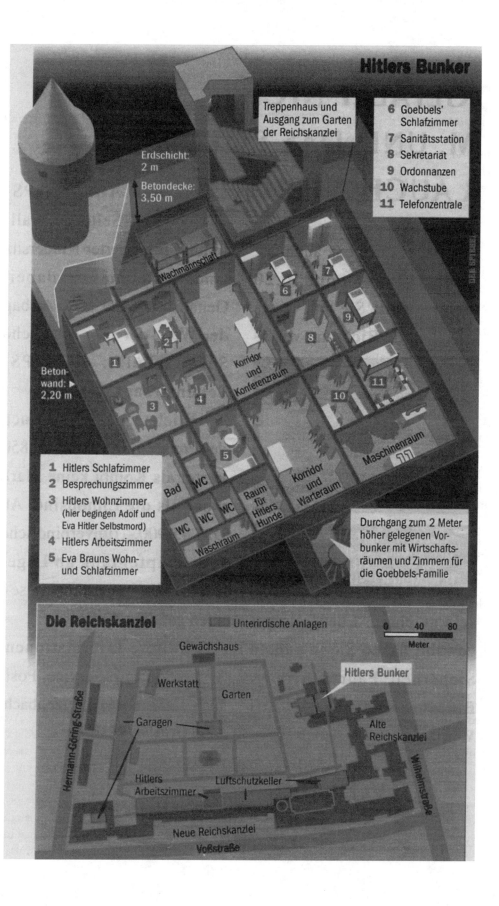

Hitlers Bunker

Treppenhaus und Ausgang zum Garten der Reichskanzlei

Erdschicht: 2 m

Betondecke: 3,50 m

6 Goebbels' Schlafzimmer
7 Sanitätsstation
8 Sekretariat
9 Ordonnanzen
10 Wachstube
11 Telefonzentrale

Wachmannschaft

Betonwand: ► 2,20 m

Korridor und Konferenzraum

Maschinenraum

Bad WC

Raum für Hitlers Hunde

Korridor und Warteraum

WC WC WC

Waschraum

1 Hitlers Schlafzimmer
2 Besprechungszimmer
3 Hitlers Wohnzimmer (hier begingen Adolf und Eva Hitler Selbstmord)
4 Hitlers Arbeitszimmer
5 Eva Brauns Wohn- und Schlafzimmer

Durchgang zum 2 Meter höher gelegenen Vorbunker mit Wirtschaftsräumen und Zimmern für die Goebbels-Familie

Die Reichskanzlei

Unterirdische Anlagen

0   40   80
Meter

Gewächshaus

Werkstatt

Garten

Hitlers Bunker

Hermann-Göring-Straße

Garagen

Alte Reichskanzlei

Hitlers Arbeitszimmer

Luftschutzkeller

Wilhelmstraße

Neue Reichskanzlei

Voßstraße

enlightenment of the people and propaganda, Joseph Goebbels, his wife, and six children.

To the left were Hitler's bedroom, living room, and work room, each measuring about three by four meters, a conference room, and the apartment of Führer-mistress Eva Braun. A room for Hitler's dogs and three bathrooms were nearby.

Martin Bormann had ordered the red carpet, which covered the floor of the corridor. An emergency exit with 37 steps led to the garden. A second exit led to an observation tower, left unfinished.

The bunker reminded Albert Speer of "the thick walls and ceilings of a prison. Iron doors and hatches closed off the few openings, and the narrow walkways between the barbed wire brought [Hitler] no more air and nature than the walkway around a penitentiary brings a convict." In fact, in size and design the bunker was quite similar to the storage cellars for corpses in the crematoria at Auschwitz. Some generals called the Führerbunker a concrete submarine.

The absence of windows satisfied Hitler's need to make day into night (Josef Stalin liked to do this also). Hitler slept from 5 or 6 A.M. to around 11 A.M.

Two dozen people were continually in the bunker. Among them were the telephone operator, Rochus Misch; the diesel generator and ventilation mechanic, Johannes Hentschel; and Eva Braun. There was also a blond Bavarian girl who, contrary to Hitler's wishes, had arrived in Berlin from Munich in a gray flecked Mercedes and liked to dance the Charleston.

Hitler had only his closest associates with him in the bunker: Chief of the Party Chancellery and Reich Leader Martin Bormann, Hitler valet and SS Sturmbannführer (major) Heinz Linge, SS Adjutant Sturmbannführer Otto Günsche, SS-Brigadeführer (major general) and bodyguard Johann Rattenhuber, with his adjutant

SS-Standartenführer (colonel) and procurator Peter Högl. Along with these men were secretaries Johanna Wolf, Traudl Junge, Gerda Christian, Christa Schroeder, and Else Krüger; diet cook Constanze Manziarly; personal physician Dr. Ludwig Stumpfegger; SS Standartenführer and chauffeur Erich Kempka; Lieutenant General and chief pilot Hans Baur.

High officials came to see Hitler in the chancellery basement or the bunker. Army Chief of Staff Hans Krebs was a frequent visitor, along with liaison people from the crumbling power organs of the reich:

- for Heinrich Himmler's SS, Eva Braun's brother-in-law, SS Gruppenführer (lieutenant general) Hermann Fegelein[54];
- for Hermann Göring's Luftwaffe, Colonel Nikolaus von Below;
- for the Navy and Grossadmiral Karl Dönitz, Vice Admiral Erich Voss;
- for Foreign Minister Joachim von Ribbentrop, the old Nazi ambassador Walter Hewel.

From his bunker in 1945 Hitler could make war only with difficulty and finally not at all. Hair graying, hands trembling, back bent, gait shuffling, saliva dripping from the corners of his mouth, the Führer appeared much older than his 55 years. He wandered aimlessly through the corridors and rooms like a ghost who could not find peace. Formerly meticulous about personal hygiene, he now did not bother to shave properly and wore a soiled, stained uniform. "You must not try to look just like old Fritz [Frederick the Great]," remonstrated Eva Braun. (The eighteenth-century Prussian king was indifferent to personal hygiene in his last years.)

In a cellar room of his subterranean labyrinth, under Vossstrasse, was a model of Hitler's favorite city, Linz. Hitler had intended to retire to Linz, with "Fräulein

Braun" and his German shepherd, Blondi. Even as Berlin exploded, burned, and crumbled around him, Hitler and architect Albert Speer discussed new building plans for Linz.

Hitler was determined to defend his bunker to the end. He himself was commandant of the government quarter, where the bunker was located. He named the military district "Citadel," after his final failed Russian offensive at Kursk.

At Hitler's order, holes were made in the concrete walls for gun barrels; grenade throwers were built in, and antitank cannon emplacements were spread throughout the garden. SS-Brigadeführer Mohnke's bunker defenders included members of Hitler's Scandinavian SS bodyguards from the Northland division, 90 French SS men from the Charlemagne division, a few Latvians, and some Spaniards.

To protect the chancellery building itself, navy cadets from the North Sea island of Fehmarn were hastily flown in. These men were being trained for the signal corps and had no other military experience. Their post was the great hall and Hitler's workroom. They were ordered to use Hitler's card table as a shield.

By April 29, 1945, conditions in the bunker reflected the destruction of the city outside. Exhaust ducts plugged, the overheated rooms stank of soldiers' sweat and chlorine. The air intake sucked in dust from artillery shelling, as well as the odor of fire and rot. In these disagreeable surroundings, Hitler married Eva Braun on April 29.

Fearful of being put on exhibit in the Moscow zoo, Hitler committed suicide April 30, with a bullet in the head from his 7.65 caliber Walther semiautomatic pistol.[55] Eva Braun swallowed poison. Josef Stalin never stopped complaining that Hitler had not fallen into his hands alive.

SS adjutants doused the bodies of Hitler and Eva Braun with gasoline and burned them. A day later they did the same to the remains of Goebbels, his wife, and their six young children. Goebbels had the children killed with injected opiates and cyanide before he and his wife poisoned themselves.

When the Soviets found the charred remains, "they stank horribly." Dr. Faust Jossifowitsch Schkarawski performed the autopsy on Hitler: "The corpse is strongly blackened and smells of burnt flesh. A piece of the calvarium is missing.... The lower jaw lies free in the singed oral cavity." Dental records confirmed that the jaw was Hitler's.

After the war Soviet army engineers razed the above-ground sections of the Führerbunker and closed off the underground rooms. When the Berlin Wall was built in 1961, the East German Secret Police moved to identify and seal off any subterranean escape hatches. Since the Führerbunker lay in no-man's land, adjacent to the wall, it was a logical place to search.

The East Germans located Albert Speer's original plans for Hitler's Reich Chancellery, along with precise drawings of bunkers and tunnels. In the summer of 1973 they explored the maze of underground passageways, made many photographs, and even found pages from Goebbels's diary.

"In one of the lower rooms, torturously, fearfully hemmed in, I give a speech in my best form," Goebbels wrote about his appearance before a group of adjutants. "The young officers are enchanted and give me a great ovation."

From 1986 to 1989 the East Germans dynamited the Führerbunker. They carted away the fragments, even the four-and-a-half meter-thick steel and concrete slabs that made up the floor. But part of the bunker complex survived. In 1990 archaeologists found undamaged rooms, along with rotted furniture decorated with swastikas, a few light weapons, abandoned gas masks, and brightly painted murals depicting eagles, SS soldiers in heroic poses, and blond Rhine maidens. These rooms probably housed SS guards and drivers.

More of the Führerbunker turned up in October 1999. Construction workers near the Wilhelmstrasse came upon a concrete slab, which may have formed part of the roof or floor. After archaeologists in the Berlin Monument Service made a cursory inspection, the excavation was filled with dirt and closed.

When the Berlin Wall came down in 1989, there was a mound of earth above the bunker site. Today the site is behind a playground in back of apartment buildings. There is no marker. At Wilhelmstrasse 90 a passageway under an apartment complex, between stores, opens into the playground area.

Bönisch, Georg, and Mathias Müller von Blumencron. Trophäen des Sieges. *Der Spiegel* 5:50–54, 1999.
Hitler's Höllenfahrt. *Der Spiegel* 14:170, 1995.
Kinzer, Stephen. Retrieve the lurid past? (Some Germans recoil). *New York Times.* February 12, 1992.
O'Donnell, James P. *The Bunker.* Houghton Mifflin. Boston 1978.
Soltis, Andy. New embassy in Berlin raises historic Führer. *New York Post.* November 24, 2000.
Stasi im Führerbunker. *Der Spiegel* 10:18, 1997.
Streider: Hitler-Bunker nicht öffnen. *Berliner Morgenpost.* October 16, 1999.
Terrance, Marc. *Concentration Camps. A Traveler's Guide to World War II Sites.* Universal Publishers 1999.
Walsh, Mary Williams. A witness to Hitler's last stand as Germany debates sealing the Berlin bunker where the Nazi leader killed himself; one of its last occupants describes the intrigues and tension of the final days. *Los Angeles Times.* April 29, 1995, p. 1.

Joseph Goebbels's Bunker. Potsdamer Platz (Behrenstrasse and Vossstrasse)

In January 1998 construction workers near the proposed site of the Berlin Holocaust Memorial unearthed Goebbels's bunker. In the bunker, 3,200 square feet in size, workers found rusted helmets, munitions, two empty safes, collapsed airshafts with torn cables, thick steel doors, and a floor covered with mud.

"The bunker is completely decayed," construction engineer Dietmar Arnold told Jola Merten, a reporter for the *Berliner Morgenpost*.[56] "For years it was filled with water, to a depth of 1.7 meters. It contains five rooms, approximately the same size, and one larger room missing a separating wall. Although the bunker is burned out, remains of wall covering are recognizable, and there is probably a parquet floor under the mud."

On account of the 1.8-meter-thick

Site of Hitler's bunker just after the fall of the Berlin Wall in 1989. The mound in the foreground lies directly over the bunker. The Reichstag is in the background.

ceiling, Arnold believes that building of the bunker began in 1941. "The roofs of the first bunkers, such as the one built under the Air Ministry in 1935, were only 80 centimeters thick. But the roof of the Führerbunker was 4.5 meters thick. At the time, bombs were falling, and concrete was the defense."

Arnold says that the *Torfklo* (peat toilet) in Goebbels's bunker was standard equipment, "without a whiff of luxury."[57] Only the thick telephone cables and many plugs indicate that the place belonged to a high Nazi official.

Six feet underground, the bunker had been connected to Goebbels's Berlin villa on the Potsdamer Platz, the former palace of the royal Prussian court marshall. The villa, in the ministry garden located between the present-day Ebertstrasse and Behrenstrasse, no longer exists.

Goebbels's bunker was not connected to the Führerbunker, which was several hundred yards away. Workmen have closed up Goebbels's bunker. Its fate is uncertain. Wilfried Menghin, a Berlin archaeologist who has examined the bunker, feels that it should be preserved as a historic artifact.

Goebbels' bunker found at Holocaust memorial site. *The Guardian*. Manchester. January 27, 1998, p. 13.

Goebbels' bunker possibly located. *Washington Post*. January 28, 1998, p. A13.

Merten, Jola. Torfklo und armdicke Telefonkabel: Was Goebbels im Bunker hinterliess. *Berliner Morgenpost*. January 29, 1998.

_____. Auf der Spur moralischer Grösse. Eine Führung zu den Orten der Hitler-Verschwörung. *Berliner Morgenpost*. July 21, 1999.

_____. Erfolg der "Bunkerküsser." Die Schaustelle führt erstmals in die Unterwelt. *Berliner Morgenpost*. June 6, 1999.

_____. Schrott-oder Zeugnis der Zeitgeschichte? Wilfried Menghin, Leiter des Archäologischen Landesamtes, zum Thema "ausgegrabene Nazi-Bunker." *Berliner Morgenpost*. February 2, 1998.

_____. Was soll aus Goebbels Bunker werden? Verein "Berliner Unterwelten" warnt vor Zerstörung und regt Diskussion an. *Berliner Morgenpost*. January 31, 1999.

Bunker of Reich Ministry for Armaments and Munitions. Pariserplatz 3 (Razed 1997)

This 250-square-meter bunker complex was discovered during excavation of a new headquarters for the DG Bank. The construction workers came on entrance holes leading into the bunker, which was filled with water. The concrete plates were up to two meters thick. Historians believe that Defense Minister Albert Speer and his staff worked here until the end of the war.

The bunker was probably quite comfortable. It had three large rooms, some smaller rooms, a kitchen, and bathroom. The walls were covered with wood paneling. Traces of smoke damage indicated that the interior was destroyed by fire.

Demolition experts drilled holes in the concrete and placed explosive charges. The resulting explosions were "small and precise." Neighboring buildings, above all the nearby Brandenburg Gate, were unshaken.

Dannenbaum, Uwe. Nazi-Bunker wird gesprengt: "Keine Gefährdung für Brandenburger Tor." *Berliner Morgenpost*. January 30, 1997.

Air Raid Shelter. Alexanderplatz (Former East Berlin)

The Nazis built this massive concrete bunker as an air raid shelter. With its warrens of dark passageways and narrow rooms, it is one of the best-preserved Berlin bunkers.

Only the upper levels have electric lights. Visitors must use flashlights to descend ramps to the bunker's main section, which was capable of sheltering 3,000 people 40 feet underground for long periods. "Ramps were built instead of stairs because there would be so many people," says Dietmar Arnold, a construction engineer who has become a local bunker authority.

The bunker was divided into separate rooms to minimize casualties if a bomb should break through and to provide more structural stability. Each room was capable of holding 80 people. There are still hooks on the walls for bunks, which could be hung three high. At the far end pipes emerge from the floor, indicating the position of toilets, long gone. Fresh air was forced in through filters, but exhaled vapor from the breath of many people collected in gullies along the walls and was drained off. "It must have been like the tropics in here," says Arnold. The stale air is now thick with dust.

After the war desperate Berliners removed anything useful in the bunker — wood, metal, pipes, generators — leaving a large, empty space. East German communist leaders began renovating the bunker for their own use as a shelter but abandoned the project in the 1970s. "They ran out of money, and it wasn't that important," says Arnold. The Alexanderplatz bunker is now locked away behind a graffiti-covered yellow door inside a subway entrance.

Geitner, Paul. Secret bunkers begin to see light of day. History: Architectural engineer works to ensure that Berlin's subterranean past is not forgotten. *Los Angeles Times*. February 16, 1997, p. 20.

POTSDAM

On March 21, 1933, a pompous ceremony celebrated the opening of the Reichstag, which had been elected on March 5, 1933, a month after Hitler became chancellor. Hitler and Goebbels picked Potsdam, the old Prussian capital outside Berlin, as the venue. They chose March 21 because 62 years earlier on that day Otto von Bismarck had convened the first Reichstag of the "Second Reich." The entire event was broadcast on radio to present the Third Reich as the legitimate heir to the kaiser's Reich and weaken objections to Hitler's seizure of power.

The Day of Potsdam was introduced with religious services. The Evangelical deputies (including Göring) worshiped in the Church of Saint Nicholas (Nikolaikirche). The Catholics had their own special mass in the parish church. But Hitler and Goebbels, both nominally Catholic, stayed away from the mass because the German bishops were upholding a ban against the Nazis.

The main event was a state ceremony in the Potsdam Garrison Church (*Garnisonkirche*), the site of

Garrison Church, Day of Potsdam, Hindenburg seated (left), Hitler speaking (right).

the Prussian royal tombs.[58] Eighty-five-year-old Reich president Paul von Hindenburg and Chancellor Hitler both spoke. Hindenburg wore his field marshal's uniform. Hitler, in a cutaway, looked like an officious headwaiter. A solemn handshake between Hindenburg, ramrod straight, and Hitler, head humbly bowed, sealed the "marriage of old grandeur and new power." This, by the way, was the same Hindenburg who, a few weeks earlier, had said he would make Hitler a postmaster so that Hitler could lick stamps with Hindenburg's picture on them.

Hindenburg laid a wreath on the Garnisonkirche tomb of Frederick the Great as a 21-gun salute was fired. Then, together with Hitler, the old field marshal reviewed a parade of reichswehr, police, SA, SS, and Steel Helmet units.[59] The festivities ended with the return of the deputies to the Kroll Opera House, where the Reichstag was convened. Two days later, the Reichstag accepted the Enabling Law and relinquished its own power.

Geisler, Kurt. Aus dunkler Ferne hallt der Ton: Üb immer Treu und Redlichkeit. *Berliner Morgenpost* October 17, 1999.

Leser-Frage: Wo befindet sich das Grab Hindenburgs? *Berliner Morgenpost*. December 9, 1999.

Lorant, Stefan. *Sieg Heil! An Illustrated History of Germany from Bismarck to Hitler.* Norton. New York 1974.

Teile des Tischaltars Wilhelm IV. gefunden. Berolinensien sollen in diesem Jahr der Öffentlichkeit zugänglich gemacht werden. *Berliner Morgenpost*. October 7, 1998.

Vor 30 Jahren wurde die Garnisonkirche gesprengt. *Berliner Morgenpost* June 23, 1998.

Weihrauch, Dieter. Vorschlag: Garnisonkirche als Ruinen-Mahnmal wiederaufbauen. *Berliner Morgenpost* July 12, 1998.

Zentner, Christian, and Friedemann Bedürftig, eds. *The Encyclopedia of the Third Reich.* English translation edited by Amy Hackett. Macmillan. New York 1991.

Schloss Cecilienhof

Located in Potsdam's Neuer Garten, this palace, which resembles an English Tudor house, was built for Crown Prince Wilhelm and his wife, Cecilie von Mecklenburg-Schwerin. Architect Paul Schultze-Naumberg (1869–1949) designed the 180-room residence. Construction began in April 1914, was interrupted by the First World War, and finished in 1917. North German Lloyd's gave Cecilie one of the rooms, which resembles a ship's cabin.

After the armistice in November 1918, only the crown prince's two sons, Wilhelm and Louis Ferdinand, remained in the Cecilienhof, along with their tutor. Louis Ferdinand later recalled this period: "We lived in a mixture of cloister and barracks" (Müller, 1997). The crown prince returned to the Cecilienhof from exile in the Netherlands on November 9, 1923, much to the annoyance of his father, ex–Kaiser Wilhelm II, who was permanently exiled in Doorn, Holland.

Hitler visited the crown prince in the Cecilienhof for the first time in 1926. The crown prince supported Hitler's rise, which made the ex–Kaiser quite angry. During the day of Potsdam, March 21, 1933, the crown prince, in gala uniform, sat in the Garnisonkirche, behind the kaiser's traditional place.

Hitler visited the Cecilienhof again in 1933 and 1935. The crown princess is said to have aired out the house after the visits.

The crown prince soon recognized that Hitler had absolutely no use for the Hohenzollern monarchy. Realizing he would have no influence in the government, the crown prince began to distance himself from the Nazis. But he played no role in the resistance to Hitler of the army and diplomatic leaders. Hitler was nevertheless suspicious of him and ordered Gestapo surveillance of the Cecilienhof after the July 20, 1944, assassination attempt.[60]

In January 1945, because of liver and gallbladder complaints, the crown prince went to Obersdorf for a cure. Cecilie fled the Cecilienhof three months later, without being able to get "anything important or of value into her vest," as she wrote in her memoirs (Müller, 1997).

When Soviet troops occupied East Germany, the crown prince and princess lost almost everything and lived on in very modest circumstances. Husband and wife had long since drifted apart and went their separate ways. Cecilie moved to Bad Kissingen, the crown prince to a Hohenzollern property in Hechingen.

Between July 17 and August 2, 1945, the Cecilienhof was the site of a meeting of the victorious Allies, represented by Winston Churchill, Josef Stalin, and Harry S Truman.

Churchill and Truman arrived July 15. Possibly having suffered a mild heart attack, Stalin came a day later. Fearful of flying, the Soviet dictator traveled in an armored train. His itinerary was secret, but Red Army soldiers guarded the entire route.

Stalin's workroom in the Cecilienhof was the mahogany paneled red salon used by the crown princess as a writing room. The white salon, once the music room of the crown princess, became the reception room of the Soviet delegation. The crown prince's smoking room was the workroom for the American delegation. The British delegation's workroom was the crown prince's former library. The royal family's breakfast room housed the secretariat of the British delegation.

The lofty conference room, 26 meters long and 12 meters high, had been the living room of the royal family. The conference table, 3.05 meters in diameter, covered with burgundy cloth, was specially built in Moscow.

Clement Attlee replaced Churchill after the Labour election victory in England, July 26. Stalin was then the only war leader still in power, as Franklin D. Roosevelt had died April 12.

Attlee and Truman lacked Stalin's experience and guile. They immediately agreed to leave to Stalin the territories of East Germany, Thuringia, and Saxony, which the Americans and British had liberated but which were part of the previously agreed-on zone of Soviet occupation.

The Potsdam Agreement established four-power (American, British, Russian, French) occupation zones for postwar Germany. A comprehensive reordering of the German economy and German institutions was also part of the agreement. The Council of Foreign Ministers was established to consider peace settlements. Finally, the conference issued an ultimatum to Japan either to surrender or risk total destruction.

The Potsdam Agreement was full of ambiguities, which the wily Stalin was later quick to exploit. The subsequent rift between the Soviet Union and the Western Allies caused consistent breaches of the Potsdam Agreement, an early manifestation of the cold war.

Today, most of the Cecilienhof is a hotel and restaurant. But the historic rooms used during the 1945 Potsdam Conference have been preserved in their original state and are open to the public.

The Concise Columbia Encyclopedia. Columbia University Press. New York 1995.
Müller, Heike. *Die Konferenz von Potsdam 1945 im Schloss Cecilienhof. Stiftung Preussische Schlösser und Gärten.* Berlin-Brandenburg. 3rd ed. 1997.
Potsdam-Infos. Gedenktafel erinnert an Hitler-Gegner. *Berliner Morgenpost.* July 20, 1997.

Gregor Mendel Strasse 26. Villa Löwenberg

The rooms in this splendid villa are a prime example of *Jugendstil*. According to an owner of the building, Margret Hansen, her grandfather was one of the July 20, 1944, conspirators.[61] The chauffeur of Colonel Claus Graf Schenk von Stauffenberg fetched the famous bomb from the basement of the Villa Löwenberg, where it had been hidden. The villa is being renovated. A club and restaurant will occupy the lower level, and the library is being restored.

Potsdam Privat. Kulturförderer. *Berliner Morgenpost.* January 19, 1997.

SCHORFHEIDE

Carinhall

Carinhall was the "hunting lodge" of Hermann Wilhelm Göring (1893–1946), the number-two Nazi, Hitler's heir apparent, economic leader of the Third Reich, and head of the Luftwaffe. During World War I Göring was commander of the Jagdgeschwader flying squadron, made famous by Manfred von Richthofen, the Red Baron. Göring was an intrepid aviator, who was awarded both the Iron Cross First Class and Pour le Mérite, the Prussian equivalent of our Congressional Medal of Honor. Kaiser Wilhelm II personally bestowed Pour le Mérite on Göring.

Göring's first wife was a beautiful Swedish aristocrat, Carin von Kantzow (née Carin von Fock), whom he married in Munich on February 3, 1922, and through whom he met Hitler. During the 1923 Beer Hall Putsch, Göring, marching at Hitler's side, was severely wounded and arrested. He escaped to Austria, Italy, and finally Sweden. During his prolonged recovery he became addicted to morphine. Carin Göring died of tuberculosis on October 17, 1931, and Hermann Göring married an actress, Emmy Sonnemann.

After Hitler came to power, Göring rose rapidly through the hierarchy of the Third Reich. His corpulent figure, love

Hitler visits Göring at Carinhall, 1935 (Library of Congress).

for uniforms, and sometimes-comic behavior made him a great hit with the German public.

In 1933, as Prussian minister president, Göring received from the government a plot of land in the Schorfheide, a heath, on which he constructed a hunting lodge at government expense. Werner March, architect of the Olympic stadium, designed the building. Göring named the lodge Carinhall, after his beloved first wife. In 1936 Göring commissioned two new architects, Friedrich Hetzelt and Hermann Tuch, to enlarge Carinhall.

Carinhall was built between two lakes, the Grösser Döllnsee and the Wuckersee. A highway, Reichstrasse 109, ran nearby. To reach Carinhall from the capital, one drove north along the Berlin-Prenzlau Autobahn. Sixty-five km from the center of Berlin, 10 kilometers north of Gross Schönebeck, an asphalt road ran east to the south bank of the Grosser Döllnsee and Carinhall.

From the exterior the building, constructed around a rectangular court, looked like a thatched-roof log cabin the size of Louis XIV's palace at Versailles. The interior was even more impressive.

Paul Schmidt, Hitler's interpreter, described a 1941 visit to Carinhall with Yosuke Matsuoka, Japan's foreign minister, who died in prison in 1946 after being arrested for war crimes.

Carinhall had been further enlarged. Among its rambling passages one sometimes got the impression of being in a small museum. In Göring's study, with its vast seats and mighty writing table, and especially, of course, in the huge hall with its heavy beams, the little man from Japan seemed even more diminutive than he had in Berlin. When we sat down in the magnificent dining room, one whole wall of which was a window, one was almost surprised that Matsuoka, sinking into his seat, could see over the edge of the vast table, with its heavy silver and floral decorations. His surroundings seemed rather to oppress Matsuoka. He gazed meditatively at the snowy landscape outside the enormous window. Looking at the snow-covered pine trees of the Schorfheide, which stood out like filigree work against the gray March sky, he said to me: "That reminds me of the pictures we love in Japan. The marvelously delicate drawing makes me feel quite homesick...."

Göring naturally took Matsuoka on a tour round the house. The master of the house, like a big boy showing his possessions to a younger

Carinhall main entrance (Bildarchiv Preussischer Kulturbesitz).

playmate, displayed with pride the treasures he had collected, the pictures, Gobelin tapestries, art, antiques, sculptures, and valuable old furniture. Göring took him through the whole house, starting at the cellar, where once he had shown the Duchess of Windsor how Elizabeth Arden's massage apparatus worked, and which now contained in addition an excellent swimming bath. "I hope that one of these gentlemen in their beautiful uniforms doesn't slip on the tiles and fall in!" Matsuoka whispered to me with a grin. Then we came to the large room on the ground floor, where a model railway had been set up.

Japanese foreign minister Yosuke Matsuoka and Hermann Göring in front of the library wing of Carinhall, 1941 (Library of Congress).

"There's three hundred square yards here," said Göring, and he went to the control station and released a Flying Dutchman, a perfect model of a German express. The train seemed to run as steadily as a main line train. The Duke of Windsor would not now have had to stand on tiptoe to pick up the trains that had run off the line. "The track is 1,000 yards long and there are 40 electric points and signals," the big boy told the small boy, who was shyly admiring this splendid toy.

Sumner Welles and Hermann Göring at Carinhall. President Franklin D. Roosevelt had sent Under Secretary of State Welles to Europe in March 1940 in a last-ditch effort to secure peace. In September 1940, Welles was returning on a train to Washington with Roosevelt and other dignitaries from the Alabama funeral of House Speaker William Bankhead. At 4 A.M. Welles, quite drunk, solicited sex from a Pullman car porter. The immensely wealthy, aristocratic, Groton and Harvard educated Welles had a huge sexual appetite for women and men, black and white, but his money, foreign travel, and cordon of servants had hitherto allowed him to disport himself without public scandal. This time, Welles came a cropper. His advances to the porter were reported to the Secret Service and the president of the railroad. Roosevelt tried to protect Welles but in 1943 had to cashier him. (Library of Congress)

Göring had a gigantic collection of baroque uniforms in pastel shades of white, blue, and gray, bedecked with medals. He adored jewelry and wore huge diamond and emerald rings on both hands. On his desk was a pot of diamonds, which he would fondle during interviews. At Carinhall he kept a menagerie, including bison, elk, and lion cubs. Occasionally wearing outlandish costumes, such as forester or sultan, Göring received his guests. Not all were as impressed as Matsuoka had been. After his visit to Carinhall, American under secretary of state Sumner Welles said, "It would be difficult to find an uglier building or one more intrinsically vulgar in its ostentatious display."

On June 20, 1934, Carin Göring's remains were transferred from Lovö, Sweden, to a lakeside vault at Carinhall. A Swedish ferry carried the massive zinc sarcophagus to a special German train. Emblems of mourning adorned the railroad line, from the Baltic port of Sassnitz, on the island of Rügen, to Eberswalde in northern Germany, 200 km distant. Thousands of Germans lined the 15 km route from the Eberswalde railroad station to Carinhall to pay their respects. In the presence of Göring, Hitler, and most of the government, 20 military pallbearers carried the massive zinc sarcophagus to the vault.

Carin Göring's tomb was no mean affair. The coats of arms of both the Fock and Göring families were chiseled in stone at the entrance. Stone steps led down to the crypt, illuminated by a small, deep-blue stained-glass window, with the image of an edelweiss, facing the lake of Döllnsee. Just beyond the vault, along the shore of the lake, was a magnificent flower garden. Göring intended that the vault should also be his last resting place.

As late as 1944, Göring's architects were drafting blueprints for expansion of Carinhall. Göring even ordered drawings of an entirely separate art museum, the Hermann Göring Museum, facing the Wuck-ersee. This building was to hold his huge art collection, much of which had been plundered from Jewish collectors.[62] To accommodate the heavy traffic to the large public museum, Göring wanted to completely rebuild the little railroad station at Friedrichswalde, which was 5 km closer to Carinhall than the larger Eberswalde station. But the war nullified these plans.

On March 13, 1945, with the Red Army closing in, Göring sent the last trainload of art objects from Carinhall south to be stored in a mineshaft in Altaussee or in his country house on the Obersalzberg. Many of these works still have not been restored to their rightful owners.

Göring ordered the destruction of Carinhall on April 21, 1945. Explosives were placed in the cellar adjacent to the load-bearing walls and detonated electrically. Only the entrance portal remained standing. During the 1950s the East Germans knocked down the portal and leveled the area with bulldozers. In 1993 someone placed a stone, inscribed Karinhall [sic], at the former entrance. Every January 12, Göring's birthday, visitors put candles on the stone.

The gatehouses with Göring's coat of arms and Carin Göring's crypt survive today, along with a maze of tunnels and a 20-square-meter bunker. In 1995 German archaeologists from Potsdam found fragments of Greek vases, thousands of years old, in the bunker. The fragments are all that is left of Göring's collection of Greek antiquities that disappeared at the end of the war.

What happened to the remains of Carin Göring? Swedish tourists visiting the site frequently ask this question. According to the report of a forest official, Herr Templin, of the provincial government of the Mark Brandenburg (Kittler, 1997):

My Herr Gierke, April 10, 1947, confirms that the mausoleum in which Carin Göring was buried was reopened. The zinc sarcophagus was broken open and the corpse was left lying on the floor of the chamber. The corpse's head has been gone for a year. The mummified feet of the corpse have been broken off and stolen. We have had talks with Herr Hesse, the responsible official, and the remainder of the corpse will be buried to prevent further desecration. As was previously determined, groups of Russians often appear around the Carinhall property to plunder and to conduct target practice.

The East German officials buried Carin Göring's remains in front of the granite stone bearing the familial coat of arms. But at the request of the Fock family the minister of the Swedish community in Berlin, Pastor Heribert Jansson, arranged for exhumation of the remains, transported them to West Berlin, and had them cremated in Wilmersdorf under an assumed name.

Pastor Jansson carried the urn containing the ashes to Sweden. On October 17, 1951, Carin Göring was reinterred in the little cemetery at Lovö, where she had lain 30 years before.

Archaeologen präsentieren Fundstücke aus Göring-Bunker. *Frankfurter Allgemeine Zeitung*. March 18, 1995.

Chronik Berlin. Chronik Verlag. Munich. 3rd updated edition 1997 Gross Schönebeck.

Jahr-Weidauer, Konrad. Auf Schatzsuche in Göring's Refugium. *Berliner Morgenpost*. April 11, 1999.

Kittler, Andreas. *Hermann Görings Carinhall. Der Waldhof in der Schorfheide*. Druffel Verlag. 82335 Berg. 1997.

Knopf, Volker, and Stefan Martens. *Görings Reich. Selbstinszenierungen in Carinhall*. Ch. Links Verlag. Berlin 1999.

Nichols, Lynn H. *The Rape of Europa. The Fate of Europe's Treasures in the Third Reich and the Second World War*. Vintage Books. New York 1995.

Schmidt, Paul. *Hitler's Interpreter*. Macmillan. New York 1951.

Welles, Benjamin. *Sumner Welles. FDR's Global Strategist*. St. Martin's Press. New York 1997.

Gross Schönebeck

Schorfheide Museum (telephone 03 33 93/6 52 72). Gross Schönebeck is an idyllic town of 2,400 inhabitants on the edge of the Schorfheide. A marble column from Carinhall is on display in the local museum.

Fülling, Thomas. Ein Ehrenbürger namens Hermann Göring. Gross Schönebeck streitet um seine Vergangenheit. *Berliner Morgenpost*. March 13, 1998.

BAYREUTH

Bayreuth is the town of Richard Wagner and still has controversial associations with Hitler. Having searched for the ideal spot to stage his operas, Wagner chose Bayreuth in 1872. With the support of the Bavarian king, Ludwig II, Wagner built a festival theater, the Festspielhaus, to his own design. In 1876 a performance of *Der Ring des Nibelungen* inaugurated the opening of the theater.

Wagner was a virulent but inconsistent anti–Semite. He treated Jews viciously in his writings and denounced their influence. Yet he chose Hermann Levi, a rabbi's son, to conduct the first performance of *Parsifal* at Bayreuth. And he entrusted the responsibility of touring *The Ring* to another Jew, Angelo Neumann.

Are Wagner's operas anti–Semitic? This question is hotly debated and does not admit of easy answers.

Hitler's connection with Wagner is complex. Wagner's first great operatic success, *Rienzi*, provides one example of this complexity. The opera tells the story of Cola Rienzi, an idealized historical personality who wrests authority from a corrupt Roman oligarchy. A performance in Linz of *Rienzi* electrified the 15-year-old Hitler, as his friend August Kubizek wrote: "My friend, his hands thrust into his coat pockets, silent and withdrawn, strode through the streets and out of the city.... Never before and never again have I heard Adolf Hitler speak as he did in that hour, and we stood there alone under the stars.... It was a state of complete ecstasy and rapture, in which he transferred the character of Rienzi … with visionary power to the plan of his own ambitions." *Rienzi* is imbued with a mission to lead his people out of servitude, a conquering hero overthrown by a mob in the opera's finale. Hitler used the Rienzi overture as the musical theme for all Nazi Party rallies. In 1945 the Führer perished in his bunker with the *Rienzi* manuscript in his possession. A few years before, he had refused to deposit the document at Bayreuth for safekeeping, and it is now lost.

From the beginning, Hitler used Wagner to present the Third Reich as the culmination of centuries of German culture and history. The operas stirred him to restore Germany to greatness.

One route was racial purification, an obsession of Wagner's. In the first act of *Die Walküre*, Siegmund and Sieglinde's intense sexual desire derives from sameness. Wagner has made them brother and sister. And their incestuous inbreeding leads here to the birth of a true hero, Siegfried. Hitler first codified racial purification in the 1935 Nuremberg Laws and later carried it to murderous extremes.

As Leon Botstein has remarked, Wagner's *Die Walküre*, in fact the entire *Ring* cycle of which it is a part, can inspire a mix of ambition and frustration with the world as it is, and it certainly did so in Adolf Hitler. Swept along by the intensity of his experience in the theater of Wagner, the disaffected, resentful young Hitler fantasized about becoming the fearless hero of the future, whom Wotan, the ruler of the gods, describes in the closing scene of Die Walküre. The desire to escape the petty limitations of middle-class life became irresistible all too easily with the help of Wagner's music and inspired in Hitler grandiosely malevolent schemes.

Wagner's English-born daughter-in-law, Winifred (1897–1980), was Hitler's early supporter during the 1920s. Gottfried Wagner, the composer's great grandson, says that Hitler proposed marriage to Winifred, and she supplied him with the paper on which he wrote *Mein Kampf* in Landsberg Prison.

As Führer, Hitler was a frequent visitor to Villa Wahnfried, Wagner's Bayreuth home. He tucked in Winifred's two children, Wieland and Wolfgang, who called him "Uncle Wolf." He attended the annual Wagner festivals in Bayreuth and enshrined the town as a temple of Nazi culture. Because of this odious association, the Allies closed down the Bayreuth Festival from 1945 to 1950 for "decontamination." Villa Wahnfried was heavily damaged during the war but was rebuilt and is now a museum.

Botstein, Leon. *Die Walküre* Analysis. Texaco-Metropolitan Opera International Radio Network. New York 1997.

Horowitz, Joseph. The specter of Hitler in the music of Wagner. *New York Times*. November 8, 1998, sec. 2, p. 1.

Kubizek, August. *Adolf Hitler, Mein Jugendfreund*. Leopold Stocker Verlag, Graz and Stuttgart. 6th edition 1995.

Walsh, Mary Williams. Heirs' Angst upstages Wagner. The Bayreuth Festival, Germany's new showcase for the composer's works, has become a gothic tale of infighting. Control of the operas, new revelations of Third Reich ties figure in the generational face-off. *Los Angeles Times*. July 31, 1998, p. 1.

White, Michael, and Kevin Scott. *Introducing Wagner*. Totem Books. New York 1995.

BERCHTESGADEN

In the Middle Ages the local population of Berchtesgaden lived by extracting and selling salt. At the end of the nineteenth century Berchtesgaden caught on as a vacation spot. German and Austrian royalty, the Bavarian royal family, and Sigmund Freud were summer guests.

Hitler began visiting Berchtesgaden in the early 1920s and wrote part of the second volume of *Mein Kampf* on the Obersalzberg, a mountaintop area that he made into his private retreat after he became chancellor. This he accomplished by having his private secretary, Martin Bormann, expell the other residents, who occupied century-old peasant farms, boarding houses, Dr. Seitz's Children's Sanitarium, and Antenberg, an old-age home for sailors. Bormann replaced several mountain farms, fiefs from feudal times, with an expanse of lawn, which is now a golf course. The area he confiscated, 2.7 square miles, extended from the top of the mountain to the valley below. The fence around the inner perimeter was almost two miles long, a second fence around the outer perimeter nine miles long. Because of the fences, the Obersalzberg was "reminiscent of an open-air enclosure for wild animals," wrote Albert Speer, and added:

On certain days the SS opened the gates of the Obersalzberg property. A column five yards wide, consisting of thousands upon thousands of admirers, filed past Hitler, who stood in a raised place, visible to all. People waved; women shed tears of exaltation. Hitler would point out one child or another to his chauffeur, [SS Colonel Erich] Kempka, and an SS man would lift the child above the crowd. Then the inevitable group picture would be taken; Hitler seemed to be avid for such pictures. The children themselves often looked rather unhappy.

Around Hitler's home (the Berghof), Bormann, Speer, and Reichsmarschall Hermann Göring had their own houses. Göring's home, with swimming pool and art treasures, was quite sumptuous. Bormann moved in to Dr. Seitz's former home. Thousands of SS men and Reich Security Service officials were quartered in barracks and bunkers that still exist. Bormann built a 2,000-seat theater, which entertained the men with movies and floorshows.

Today Berchtesgaden is still a miniature Third Reich and a magnet for neo–Nazis. It is illegal in Germany and Austria to deny the reality of the Holocaust. But there is no law against writing books

that proclaim Hitler a great man and a regular guy, too. In Berchtesgaden there is no shortage of such books or publishers to print them. From Austria and Germany, especially the former East Germany, Hitler-loving visitors come to buy this repugnant stuff. Kiosks scattered along the paths sell the books and other Hitler kitsch, such as photos of the Führer posing with "Bernile," the "German girl of 1934." Nothing sold, of course, conflicts with the alpine idyll.

But, mirabile dictu, the Obersalzberg has acquired a "conscience," in the form of a documentation center. The center was established specifically to contradict the plethora of nauseating neo–Nazi hagiographies hawked by local vendors.

The documentation center is made up of a pavilion, a tunnel, and part of a bunker. The historic exhibit begins in the pavilion, a wood and glass building constructed on the foundation of a former Nazi guesthouse.[63] The visitor encounters scenes of terror. A projector casts the Star of David on Nazi propaganda posters. A loudspeaker blares the strident voice of People's Court Judge Roland Freisler, condemning to death opponents of the regime. Large photographs document Nazi mass murders.

"We want to lead the visitor from a glowing image of the Third Reich to the awful reality, from perpetrators to victims," says Volker Dahm, of Munich's *Institut für Zeitgeschichte. Berliner Morgenpost* reporter Robert Zsolnay interviewed Dahm in front of a placard showing Hitler striding energetically forward with a swastika banner, flanked by joyous girls, arms raised in the Hitler salute. Nearby were other pictures: civilians hanged by Wehrmacht soldiers, the snow-covered face of a dead German soldier at Stalingrad, and corpses of murdered Jews at Bergen-Belsen.

In the tunnel the visitor sees photos and text documentation of the resistance to Hitler, emigration, Hitler's aggressive foreign policy, and World War II. There is even a photo of Volker Dahm, who created the exhibit. The picture shows Dahm in October 1944, age six months. His father had been killed in France two months earlier. "A common German destiny," Dahm told reporter Zsolnay.

The damp tunnel leads into the bunker, dug by slave laborers. A darkened cavern serves as an auditorium. The visitor hears the voices of two women describing how they survived the concentration camps.

A photo of the partially completed pavilion, hanging in the tunnel, makes clear the need for the new documentation center. The photo shows the unfinished walls, which vandals had smeared with swastikas.

Berchtesgaden teems not only with young neo–Nazi vandals but with elderly

Hitler and Bernile (Bernhardine Nienau), the "German girl of 1934." Hitler had come upon this child at a rally in Munich and invited her to the Obersalzberg to be photographed. Afterward, Hitler discovered that Bernile's birthday was April 20, his own birthday, and a four-year correspondence ensued. Photographer Heinrich Hoffmann's pictures of Hitler and Bernile were a huge commercial success and are among the most famous photos of Hitler with a child. Yet as early as December 1933, someone had tattled to the Bavarian Political Police and Martin Bormann that Bernile's grandmother was Jewish. But Hoffmann was making so much money hawking his Bernile photos that he rejected all demands to yank them from the stores. Moreover, even though Hitler knew about grandma, the correspondence between "the Führer's child Bernile" and her "Uncle Hitler" continued, as did Bernile's visits to the Obersalzberg. Finally, in May 1938 the Führeradjutantur scotched further contact between Hitler and Bernile. Simultaneously, Philipp Bouhler, head of the Führer Chancellery, stopped the sale of Hoffmann's photos (Süddeutscher Verlag Bilderdienst).

Nazis as well. In 1996 Walter Mayr, a reporter for *Der Spiegel*, interviewed Göring's former adjutant, "Hegeler" (not his real name), a pleasant man in his eighties.

"Come in, sit down," said Hegeler, in his Berchtesgaden living room; "over there is the chief's seat." He pointed to an armchair that had belonged to Göring.

Hegeler has preserved Göring memorabilia such as tunic buttons with Göring's coat of arms, an iron fist grasping a ring. Over the bed hangs a black and white photo of Hegeler in a Luftwaffe leather jacket, clasping the right hand of Frau Emmy Göring and holding little daughter Edda Göring. Nearby stands a smiling Hitler.

"June 2, 1943," said Hegeler, "Edda's fifth birthday." The photo was taken on the terrace of the Berghof. Four years earlier, in the same place, Hitler had informed his generals about the invasion of Poland and then added, "I will make a propaganda event to justify the outbreak of war. It's all the same to me whether anyone believes it or not" (see Anatomical Institute, University of Vienna).

Hegeler claims he was not a party member and thus had no responsibility for a conflict in which 55 million perished. But he did partake of Göring's elaborate lifestyle, Göring's Obersalzberg villa, trips in Göring's special train to Bayreuth, Capri, and Verona. Hegeler listened to the whining of agitated Luftwaffe generals, though their vociferous complaints did not in the least unsettle the obese, morphine-addicted Göring.

Hegeler was a drinking companion of Ernst Udet, the World War I flying ace and chief air inspector of the Luftwaffe, whom Hitler and Göring held responsible for the failure of the air war against Britain in 1940 and the Soviet Union in September 1941. Udet committed suicide November 17, 1941, with a single pistol shot to the head in his Berlin apartment, Stallupöner Allee 11, Charlottenburg 9, and was buried in Berlin's Invalidenfriedhof. Hitler ordered that Udet's death be attributed to an accident while testing a new weapon.

"They were good times, back then," said Hegeler. "But afterward we were war criminals." He looked bitter as he pulled out a leather binder, in which Göring, on trial at Nuremberg, had penciled "observations for a closing address."

In May 1945 the Americans took over the Obersalzberg. The citizens of Berchtesgaden welcomed their conquerors, for the presence of the victors served as a symbol of absolution for past sins. The U.S. Army used Hitler's buildings for rest and recreation. In 1991 U.S. soldiers came directly from "Operation Desert Storm" in Kuwait to the Obersalzberg. Martin Bormann's property became a golf course.

There is no need to worry about Herr Hegeler. While the U.S. Army was in Berchtesgaden, he worked as an elevator operator, though he hardly ever saw his American employers. Now he receives a fat pension from the Bundeswehr, the new German Army. And why shouldn't he? As Emmy Göring said, "He was always loyal and industrious."

Herr Hegeler spends his days playing golf or hobnobbing with old Göring intimates. On the anniversary of Emmy Göring's death, Göring's personal physician, valet, chief cook, and daughter Edda, who lives in nearby Munich, gather to toast the late Reichsmarschall. Among Hegeler's other friends is a former SS officer who spent time in prison for his crimes.

Holzhaider, Hans. Grosser Andrang auf dem Obersalzberg. *Süddeutsche Zeitung*. February 9, 2000.

Jäckel, Hartmut. *Menschen in Berlin. Das letzte Telefonbuch der alten Reichhauptstadt 1941*. Deutsche Verlags-Anstalt. Stuttgart München 2000.

Mayr, Walter. "Soll' mer'n wegsprengen?" *Der Spiegel* 33:101–11, 1996.

Möller, Horst, Volker Dahm, Hartmut Mehringer. *Die tödliche Utopie*. Institut für Zeitgeschichte. Munich 1999.

Speer, Albert. *Spandau. The Secret Diaries.* Translated by Richard and Clara Winston. Pocket Books. New York 1977.

Zsolnay, Robert. Mahnmal in Hitlers Alpenfestung. Auf dem Obersalzberg wurde eine ständige Ausstellung über die NS-diktatur eröffnet. *Berliner Morgenpost.* October 21, 1999.

Hotel Zum Türken

The writer Ron Rosenbaum visited Berchtesgaden while researching his book *Explaining Hitler.* He spent the night in this inn, also called the "Gestapo Cottage," and describes the experience in his book:

The place felt only slightly less sinister than it sounded. It was a compact little inn not far down the mountain from the Hotel General Walker, a place that had been built before Hitler began building his private preserve, a little inn known as far back as the twenties as Zum Türken because of the Turkish nationality of its original owners. In the thirties, to the great credit of the owners, their clear lack of Nazi sympathies caused Bormann to seize it from them and turn it into a dormitory residence for Hitler's Gestapo bodyguards. After the war it was returned to the ownership of the original family, whose descendants run it now…. Despite the proprietor family's lack of sympathy, the place, because of its location, attracts those obsessed with and sympathetic to the era, who want to stay in a place that has changed less than any other Hitler landmark except perhaps the Männerheim [q.v.]. By the registration desk, one can find books filled with cheerful photographs of a relaxed, genial Hitler taken at various sites on the mountain top: Hitler with his beloved dog Blondi (the one he killed with cyanide when he was testing the poison he would take himself); Hitler with blond children; Hitler with Eva Braun; Hitler posing with Alpine-garbed Nazi visitors; Hitler hiking through the wildflowers; Hitler relaxed in front of the breathtakingly picturesque crags. Hitler, in other words, in slippers. And in the Gestapo Cottage's cozy common room … there is still a picture on the wall of Eva Braun, one that could well have been put there to brighten up the off-duty hours of the Gestapo bodyguards while she and Hitler were still alive.

There is an entrance to the bunkers, a door on the side of the hotel facing the parking lot. The entrance fee is 5 DM, and the visitor must have a 5 DM coin for the turnstile. No one will make change.

Terrance, Marc. *Concentration Camps. A Traveler's Guide to World War II Sites.* Universal Publishers 1999.

The Berghof

In 1916 a north German businessman from Buxtehude, Otto Winter, built this chalet, originally called Haus Wachenfeld, on the Obersalzberg. In 1928 Hitler rented Haus Wachenfeld. When he became Reich Chancellor in 1933, he bought Haus Wachenfeld, and it became his alpine home.

In 1935 Hitler decided to enlarge the modest structure. He borrowed drawing board, T-square, and other drafting tools from architect Albert Speer and drew ground plans, renderings, and cross sections of the renovations to scale, refusing any help from Speer. Understandably, there were some major defects that were never corrected, despite the contributions of another architect, Alois Degano.

Hitler's plan preserved the original house within the one he designed. The living room of the old house joined the new house through a large opening. But the ground plan was awkward for receiving official visitors. Their staffs were confronted with an entry hall that was too small.

Another fault was the stairway location. During state conferences Hitler sent his private visitors upstairs. But because the stairway was in the entry hall, a guard had to vet the upstairs visitors before they could pass through the hall if they wanted to leave the house while the conference was in progress.

Albert Speer in *Inside the Third Reich* describes the living room of the Berghof as being furnished sparsely, but with furniture

The Berghof, Hitler's Obersalzberg mountain retreat. Nazi supporters (mid–1930s) wait for Hitler to receive them (Süddeutscher Verlag Bildderdienst).

he calls, "monumental" and "massive," including a twenty-foot table where Hitler often worked. The walls were hung with large oil paintings. Red-upholstered chairs made a sitting area around a fireplace, and movie projection equipment and a movie screen were concealed by hanging tapestries. A film was often shown after supper:

We found places on the sofas or in one of the easy chairs in either of the sitting areas; the two tapestries were raised; and the second part of the evening began with a movie, as was also the custom when Hitler was in Berlin. Afterward the company gathered around the huge fireplace. Some six or eight persons lined up in a row on the excessively long and uncomfortably low sofa, while Hitler ... ensconced himself in one of the soft chairs. Because of the inept arrangement of the furniture the company was so scattered that no common conversation could arise.... Later, during the war, Hitler gave up the evening showings, saying that he wanted to renounce his favorite entertainment "out of sympathy for the privations of the soldiers." Instead records were played.

Hitler was quite proud of the enormous picture window in the living room of the Berghof, which could be raised and lowered electrically. It gave a commanding view of Berchtesgaden, Salzburg, and the Untersberg, where, according to legend, Charlemagne still sleeps but will one day arise to restore the German Empire. Believing himself to be another Charlemagne, Hitler told Speer, "You see the Untersberg over there. It is no accident that I have my residence opposite it." But Hitler had clumsily placed his garage under the picture window, and the wind often brought the strong odor of gasoline into the living room.

After the war began, the Obersalzberg was heavily fortified. Below the Berghof, bunkers were dug, augmented by antiaircraft guns and smoke-screen generators. The defenders stocked enough provisions, weapons, and ammunition to hold out for 18 months. The Berghof itself was covered with camouflage netting that, according to Albert Speer, "made even a sunny morning seem like a dark late afternoon."

The British air raid of April 24, 1945, ruined the Berghof. The house suffered three direct hits, destroying the main building and severely damaging both wings. On the morning of May 4 SS guards doused the Berghof with gasoline and set it on fire. That afternoon, units from the U.S. Third Infantry Division captured Berchtesgaden. French troops followed. On May 5 U.S. soldiers raised the American flag on a hill above the Berghof.

The U.S. Army closed off the entire Obersalzberg because of its connection with the Nazis. But in late 1951 the army opened the area again, after German demolition crews had leveled the ruins of the Berghof, as well as the houses of Hermann Göring and Martin Bormann.

Today the land on which the Berghof stood, a few meters down the hill from the Hotel zum Türken, is marked with a sign

Unfallgefahr
Betreten Verboten

(danger of accident
no entry)

The ruins of the Berghof foundation and retaining walls are overgrown with weeds and trees.

Speer, Albert. *Inside the Third Reich.* Translated by Richard and Clara Winston. Avon Books. New York 1971.
Terrance, Marc. *Concentration Camps. A Traveler's Guide to World War II Sites.* Universal Publishers 1999.

The Teahouse

On the Obersalzburg property, some distance from the Berghof main house, was the teahouse, which Albert Speer (in *Inside the Third Reich*) describes as "a round room about twenty-five feet in diameter, pleasing in its proportions, with a row of small-paned windows and a fireplace along the interior wall." Hitler and his company would walk to the teahouse after dinner for conversation over hot drinks and desserts. During these conversations, Speer writes, "Hitler was particularly fond of drifting into endless monologues.... Occasionally Hitler himself fell asleep over one of his monologues. The company then continued chatting in whispers, hoping that he would awake in time for the evening meal. It was all very familial." The ruins of the teahouse still stand on the Mooslahnerkopf.

Speer, Albert. *Inside the Third Reich.* Translated by Richard and Clara Winston. Avon Books. New York 1971.

The Eagle's Nest (Also Called Adlerhorst or Kehlstein House)

In autumn 1936 Martin Bormann selected the peak of the 6,017-foot Kehlstein Mountain for the Eagle's Nest, a teahouse cum conference center. Bormann said he wanted to present the house to Hitler as a fiftieth-birthday present, but he actually built the Eagle's Nest mainly for his own purposes.

One purpose was to ingratiate himself with the boss. Bormann noticed that Hitler liked taking walks after meals to the small teahouse below the Berghof on the Mooslahnerkopf. What better way was there to gratify Hitler than to build another teahouse, unique in the entire world?

Bormann's second purpose was served by the isolated location of the Eagle's Nest. Away from the heavily guarded Obersalzberg area, Bormann could meet with Hitler undisturbed by anyone who might diminish his influence.

The Munich architect Roderich Fick designed the Kehlstein House. The large meeting rooms in Fick's plans indicate that the building was intended as a conference center rather than another modest teahouse.

The 3,000 workmen who built the Kehlstein House were mostly German, except for some men Mussolini sent. The builders erected a temporary cableway from the Obersalzberg to the Kehlstein summit to ferry building materials. Because Bormann was in a hurry, the construction site was lit with floodlights, and work went on day and night. Completion of the house required 13 months, and cost 30 million reichsmarks (about $150 million today).

Inside the house, a modest, pine-paneled tearoom was called the Scharitzkehl or Eva Braun Room. SS guards had a small duty room across from the kitchen. There was a study, a hallway with 24 bronze hat

Berghof: Hitler's Study

and coat hooks, and a cellar with supply and machinery rooms. A terrace and colonnade on the south side of the building were later enclosed with glass. A long conference room was originally furnished with an oak table and 26 chairs.

A rotunda was the centerpiece of the Kehlstein House. It had five picture windows affording a breathtaking view and a huge fireplace, all red marble and bronze tiles, which Mussolini gave Hitler as a birthday present. In the center of the room was a broad circular table, surrounded by armchairs. In 1945 souvenir hunters cut up the Oriental rug, a gift from Japanese emperor Hirohito, and broke off pieces of the fireplace. The only original piece of furniture still in the house is the buffet in the dining room, which was too massive to haul off.

A six-foot fence surrounded the entire pinnacle on which the house was built. Called "prohibited zone III,"

Kehlstein House interior today. The rotunda is now the main dining room of a restaurant (Plenk Verlag, Berchtesgaden).

Kehlstein House exterior today. Except for the television antenna, the building is unchanged (Plenk Verlag, Berchtesgaden).

Year's Eve, 1938, Bormann, decidedly tipsy, bullied a few unlucky revelers to drive with him up the icy Kehlstein road to the house. Very little snow had fallen on the road, and the car made it to the parking lot outside the house. But then Bormann's frightened companions had to shovel deep snowdrifts in order to reach the doors to the entrance tunnel. All told, the experience was not felicitous.

Most of Hitler's top subordinates came to the Kehlstein House. Foreign Minister Joachim von Ribbentrop visited at least three times, Heinrich Himmler and Joseph Goebbels twice.

In 1938 Hitler invited French foreign minister André François-Ponçet to the Kehlstein House. François-Ponçet, who spoke grammatically perfect German and was author of a book on Goethe's politics, wrote the following description of his visit (Frankel, 1985):

the area was patrolled by guards. Concealed, remote-controlled gas capsules had been installed for additional protection. Gas masks were in containers nearby.

There is controversy over how often Hitler visited the Kehlstein House. Hitler's valet said that Hitler did not like the house and forced himself to enter the place to please Bormann and Eva Braun. The dictator claimed that the change in altitude caused him shortness of breath and palpitations. But an SS guard, who was stationed at the doors leading to the entrance tunnel, claimed that Hitler visited frequently.

However Hitler may have felt about the house, Bormann and Eva Braun loved it and used it regularly. Bormann liked to show it off to people he wanted to impress, among them his secretary and his mistress.

Not every visit was agreeable. On New

On the day of the invitation, October 17, Hitler placed his personal airplane at my disposal. I arrived in Berchtesgaden the next day at 3 p.m., continuing the journey by car. The house looked like an observatory from the distance, standing on a mountain ridge. I drove along a winding road to the top.... The road leads to the beginning of a long tunnel, blasted into the living rock, the entrance of which was provided with double doors of solid bronze. A roomy, brass-fitted elevator was waiting for me at the end of the tunnel.

I arrived in a low-ceilinged, solidly constructed building. It consisted of a gallery with Roman columns and a gigantic glazed rotunda. Huge logs were burning in a large open fireplace and there was a long table with some 30 seats. The panorama of the mountains was like an amphitheater, and there were many small towns and countless mountains, meadows and woods as far as the eye could see. Hitler's house gave me the impression of being in a building that was floating in space.

The view, bathed in the half-light of the autumn evening dusk, seemed incredibly wild, like an illusion. Was it Monsalvat Castle, inhabited by the Knights of the Grail, or Mount Athos, where the cenobites meditate?

The Prime Minister greeted me in a charming and polite manner. His face was pale and marked by fatigue.

Hitler led me immediately to a side window of the main room and was pleased to see the unconcealed surprise and amazement on my face at the sight of the wonderful panorama. As we paid each other compliments, he said that he was sorry that I would be leaving soon. He ordered tea to be served in an adjacent room, in which Ribbentrop was also present. Other people were gathered in the dining room.

The servants were asked to leave, the doors were closed and the meeting began. Ribbentrop took part in the conversation only to repeat or lay stress on what Hitler had already said.

Hitler allowed me to ask him questions for two hours. He answered candidly, sincerely, directly.

The Eagle's Nest now lay in the shadow of the mountains. I took my leave. The Führer expressed his wish to see me again soon. Several times he grasped my hands and shook them warmly.

François-Ponçet called the Kehlstein House "un nid d'aigle," an eagle's nest, a name that stuck because of its appeal to American and British journalists.

A notable social occasion in the Kehlstein House was the wedding reception for Gretl Braun, Eva's promiscuous younger sister, and SS Gruppenführer (lieutenant general) Hermann Fegelein, who was the liaison officer between Hitler and Himmler, as well as a friend of Martin Bormann. Gretl had become pregnant by an SS captain, who requested posting to the eastern front to avoid marrying her. The gallant Fegelein, who was keeping a mistress at the time, stepped forward to rescue Gretl's honor. (Fegelein had his brains in his scrotum, commented Bormann.) Gretl and Hermann married on June 5, 1944, in the Salzburg City Hall. Bormann

Wedding dinner of Gretl Braun and Hermann Fegelein, rotunda, Kehlstein House, June 5, 1944 (Bayerische Staatsbibliothek).

and Himmler were witnesses. That afternoon, Hitler gave the newlyweds an elaborate reception at the Berghof. In the evening there was another reception with more than 50 guests in the Kehlstein House. An SS orchestra played, and the revelers quaffed champagne and liqueurs. Bormann imbibed so freely that aides had to point him to the elevator and help him into his car.

Hitler was not at the party. He was listening to the radio for reports of the Allies' landings on the French coast.

On April 25, 1945, 318 British Lancaster bombers dropped 1,232 tons of bombs on the Obersalzberg. The British came in two assault waves 90 minutes apart. Nearly every building was severely damaged, except for the Kehlstein House, which was a small target, difficult to distinguish from the mountain terrain.

On May 6, 1945, after having captured the Obersalzberg, 12 soldiers in a U.S. combat patrol tried to reach the Kehlstein House. But the snow was so deep that the men had to abandon their jeep halfway up the Kehlstein Road.

Many Allied military leaders visited the Kehlstein House. Among them were General George S. Patton, General Mark Clark, General Omar Bradley, General Dwight D. Eisenhower, and Russian Field Marshal Georgi Zhukov. Eisenhower pointedly removed a sign saying that only field officers could ride in the elevator.

The Americans wanted to raze the undamaged Kehlstein House. But Dr. Wilhelm Högner, the Bavarian prime minister, objected and allowed the Alpine Society of Berchtesgaden to lease it. Today the Kehlstein House is a popular tourist destination, with an excellent restaurant. A bus runs regularly on the Kehlstein Road from May to October, and there is also a footpath to the house.

Frankel, Andrew. *The Eagle's Nest. From Adolf Hitler to the Present Day*. Plenk Verlag. Berchtesgaden 1985.

O'Donnell, James P. *The Bunker*. Houghton Mifflin. Boston 1978.

Kehlstein Road, Parking Lot, and Elevator

Martin Bormann appointed an eminent engineer, Dr. Fritz Todt, Hitler's armaments minister and designer of the Autobahn, to build a road to the Eagle's Nest. In spring 1937 Bormann and Todt climbed the Kehlstein to lay out the road. In August 1937 Bormann himself drove into the ground the wooden pegs to mark the road.

The Kehlstein road is a masterpiece of civil engineering, four miles long, with seven tunnels and a hairpin turn. Todt built a secondary road to carry rubble down the mountain; it was converted to a footpath after the completion of the main road. Several guardhouses were placed along the road, and the tunnels were used as gates to exclude the unwelcome. Because of snow and ice the road is passable only from May to October. Bormann wanted to heat the road with pipes and hot water so that it could be used year round, but this plan was impractical.

The top of the road ends at a large parking lot. A 136-yard-long tunnel into the center of the mountain leads from the parking lot to the bottom of an elevator shaft, with a parallel tunnel for water pipes and electrical cables.

The 400-foot-tall elevator shaft ascends directly into the Kehlstein House. Workmen bored the shaft, which took three months to finish, before winter so that work could be continued inside despite the severe cold.

The Flohr Company, acquired by Otis after the war, built the elevator. The heated cab is adorned with highly polished brass fittings, Venetian mirrors, and rich green leather. The ride to the top lasts 45 seconds. Flohr added a lower tier to the cab for transporting goods, but this tier has now been removed. In case of a power failure, a Man submarine diesel engine connected to a generator could produce emergency electricity for the elevator and the house. Today the functioning of the engine is still *perfekt*.

Hitler was less enthusiastic about the entire Kehlstein project than Bormann and during construction did not allow blasting in the early morning hours. Worse, the Führer became claustrophobic in the elevator and was terrified lightning might strike the cable.

Frankel, Andrew. *The Eagle's Nest. From Adolf Hitler to the Present Day*. Plenk Verlag. Berchtesgaden 1985.

Top: **Entrance to Kehlstein House tunnel. Kehlstein House is visible on the mountain peak (Plenk Verlag, Berchtesgaden).** *Left:* **Kehlstein House elevator (Plenk Verlag, Berchtesgaden).**

Greenhouse

A greenhouse held rare plants and flowers. Bormann grew mushrooms in the basement after Hitler's doctor, Theodor Morrell, recommended them for the Führer's diet. During the war a heavy hailstorm broke the glass and ruined the plants. Despite the shortages of glass and building materials, the Führer's Office of Special Construction Programs approved reconstruction. On April 25, 1945, the

Man submarine diesel engine connected to a generator can provide emergency electricity for the Kehlstein House and elevator (Plenk Verlag, Berchtesgaden).

British bombing raid destroyed the greenhouse. The ruins of the foundation are adjacent to a parking lot.

Gutshof (Farmhouse)

Bormann raised Haflinger mountain horses and had 60 to 80 mares. He also bred hogs and kept milk cows in modern stables. The buildings were only slightly damaged in the 1945 air raid and were converted to a hotel and recreation center, The Skytop, after the war. The ruins of the pig farm are nearby.

Hotel Platterhof and Bormann Guest House "Hoher Goell"

Hitler ordered Bormann to turn the Hotel Platterhof into a guesthouse, where, for one mark, every citizen of the Reich would be able to spend "a night close to the Führer" (Rosenbaum, 1998). In 1936 the renovated 150-room guesthouse was completed. But high Nazi officials were the main patrons.

Another guesthouse, "Hoher Goell," had Bormann's offices and accommodations for his visitors. Hoher Goell was severely damaged in the 1945 air raid and is now a ruin.

The Platterhof was also damaged in the raid. After the war the U.S. Army rebuilt it, closed it to civilians, and renamed it the Hotel General Walker.

The army pulled out of Berchtesgaden in June 1996. The Platterhof and the other Nazi buildings became the property of the Free State of Bavaria (which also owns the copyright of *Mein Kampf*).

In 1998 the Bavarian government turned the Platterhof over to a construction firm, *Gewerbegrund*, which intended to raze it and build a sport hotel. But there was considerable public resistance.

Preservationists pointed to a small part of the Platterhof, which occupied a piece of land once the site of a little inn, the *Pension Moritz*. Johannes Brahms, Clara Schumann, and Sigmund Freud had been summer guests at the Pension Moritz.

The name Platterhof originated with another guest at the inn. The novelist Richard Voss used the owner of the *Pension Moritz*, Mauritia ("Moritz") Mayer, as a model for a character in one of his books and named her Judith Platter.

When preliminary demolition of the Platterhof began, the architect Herbert Kochta discovered that ceiling beams in the Pension Moritz section of the Platterhof had apparently come from the inn itself. The Bavarian government must now decide whether demolition of the Platterhof can proceed, or whether the construction firm should be compensated and the Platterhof preserved.

Holzhaider, Hans. Grosser Andrang auf dem Obersalzberg. *Süddeutsche Zeitung*. February 9, 2000.

Möller, Horst, Volker Dahm, Hartmut Mehringer. *Die tödliche Utopie*. Institut für Zeitgeschichte. Munich 1999.

Rosenbaum, Ron. *Explaining Hitler*. Random House. New York 1998.

Albert Speer's Studio

Hitler had Bormann build this chalet from Speer's design. It was finished in May 1937. Speer drafted his architectural plans here. The studio currently houses a youth hostel. It had been a VIP guesthouse for the U.S. Army.

Albert Speer's Family Villa

Speer rented this elegant home in 1937 from the actor Gustav Fröhlich, who had played the lead character, "Freder," in Fritz Lang's film classic, *Metropolis* (1926). The house now belongs to a retired couple from the Rhineland and is unchanged from Speer's tenancy. The four rooms downstairs are used exactly as in Speer's time, the owners told Gitta Sereny in 1991. At the front of the house, which overlooks the studio below, a modest kitchen adjoins a sewing room–playroom. Next door a sitting room furnished in peasant style contains a lovely white-tiled cylindrical stove, which Speer designed. The opposite side of the house, overlooking the mountains, has a living room and a library with square-paneled ceilings, resembling those Speer had installed in his studio.

"I had no wish whatsoever to have us live too close to anyone else, including the Berghof," Speer told Ms. Sereny. Although the Obersalzberg was thickly populated and policed, his property was quite private.

"Even now," the current owner told Ms. Sereny, "in the winter it's quite a trick to drive up the 30-percent incline of the drive. When the Speers lived here there was no drive. I always wondered why."

"I never liked to live in places where I look out on houses or where people can, heaven forbid, drop in," Speer said to Ms. Sereny. "I like waking up to the smell of grass and the sight of mountains, and I like to choose who I see, in my own house or elsewhere."[64]

Sereny, Gitta. *Albert Speer: His Battle with Truth*. Alfred A. Knopf. New York 1995.

Klaushoehe and Buchenhoehe

Bormann built Klaushoehe, the first large settlement on the Obersalzberg, to house his friends and Hitler's faithful retainers. Klaushoehe had four rows of eight two-or-three-family houses. The apartments were spacious, modern, and comfortable. The rents were very reasonable.

Some of the houses were destroyed during the war. Others are still in use.

Buchenhoehe, Bormann's second settlement, had 40 houses with two to four apartments each. Before he could build on the difficult terrain, Bormann had to move thousands of cubic meters of earth, cut down woods, bridge gorges, and build roads. Buchenhoehe had an inn, a kindergarten, a swimming pool, a school, a gymnasium, a firehouse, and a central heating system that provided all of the buildings with hot water and heat. Albert Speer tried unsuccessfully to convince Bormann to stop building because of the desperate need for war materials. Only the April 1945 air raid put an end to construction.

Bunkers

The Nazis honeycombed the Obersalzberg with underground rooms and tunnels. There are 79 rooms, with a total floor space of 4,120 square meters. The total length of all the tunnels is 2,775 meters.

Hermann Göring built the first Obersalzberg bunker in 1941. The entrance was at the end of a short footpath behind his house. The walls were three-meter-thick reinforced concrete. Göring's bunker is now locked shut with a heavy steel plate.

In August 1943, as Allied bombing of Germany intensified, Hitler ordered the building of additional bunkers. The first was dug next to the Berghof. Another was built adjacent to Martin Bormann's house. Underground tunnels and rooms for offices and storage connected the Berghof and Bormann bunkers, which had external ventilation and air-conditioning.

Hermann Göring wanted his bunker attached to the others. But the closest, 10 meters away, belonged to Bormann, who refused to join his tunnel to Göring's.

As digging progressed, the accommodations became more and more elaborate.

Hitler's German shepherd, Blondi, had her own room. Eva Braun wanted her own bathroom. Hitler's cooks got a fully equipped kitchen. Emergency generators were installed.

Bormann got a special dining room and appropriated rooms that had been intended for antiaircraft gunners. He used the space for cabinets filled with heavy silver candlesticks, silver plates, jewelry, and 36 tailor-made suits. According to one of the builders, Josef Geiss, Bormann had hoarded enough food to feed himself, his wife, and their nine children for more than 200 years.

Bormann did not want plain concrete walls and floors. He demanded marble walls with wainscoting and heavy oriental rugs. The doors and doorframes were lacquered, highly polished wood. The living rooms, bedrooms, and nursery looked like the rooms in his above-ground chalet. His offices were outfitted with hardwood furniture, heavy desks, file cabinets, and upholstered armchairs. Safes were built into the stone walls.

Connected to other Obersalzberg buildings were more tunnels and rooms. Water dripped through their walls onto muddy floors. Benches were scattered about.

Today, the only open bunker entrances are those of the new documentation center, Platterhof, and the Hotel Zum Türken.

Plenk, Anton. *The Obersalzberg and the Third Reich*. Verlag Plenk. Berchtesgaden 1984.

Bischofswiesen. Second Reich Chancellery

Though this building is located only 10 kilometers from the Berghof, most tourists ignore it. According to records, plans, and photos in the Bundesarchiv and the Munich State Archives, the building was known officially as Hitler's "Berchtesgaden office" (*Dienstelle Berchtesgaden*).

Bischofswiesen. Second Reich Chancellery (Bayerische Staatsbibliothek, Munich).

The Führer himself wanted this Second Reich Chancellery because he was increasingly using his Obersalzberg refuge as a seat of government. On February 21, 1936, he commissioned Alois Degano, an architect of the Berghof, to design the structure, and it was completed in a year and a half. The interior conformed slavishly to Hitler's taste: hallways with columns, swastika emblems in the floor, walls paneled in dark wood, kitschy landscape paintings with toiling farmers, and a Franz von Lenbach bust of Bismarck.

The *gauleiter* of Bavaria, Adolf Wagner, complained to Hans Heinrich Lammers, head of the Reich Chancellery, that Degano's building looked like "an upper Bavarian farm house." Lammers ignored Wagner's carping and, when Hitler was in Berchtesgaden, made certain that the dictatorial bureaucracy continued to function smoothly.

High Nazi officials, such as Field Marshal Wilhelm Keitel and Albert Speer, frequently came and went. Degano's work so deeply impressed Speer that in 1944, "for further ornamentation," Speer asked Lammers to commission sculptor Arno Breker to cast a "Führer relief in iron."

In May 1945 the U.S. Army captured Berchtesgaden. With considerable fanfare, in Hitler's Mercedes touring car, General Omar Bradley was chauffeured to Degano's chancellery, where U.S. soldiers made speeches honoring their commander.

After the war the U.S. Army took over the building, and it became the headquarters of the Armed Forces Recreation Center. An amateur historian, Gunther Exner, is responsible for unearthing the information about the building's past.

Little today in the building reminds the visitor either of Lammers or the Third Reich, other than the conference table in Hitler's workroom and the telephone installation. On the plug board's connection

list one circuit is labeled, "Der Führer —
Reichskanzlei Berlin."

The former second chancellery's future
is uncertain since the army moved out. "No
way will it become an old age home," says
Simon Schwaiger, the mayor of Bischofswiesen. "We already have plenty of those
in Berchtesgaden."

Mayr, Walter. "Soll' mer'n wegsprengen?" *Der
Spiegel*. 33:101–11, 1996.

NUREMBERG

Before World War II Nuremberg was
one of the most beautiful medieval walled
cities in Germany, with its blocks of half-
timbered burghers' houses adorned by em-
bellished gables. The artist Albrecht Dürer's
house is here. But Hitler left an indelible
imprint.

From 1933 to 1938 Nuremberg was the
city of the annual Reich Party Day, a cele-
bration in which Hitler himself participated. Carnival wagons were emblazoned
with the slogan, "Off to Dachau." Policemen whipped men dressed as Jews, to the
great delight of the crowds.

Nuremberg was home to a corrupt
Nazi clique, led by the rabid anti–Semite
Julius Streicher. He went to the gallows in
1946 for his crimes against humanity.

The 1935 Nuremberg Laws surely rank
among the cruelest statutes of the twentieth
century. Two of the three decrees, the *law*

In 1945, General George S. Patton presents the original Nuremberg laws to Robert A. Millikan, president of the Huntington Library. Millikan, who was also president of the California Institute of Tech-
nology, had won the 1923 Nobel Prize in physics for the oil drop experiment, which allowed him to
determine the charge on the electron (Huntington Library).

for the safeguarding of German blood and German honor, and the Reich citizens' law, legally excluded Jews from German life, helping to set the Holocaust in motion.

Copies of the laws were widely reprinted. But until the June 1999 opening of an exhibit in Los Angeles, the original document, signed in Hitler's hand, had never been publicly displayed.

German leaders quickly drafted the laws in a Nuremberg police station in September 1935. Invading American soldiers found the originals in the closing days of World War II in a basement vault in a Nuremberg suburb. The soldiers turned the document over to General George S. Patton, the Third Army commander. He in turn presented it in 1945 as a gift, along with a confiscated limited edition of Hitler's *Mein Kampf,* to the Huntington Library in Pasadena, California. The Huntington Library has lent the Nuremberg Laws to the Skirball Cultural Center in Los Angeles, where they are on display.

Upon giving the Nuremberg Laws to the Huntington Library in 1945, General Patton dictated this statement of explanation:

When the Third Army entered the city of Nuremberg there was quite a fight going on and the city was burning. Some troops of the 90th Infantry Division fighting through the town came to a stairway that they went down with grenades, in case there were any Germans. There were no Germans. They found a vault, not open, and persuaded a German to open it for them. In it they found this thing. That was all that was in the vault. These soldiers of the 90th Division were very fond of me and I was very fond of them. They thought they would like to do something for me, they sent for me, and we had a great public presentation. The former commanding officer of the 90th Division, now commander of the Third Corps, General [J. A.] Van Fleet — he actually made the presentation to me. So it is my property. They have given me a lot of other things but this is the important one. This [document] was taken the day we captured Nuremberg, about the 14th of March

[1945]. We captured so many towns I have forgotten just which day. The presentation must have been about the 27th of May.

And Patton offered this information about the rare volume of *Mein Kampf.* The book's publisher, Max Amann, was ultimately condemned to 10 years hard labor in 1948 and died in 1957, age 63. But here Patton exaggerates Amann's importance within the Third Reich, while implying with some swagger that Amann faced the gallows: "That book was alleged by a talkative German to be one of a limited edition of the unexpurgated text. There were alleged to have been 100 copies. A man named Emman [*sic*] published it. He is the No. 3 bad man in Germany. I have him in jail now. We'll stretch him pretty quick!" From 1945 to 1948 the Allies held the war crimes trials of the Nazi leaders in the courtroom of the old Nuremberg Palace of Justice. Nuremberg today has many memorials to Nazi victims: a plaque in the Neuer Israelitischer Friedhof (cemetery), a monument in Leopoldhain, a memorial in Lorenzer Platz, other memorial stones, and a memorial wall and relief in Neutor dedicated to Germans driven from their homeland.

Kuntz, Tom. Word for word; the Nuremberg Laws; on display in Los Angeles: Legal foreshadowing of Nazi horrors. *New York Times.* July 4, 1999.

Reich Party District (Reichsparteitaggelände)

This concrete reminder of Nuremberg's Nazi past is spread over 10 square miles at the city's southeast edge, the ruin of one of Hitler's most grandiose construction projects. The annual Nazi Party rallies were held here. The Reich Party District is part of the Luitpoldhain Park.

Hitler organized his Reich Party Congresses (Reichsparteitage) to proclaim slogans and demonstrate the Nazi Party's power. The first congress took place January 27–29, 1923, in Munich. The second, when the party was reestablished after the failed Beer Hall Putsch, was held in Weimar on July 3–4, 1926.

In 1927 Hitler changed the venue to Nuremberg. From 1933 to 1938 the congresses took place annually at the beginning of September, lasted for a week, and had a title:

- August 31 to September 3, 1933, "Victory of Faith," to commemorate Hitler's seizure of power
- September 4 to 10, 1934, "Triumph of the Will," after the creation of Hitler's dictatorship

- September 10 to 16, 1935, "Reich Party Congress of Freedom," to celebrate the Nuremberg Laws
- September 8 to 14, 1936, "Reich Party Congress of Honor," celebrating the Berlin Olympic Games and the Rhineland Occupation
- September 6 to 13, 1937, "Reich Party Congress of Labor," to announce the four-year plan
- September 5 to 12, 1938, "Reich Party Congress of Great-Germany," celebrating the annexation of Austria

The congress planned for 1939 (the eleventh), the "Reich Party Congress of Peace," did not take place because of the outbreak of war, September 1, 1939.

The stadium Albert Speer designed to accommodate 450,000 onlookers was never built. But the incomplete remnant of a huge congress hall, resembling the Colosseum in Rome, still stands. Ludwig Ruff designed the hall in 1933. It is built of granite blocks from the Flossenbürg concentration camp quarry. Nearby is a marble-faced grandstand where a spotlighted Hitler, amid flaming torches, harangued his followers, rousing them to a frenzy.

There is a steel rail on the balcony platform at the top of the stairs where Hitler once stood and was photographed by Leni Riefenstahl in *The Triumph of the Will*, the prize-winning propaganda film of the 1934 party rally. Endless rows of troops goose-stepped for Riefenstahl's cameras. The huge grandstand, draped with swastika banners, provided a backdrop. One witness, the French ambassador, wrote that the atmosphere was "amazing and indescribable, a peculiar state of euphoria in which hundreds of thousands of men

Hitler in Nuremberg for the Reich Party Congress of Freedom, September 1935.

Top: Nuremberg. Incomplete remnant of huge congress hall. Ludwig Ruff designed the hall, resembling the Colosseum in Rome, in 1933. It is built of granite blocks from the Flossenbürg concentration camp quarry (Heiner Wessel). *Bottom:* Model of completed congress hall.

stand, called the Führertribune (or Zeppelin Tribune because Count Ferdinand von Zeppelin once landed a blimp nearby), is used by tennis players as a practice wall. It is defaced by obscene and anti–Turkish graffiti. Only the central section grandstand remains. The towers and imposing colonnade were demolished in the 1960s. Weeds are everywhere.

"The Nazis claimed they would build for 1,000 years, but they couldn't even put something up for fifty years without the roof leaking," said Eckart Dietzfelbinger, who has placed a historical exhibit inside the grandstand,

Top: Hitler on the Führertribune. On this marble-faced grandstand, a spotlighted Hitler, amid flaming torches, harangued his followers, rousing them to a frenzy. *Right:* Reich Party Day, Nuremberg, 1935. Consecration of the standards and honoring of the dead. Hitler on the Führertribune at center.

and women are gripped by the romantic excitement, the mystic ecstasy of a kind of holy mania they have become slaves to."

According to Albert Speer, the entire area was to acquire a mythic significance (Speer, 1977):

The Party Rally terrain was also intended, in the course of generations, to grow into a district given over to spiritual ceremony. The rally area itself was only to be the first stage and the nucleus of the whole. Oak groves had already been planted or staked out. All sorts of buildings of a religious nature were to be erected within them: monuments to celebrate the concept of the Movement and its victories; memorials to outstanding individuals.... I secretly decided to place my own tomb by the grand processional avenue, just where the avenue crossed the artificial lake.

The police now store towed cars in the congress hall courtyard. The marble grand-

in an impressive hall with a mosaic ceiling, the "Hall of Honor." Here Hitler received high-ranking visitors.

"There's a big discussion about what to

Nuremberg. Führertribune today (Heiner Wessel).

do with the place," said Dietzfelbinger, "but there are no ready answers."

Gruber, Ruth Ellen. Standing on Hitler's Grandstand. *New Leader.* January 26, 1998, pp. 9–10.

Gumbel, Peter. War's End (A special report): Europe — The Haunting: How should Germany deal with the crimes of its past? *Wall Street Journal.* April 24, 1995, R10.

Kuntz, Tom. On display in Los Angeles: Legal foreshadowing of Nazi horror. *New York Times.* July 4, 1999, sec. 4, p. 7.

Lehrer, Steven. *Wannsee House and the Holocaust.* McFarland. Jefferson, N.C. 2000.

Leser-Frage: Haben Nürnberg, München und Bonn Denkmäler für Nazi-Opfer? *Berliner Morgenpost.* October 12, 1999.

Speer, Albert. *Inside the Third Reich.* Translated by Richard and Clara Winston. Avon Books. New York 1971.

———. *Spandau. The Secret Diaries.* Translated by Richard and Clara Winston. Pocket Books. New York 1977.

Zentner, Christian, and Friedemann Bedürftig, eds. *The Encyclopedia of the Third Reich.* English translation edited by Amy Hackett. Macmillan. New York 1991.

Palace of Justice

This group of gabled government buildings is at Fürtherstrasse 110 (U-Bahn stop Barenschanze), the main thoroughfare running northwest toward the nearby city of Fürth-im-Bayern. The large, heavily built complex includes a jail, an office building, and a courthouse, which had been the seat of the court of appeals for the Nuremberg region.

During the Nuremberg war crimes trials here, the defendants were incarcerated in the jail. Each one had a bedspread, a straw mattress, blankets, a small table, and chair. A typical cell had a narrow window in the door, allowing constant observation of a prisoner, except on the toilet, which was situated in a niche adjacent to the door. On October 25, 1945, Robert Ley, head of the German Labor Front, hanged himself in the toilet niche. He made a noose from the stripped edges of an army towel tied together and fastened it to the toilet pipe. He wrote in his suicide note that he could not stand the shame any longer.

"It's just as well that he's dead," Hermann Göring told prison psychologist G. M. Gilbert, "because I had my doubts about how he would behave at the trial. He's always been so scatterbrained — always making such fantastic and bombastic speeches. I'm sure he would have made a spectacle of himself at the trial. Well, I'm not surprised that he's dead, because he's been drinking himself to death anyway."

Göring had one of the highest IQs of all the defendants (138). After U.S. Army doctors had weaned him from narcotics, an addiction of 20 years' standing, he showed considerable poise, skill, and candor as a witness. In contrast, Supreme Court Justice Robert H. Jackson, the chief prosecutor, seemed deficient. As *New Yorker* writer Janet Flanner reported (Taylor, 1992), Jackson, recognized as a great humanitarian, nevertheless held a "burning private conviction that the Nazi prisoners [were] mere common criminals." For this reason he treated them in "a blustering police court manner, which was successful with the craven small fry but disastrous for him in cross-examining that uncommon criminal, Göring, himself accustomed to blustering in a grander way."

Göring stung Jackson repeatedly, as prosecutor Telford Taylor recalled:

Jackson asked Göring whether the German remilitarization of the Rhineland, on March 7, 1936, had been planned long in advance. Göring replied "at most 2 to 3 weeks," whereupon Jackson produced the record of a meeting of the Reich Defense Council on June 26, 1935, which called for (as worded in the English translation) "preparation for the liberation of the Rhine."

Göring at once pointed out that the reference was to the Rhine River and not the Rhineland and that the German word had been erroneously translated "liberation," while its correct meaning was "clearing." The document,

Göring explained, did not involve a plan to militarize the Rhineland, but comprised basic directions for military mobilization in the event of war and provided that the Rhine must be "cleared" of civil river traffic to clear the way for military shipping.

In a feeble effort to save face Jackson then asked: "But [these preparations] were of a character which had to be kept entirely secret from foreign powers?" To which Göring replied: "I do not think I can recall reading beforehand the publication of the mobilization preparations of the United States."

Despite his formidable verbal agility, Göring had no illusions about his fate.

"Well, we'll have plenty of time to talk things over some more before the verdict," Dr. Gilbert said to Göring one evening during a visit to his cell.

"The death sentence, you mean," Göring replied.

Göring escaped the noose by swallowing cyanide the night before he was to be executed. His body was cremated in the oven of the Dachau concentration camp and the ashes flushed into an unnamed river.

Master Sergeant John C. Woods, a professional executioner with 15 years' experience, and two GI assistants, dispatched the other condemned defendants. The gallows was set up in the jail gymnasium. But Sergeant Woods, for all his lethal *savoir-faire*, was severely criticized after the corpses' photographs had been made available to the press. Cecil Catling of the *London Star*, a veteran crime reporter, said that the drop was not long enough and that the men had not been properly tied. They struck their heads on the platform as they fell, and "died of slow strangulation." Woods made lame excuses, but the public had seen the pictures, which were distressing and reminiscent of the slow strangulation Hitler had meted out to his would-be assassins at Plötzensee two years earlier.

Room 600, the courtroom in which the trials took place, is still in use today. It is not a museum, and the 1945 furniture is long gone.

Gilbert, G. M. *Nuremberg Diary.* DaCapo Press. New York 1995.

Taylor, Telford. *Anatomy of the Nuremberg Trials.* Little, Brown. Boston 1992.

Terrance, Marc. *Concentration Camps. A Traveler's Guide to World War II Sites.* Universal Publishers 1999.

Hotel Deutscher Hof. 29 Frauentorgraben (Two Blocks from Train Station)

High party officials liked this hotel, which was divided into two sections. Hitler preferred the older, quiet section. Noisier Nazis liked the newer section. Hitler always stayed in suite 105, a group of rooms with a balcony, and often reviewed the troops

Nuremberg. Hitler at the window of his room, Hotel Deutscher Hof, ca. 1934/5.

when they paraded along the wide street below.

Haddock, Charles, and Charles E. Snyder. *Treasure Trove. The Looting of the Third Reich.* Snyder's Treasures. Bowie, Md. 1998.

Art Bunker, Beneath Nuremberg Castle

Kings and emperors once lived in Nuremberg Castle, atop a hill, the Kaiserburg. In a bunker beneath the castle the Nazis stored artworks of immense value.

The concrete bunker walls are crumbling. Water drips from the ceilings, and rust eats through the exposed pipes. The bunker was opened to public tours in 1995. A thousand people visit yearly.

Massive armored steel doors lead into the rooms, which once held more than 1,000 art objects, among them works of Albrecht Dürer, the Angel's Greeting of Veit Stoss, the kaiser's crown, and the Behaim Globe.[65] The golden royal treasures were kept in the deepest room, 900 cubic meters in size, 24 meters within the mountain on which the castle stands. No conventional bomb could ever have damaged them.

The art bunker was one of the few climate-controlled spaces in the entire country. With two air-conditioners and two heaters, air sucked in from outside could be maintained at a constant temperature of 18°C and 70 percent humidity. The machinery functioned well for 30 years, until the 1960s, when the artworks were returned to museums. A Nuremberg writer, Jan Beinssen, set part of one of his thrillers, *Two Women Against Time,* in the bunker.

Artworks were not the only stored objects. Albert Speer's building plans for the Berlin Reich Chancellery and the Nuremberg Reich Party Day District also resided in the vault-like rooms. Curators maintained

a record of the entire bunker inventory on file cards.

Bombensichere Schatzkammer der Diktatur. *Süddeutsche Zeitung.* September 26, 1997.

WUNSIEDEL

(Located in Bavaria, 93 km northeast of Nuremberg), Wunsiedel is the site of the grave of Rudolf Hess (1894–1987). Hess was deputy to the Führer and Hitler's appointed successor after Hermann Göring. Hess had marched at Hitler's side during the Beer Hall Putsch, November 1923, and was incarcerated with Hitler in Landsberg Prison. He aroused Hitler's interest in world politics and took down *Mein Kampf* from Hitler's dictation.

On May 10, 1941, Hess flew from Augsburg and parachuted to earth in Scotland. He apparently hoped to reach Tories in England who would make peace with Hitler before the German invasion of the Soviet Union. Hitler promptly pronounced Hess insane. In 1946 the military tribunal at Nuremberg gave Hess a life sentence. At 93, Hess, the last inmate in Spandau Prison, committed suicide by hanging himself with an electrical cord.

Hess's grave is now the most closely watched burial plot in all Germany. In Wunsiedel, a town of 10,000 souls, the police constantly monitor the cemetery with video

Top: Rudolf Hess, the "Führer's deputy," greets Hitler as the dictator arrives at the congress hall in Nuremberg for the Reich Party Day, 1938 (Süddeutscher Verlag Bilderdienst). *Bottom:* Grave of Rudolf Hess, a favorite gathering place for neo–Nazis and the most closely watched tombstone in all Germany (Süddeutscher Verlag Bilderdienst).

cameras. Only persons who tend Hess's grave are allowed to approach his granite tombstone, engraved with the epitaph "I dared to do it," a quote from Ulrich von Hutten.[66] A flower bouquet with a red, black, and gold ribbon reminds visitors that Hess's grave is unlike others in the cemetery and has been the site of political demonstrations.

German neo–Nazis and right-wing extremists descend on Wunsiedel every August 17, the date of Hess's death. Their destination is not only Hess's grave but also a decaying villa in Reicholdsgrün 15 km from Wunsiedel, Hess's former summer residence. To deter these misguided pilgrims and prevent their torchlight parades, the police deploy forests of barbed wire and block the side streets with heavy, sand-filled barricades. Since 1991 the authorities have prohibited Hess-inspired marches, and a massive police presence has quelled most disturbances.

Kreiss, Stefanie. Noch Grabesruhe an Hess-Ruhestätte in Wunsiedel. AP Worldstream. August 15, 1995.

HITLER'S FIELD HEADQUARTERS

During the course of the war the Germans built 16 field headquarters for Hitler. The dictator used only six of these. Even as the Wehrmacht was capitulating in May 1945, four field headquarters were under construction. (In the interest of having Hitler's field headquarters listed in one place, those that were located in Belgium, France, Poland and the Ukraine are included here.) A description of all of these redoubts is beyond the scope of this book. Interested readers are referred to the monograph by Seidler and Zeigert (see Bibliography).

Throughout history generals have used luxurious mansions and other cushy digs as their field headquarters. Not Adolf Hitler. Hating all aristocrats and the trappings of aristocracy, Hitler disdained castles, palaces, and country houses. Albert Speer discovered this fact in 1939 when he designed and built Alderhorst, which was intended to be Hitler's first permanent field command post. As Speer reports in *Inside the Third Reich*, Hitler sent him to scout a location in the area of Frankfurt-am-Main. Speer looked to the Taunus Mountains, a rolling hill country he had hiked in his youth. About a mile north of the village of Ziegenberg, Speer and his staff found "a large Gut,[67] a kind of manorial country house," which they "requisitioned." Speer redesigned the home with Hitler's comfort in mind, and made plans for Hitler's staff to be "housed inconspicuously " in surrounding villages. Speer was proud of his arrangements, in which "all suspiciously military installations … were in underground shelters, with cows grazing over such things as the subterranean garage."

In September 1939, Hitler returned from the Polish campaign,[68] saw the headquarters, and promptly refused to stay there even for a single night:

It was too luxurious, he fumed, not to his style, too grand, something for a "horse-loving aristocat." In wartime, he said, he as Führer must inspire the soldiers at the front with the Spartan simplicity of his daily life. Perhaps, says Speer, the "simple-life pose" was not without sincerity, but it rang a bit hollow with the staff members left to count the costs of the initial renovations and of moving the headquarters (along with its extensive communications network involving "many hundreds of mile of cable") to another location.

Hitler built two more field headquarters in the west, code named Felsennest and Tannenberg.

O'Donnell, James P. *The Bunker.* Houghton Mifflin Company. Boston 1978.

Felsennest

Felsennest (cliff aerie) was at Rodert, 17 kilometers from Münstereifel in the Eifel

Mountains on the Belgian border. In autumn 1939 Hitler spent a few weeks in Felsennest before he called off his planned invasion of the Low Countries and France.

Hitler returned to Felsennest for the rescheduled invasion. On May 9, 1940, at 5 P.M., he boarded his special train in Berlin's Finkenkrug station with his retinue, which included Reichsleiter Martin Bormann and Field Marshal Wilhelm Keitel, head of the Wehrmacht.

Even Hitler's secretaries did not know the train's destination. The next morning, May 10, the train arrived at a little station near Euskirchen. Cars were waiting to take the company to Felsennest. Simultaneously, Wehrmacht motor divisions and airplane squadrons were crossing the German border, heading west. *Fall Gelb*, Case Yellow, the campaign against the three neutrals, Belgium, Luxembourg, and the Netherlands, had begun.

Except for short absences, Hitler was at Felsennest for the next four weeks. Of all his command posts, Felsennest was the most attractive because of the pleasant wooded surroundings. According to his secretary, Christa Schröder, Hitler felt very well in this environment. Since his bunker room was quite small, he held most of his meetings outside and seldom went to bed before 3 A.M.

The two secretaries, Christa Schröder and Traudl Junge, were not housed within Hitler's fenced-off *sanctum sanctorum*. They lived in the town of Rodert, where the Germans had built 80 bunkers for guards and ancillary personnel.

The actual Felsennest, on the summit of a mountain, the Eselsberg, was quite small, an 18-person headquarters. It consisted of a bedroom, a workroom, two little rooms for servants and adjutants, and rooms for Field Marshal Keitel, General Alfred Jodl, and Hitler's personal physician, as well as a kitchen and a bath. Nearby was a storage bunker. A dining bunker held a table accommodating 20 persons. Hitler would invite his general staff officers from Rodert, one at a time, to join him for meals.

On Tuesday evenings Hitler visited the dance hall of the one inn at Rodert. "His large visored cap covered his eyes," remembers one witness. "He held himself erect, was of average height in his tall boots, and wore a simple belted military coat. He was completely unprepossessing."

On the night of May 24–25 an enemy plane flew over Felsennest. The antiaircraft fire was deafening. The army hastily installed more guns, as well as 10 officers and 224 men from the guard regiment in Berlin. Among these troops were soldiers specially trained to combat enemy parachutists. The Wehrmacht also required the local people to show identification whenever they wanted to come or go, until Hitler left Felsennest, June 6, 1940, for Brûly-de-Pesche, 175 km southwest.

In early 1945 the retreating Wehrmacht dynamited the Felsennest bunkers as the U.S. Fifth Army approached; the remains still exist. The guest bunker survives, as do some ammunition bunkers and foxholes in the forest.

Knigge, Jobst. Unbequeme Erinnerungsstätte-Vor 60 Jahren in der "Wolfsschlucht." Deutsche Presse-Agentur (DPA) — Europa. June 25, 2000.

Tannenberg

Tannenberg, which Hitler visited but did not use, was under a mountain called Kniebis, west of Freudenstadt, in the Black Forest. Tannenberg faced French Alsace from across the Rhine, at the southern end of the Maginot Line. Historians presume that the Germans might have considered circumventing the French defenses at this point. But in the event, they made their breakthrough into France at Sedan, 280 kilometers to the northwest, as part of the now famous Manstein Plan.

Brûly-de-Pesche (Wolfschlucht 1, Wolf's Gorge 1)

Brûly-de-Pesche (*Wolfschlucht 1*, Wolf's Gorge 1) is a Belgian village 46 kilometers northwest of Sedan and 5 kilometers north of the French border. Hitler and his army chiefs were here for three weeks (June 6–28, 1940).

Brûly-de-Pesche is tiny — a dozen houses, a church, and a cafe. A sign on the edge of town points to a shadowy path leading to Hitler's former headquarters. When Hitler arrived, the Germans quickly built a seven-meter-long, five-meter-high concrete bunker, to be used in case of an air raid. The bunker is preserved as a souvenir. A few meters away a new barracks exhibits photographs of Hitler and his minions. The two original barracks buildings the Germans built have disappeared. Hitler and his generals drafted the French surrender terms in the village church.

To make room for the Nazi high command, the Wehrmacht forced the occupants of Brûly-de-Pesche to vacate their homes. In the fall of 1940 the locals were finally allowed to move back in. Postcards sold in the village show the famous Nazis who came to Brûly-de-Pesche: Hess, Göring, Bormann, and Speer.

Barbed wire and antiaircraft guns surrounded Wolfschlucht 1. Despite the thick foliage, the British probably knew where Hitler was, and British reconnaissance flights over Brûly-de-Pesche were frequent. But only once did a British plane drop a bomb, which landed three kilometers away.

The Belgians have no qualms about maintaining Hitler's headquarters and also have an exhibit at Brûly-de-Pesche documenting the anti–Hitler resistance. But they are still a bit touchy about their King Leopold III's supposed desire to meet with Hitler at Brûly-de-Pesche. In fact, according to historian René Mathot, this apocryphal story arose after a German liaison officer at Leopold's court misunderstood the king and sent a dispatch to Brûly-de-Pesche, indicating that Leopold wanted to come to Wolfschlucht 1.

Margival (Wolfschlucht 2, Wolf's Gorge 2, W2)

In summer 1940 Hitler ordered the construction of another field headquarters in France at Margival, 8 km northeast of Soissons. He intended to use this headquarters when he directed Operation Sea Lion, the invasion of England. But the failure of the Luftwaffe to destroy the Royal Air Force in August and September 1940, the celebrated Battle of Britain, caused Hitler to call off Sea Lion in October.

Had German troops managed to land at Dover, Hitler would have moved to a headquarters further west, built into the chalk cliffs above Calais. The French grow mushrooms in this cave today.

In 1941 Hitler directed the Balkan Campaign from a field headquarters in his special train near the Austrian town of Mönichkirchen.

Hitler moved on to quarters called Wolfschanze and then Vinnitsa (see both described below), but on June 17, 1944, 11 days after the D-Day invasion, Hitler returned to Wolfschlucht 2. Albert Speer describes the waste involved in its renovation:

Before the invasion Hitler had emphasized that immediately after the landing he would go to France to conduct operations in person. In view of this, at an expense of countless millions of marks, hundreds of miles of telephone cables were laid and two headquarters built by the Todt Organization, employing large quantities of concrete and expensive installations. Hitler himself had fixed on the location and the size of the headquarters. He justified the tremendous outlay during this period, when he was losing France, by remarking that at least one of the headquarters was situated precisely at the future western border of Germany and therefore could serve as part of a system of fortifications. On June 17, he visited this headquarters, called W2, situated between Soissons and Laon.

Despite the expense, Hitler told Speer he was not happy with his headquarters: "He remarked to me that W2 seemed to him too unsafe, situated as it was in the heart of partisan-ridden France." After the war the French Army occupied the 270 blockhouses the Germans had built. In 1995 the army put the site up for sale. Developers wanted to turn it into a sporting arena, a war games venue, a museum, or a logging camp. But many people, especially the 300 villagers who lived in nearby Margival, feared that the area could become a neo–Nazi shrine. The buildings and bunkers are vacant and decaying.

Speer, Albert. *Inside the Third Reich.* Translated by Richard and Clara Winston. Avon Books. New York 1971.

Wolfschanze

Hitler's most well-known field headquarters, Wolfschanze (Wolf's Lair), was located in Rastenburg (Kętrzyn), East Prussia (now Poland), 200 km north of Warsaw. It was built in 1941 and enlarged in 1944.

The German invasion of the Soviet Union began June 22, 1941. Hitler arrived at Wolfschanze on June 24. Whereas the dictator stayed only a few weeks in his other redoubts, he spent three years at Wolfschanze, a place Colonel General Alfred Jodl described as "a cross between a cloister and a concentration camp." Hitler left Wolfschanze November 20, 1944, as the Red Army approached. On January 24, 1945, German soldiers dynamited the bunkers.

Of all Hitler's field headquarters, Wolfschanze is most popular with tourists, despite the fact that it is nothing but a heap of ruins. Nevertheless, the site is quite open and accessible. Visitors numbering 250,000 arrive yearly, mainly Poles and Germans, singly and in groups. Swarms of ravenous mosquitoes greet them.

The standard tour passes Martin Bormann's bunker number 11, Hitler's bunker 13, Hermann Göring's bunker 16, Colonel General Alfred Jodl's bunker 17, and Field Marshal Wilhelm Keitel's bunker 19. Fritz Todt, who built Wolfschanze, had his own bunker, which Albert Speer inherited after Todt's death in a mysterious plane crash, February 8, 1942. In all, there were more than 80 bunkers and buildings, among them a railroad station, two airfields, and a power plant. Still present are the ruins of the barracks where Claus von Stauffenberg's bomb exploded (see Bendlerblock).

Wolfschanze housed 2,100 officers, soldiers, and civilians. Barbed wire, mine fields, ordnance, guardhouses, road barricades, and the East Prussian forests separated this workforce from the outside world.

Wolfschanze was freezing in winter, stifling in summer. To eliminate mosquitoes, the Wehrmacht poured oil on the nearby lakes, but this killed all the frogs along with the mosquitoes. Hitler was peeved. The croaking frogs serenaded him to sleep, he said. So his minions had to bring in more frogs.

Hitler's bunker had an external concrete shell, like a nuclear power plant, covering a huge concrete block. His chamber was windowless, completely closed off from the outside, illuminated only by electric light.

Albert Speer described Hitler's bunker as resembling an ancient Egyptian tomb. In these surreal, cramped surroundings, the Führer would hold forth for hours on end, torturing his minions with long-winded disquisitions in the wee hours of the morning. Only courtesy and a sense of duty, according to Speer, enabled Hitler's exasperated listeners to stay awake.

A private company currently maintains Wolfschanze. Officials insist that they will never turn it into a Hitlerian Disneyland.

Top: Entrance to Wolfschanze. *Bottom:* Wolfschanze. Ruins of German bunker.

Flottau, Heiko. Die Bunkertrummer bei Rastenburg wo das Attentat auf Hitler misslang. Eine
Privatfirma betreibt heute die Touristenattraktion Wolfschanze. *Süddeutsche Zeitung*. July 20,
1994.

Speer, Albert. *Inside the Third Reich*. Translated by
Richard and Clara Winston. Avon Books. New
York 1971.

Vinnitsa (Werewolf)

The initial success of the German invasion allowed Hitler to transfer his field
headquarters 720 kilometers southeast, to
Vinnitsa, a small pine forest in the Ukraine,
on July 16, 1942. Code named Werewolf,
this redoubt was closer to Moscow (930
kilometers) than to Berlin (1,100 kilometers).

The Vinnitsa command center was
partly underground. Two dining halls, a
gymnasium with shower, housing for
officers, and a subterranean bunker with
three-meter-thick walls were part of the
complex. Two armored telephone cables
connected Werewolf directly with Berlin.
The generals had their own 10-by-20-meter
swimming pool, which the local people still
use. Hitler had a wood-framed bungalow,
sheltered by trees. Several winding walkways suggested a park-like, gardened area.
"It was all in strange contrast to the miserable villages and the dirty town of Vinnitsa," wrote Albert Speer, who built the
complex. To maintain total secrecy, the
Germans may have shot the Russian
prisoners of war who constructed Werewolf.

Hitler shuttled by plane between
Werewolf and Wolfschanze until March
13, 1943, just after the Russians had anni-
hilated the entire German Sixth Army at
Stalingrad. Hitler then abandoned Werewolf.

Speer, Albert. *Inside the Third Reich*. Translated by
Richard and Clara Winston. Avon Books. New
York 1971.

Adlerhorst, Riese, and Pullach

From December 10, 1944, until January 16, 1945, Hitler conducted the Ardennes
Offensive (the Battle of the Bulge) from
Adlerhorst, at one end of a solitary grassy
valley near Bad Nauheim, a mile northwest
of Ziegenberg. Hidden in the woods
and camouflaged, the command bunkers,
which Albert Speer had built in 1939, had
the usual massive concrete ceilings and
walls. Speer visited Hitler here on January
1, 1945:

Two hours of this year of 1945 had passed when
I at last, after passing through many barriers,
arrived in Hitler's private bunker. I had not
come too late: adjutants, doctors, secretaries,
Bormann — the whole circle except for the
generals attached to the Führer's headquarters,
were gathered around Hitler drinking champagne. The alcohol had relaxed everyone, but
the atmosphere was still subdued. Hitler seemed
to be the only one in the company who
was drunk without having taken any stimulat-
ing beverage. He was in the grip of a permanent
euphoria.

Speer told the writer James P. O'Donnell about one more field headquarters,
called Giant (*Riese*), probably the largest
Hitler built. Giant, a series of underground
catacombs, cost 150 million reichsmarks,
four times as much as Wolfschanze. Construction work began in 1944, in the Lower
Silesian spa town of Charlottenbrunn
(Jedlina-Zdrój), now part of Poland, 7 km
SE of Wałbrzych.[69] Hitler vainly hoped to
stop the Soviets before they reached this
highly industrialized region. Neither Hitler
nor anyone else ever occupied Giant. But in
nearby Kreisau (Krzyzowa, 18 km northeast
of Wałbrzych), Helmuth James Graf von
Moltke and other members of the "Kreisau
Circle" met at Moltke's estate to plan
the July 20, 1944, attempt on Hitler's life
and were executed for their role in the plot.
The renovated Moltke estate became a

Polish-German youth encounter center in 1998.

In 1943 Martin Bormann ordered the building of a field headquarters in Pullach, a suburb of Munich, "in case the Führer is there during a bombing raid and cannot get back directly to Berchtesgaden." This headquarters, code named Hagen, was on Heilmannstrasse. The U.S. Army occupied the buildings and underground bunkers from 1945–47. Afterward, the German Federal Intelligence Service (*Bundesnachrichtendienst*) moved in and remains there today.

Flottau, Heiko. Die Bunkertrummer bei Rastenburg wo das Attentat auf Hitler misslang. Eine Privatfirma betreibt heute die Touristenattraktion Wolfschanze. *Süddeutsche Zeitung.* July 20, 1994.

Isnard, Jacques. Le quartier general de Hitler en France est a vendre. *Le Monde.* November 22, 1995.

Knigge, Jobst. Unbequeme Erinnerungsstätte-Vor 60 Jahren in der "Wolfsschlucht." Deutsche Presse-Agentur (DPA)—Europa. June 25, 2000.

Kohl von polnischem Ministerpräsidenten begrüsst. Eröffnung von Jugendbegegnungsstätte in Kreisau. AP Worldstream. June 11, 1998.

Leser-Frage: Wann wird ein landwirtschaftlicher Betrieb als Gut bezeichnet? *Berliner Morgenpost.* August 8, 1999.

Makartsev, Alexei. Picknick auf dem Bunker. Kuhfladen, Betontrümmer und ein böser Fluch: Ortstermin in den Ruinen von Hitlers Hauptquartier "Werwolf" bei Winniza in der Ukraine. *Berliner Morgenpost.* July 17, 1999.

O'Donnell, James P. *The Bunker.* Houghton Mifflin. Boston 1978.

Schmidt, Walter. Schweigen über dem Felsennest. *Hamburger Abendblatt.* May 20, 2000.

Seidler, Franz W., and Dieter Zeigert. *Die Führerhauptquartiere. Anlagen und Planungen im Zweiten Weltkrieg.* Herbig Verlag. Munich 2000.

Speer, Albert, *Inside the Third Reich.* Translated by Richard and Clara Winston. Avon Books. New York 1971.

_____, *Spandau. The Secret Diaries.* Translated by Richard and Clara Winston. Pocket Books. New York 1977.

Webster, Paul. Nazi HQ sale raises fears of 'Hitlerpark.' Guardian; Manchester. November 25, 1995, p. 13.

Hitler hoists the first shovel of dirt to initiate the building of the Autobahn.

THE AUTOBAHN ("STREETS OF THE FÜHRER")

This nationwide system of superhighways was planned in detail during the 1920s. Hitler ordered it built after he came to power. Fritz Todt, the *Reichsautobahninspektor*, intended to use 600,000 workers, but the maximum number employed never exceeded 124,000. Thus, Autobahn construction hardly made a dent in German unemployment of almost 4,000,000 during the early 1930s.

Reichsautobahn in Germany. Reichsbahncentrale für den deutschen Reiseverkehr, 1936.

orient bomber pilots. At the end of the war Hitler ordered many of the highway bridges destroyed to thwart the Allied invasion.

Krump, Hans. Die "Strassen des Führers"-eine Sackgasse? *Berliner Morgenpost.* March 23, 1997.

Schütz, Erhard, and Eckhard Gruber. *Mythos Reichsautobahn. Bau und Inszenierung der "Strassen des Führers" 1933–1941.* Ch. Links Verlag. Berlin 1996.

THE SIEGFRIED LINE (WESTWALL)

More than 14,000 bunkers and numerous tank traps once formed what Hitler's propaganda called an insurmountable bulwark. The Siegfried Line was 630 kilometers long, extending from Basel to the lower Rhine. Between 1938 and 1940, half a million workmen laid down eight million tons of cement and 1.2 million tons of steel to build it.

Militarily, Hitler made use of the Siegfried line only once, during his 1939 invasion of Poland, to defend against a French attack. But the French remained immobile inside their Maginot Line redoubts. In fact, the Siegfried Line would have been quite vulnerable to a French air assault.

After the fall of France in 1940, the Siegfried Line had no further military significance. The Germans closed up the bunkers and removed most of the armaments. When the Wehrmacht began its retreat to the Siegfried Line in 1944, the fortifications were almost worthless. Many

Nonetheless, Todt declared the Autobahn equivalent to the pyramids and the Great Wall of China, a "grand collective work in the rebuilding of the Reich" (Schütz and Gruber, 1996).

The Autobahn was of negligible military value. Until the end of the war, almost all troop transport was by rail. Moreover, during the 1930s the German generals were quite fearful that the highly motorized French Army could use the superhighways during an invasion. After Allied bombing of Germany began, the Wehrmacht tried to disguise the Autobahn in order to dis-

of the keys to the sealed bunkers had been lost, and other bunkers were under water or indefensible. General George Patton's troops were the first Allied soldiers to break through the Siegfried Line.

In 1949 more than 500 tons of Wehrmacht munitions exploded in a Siegfried Line bunker in Kavalierenberg, in the Eifel region. A large part of the nearby city of Prüm was destroyed. Eleven people were killed, another 150 badly injured.

Vor Kriegsende abgerüstet. *Berliner Morgenpost.* March 15, 2000.

III

FRANCE

THE MAGINOT LINE

This series of fortifications on the French-German border contributed significantly to French complacency in the face of resurgent German military might after Hitler's rise to power in 1933.

Running from Longwy in northeast France to Basel, Switzerland, the Maginot Line was named after French war minister André Maginot (1877–1932).

Because certain modern fortresses had held out against German artillery during World War I, and saved military manpower too, Maginot urged the French government to build a permanent fortified line to guard against German attack. In 1929, during Maginot's second term as minister of war, construction began on the French northeast frontier. Maginot died in early 1932, but his project continued and was completed in 1938.

The Maginot Line had concrete thicker than in any fortress ever built, and its guns were heavier. It had air-conditioned areas for the troops and was said to be more comfortable than a modern city. There were recreation areas, living quarters, supply storehouses, and underground rail lines connecting various portions of the line. Strong points could be defended by troops moved through its tunnels by rail. The tunnels extended over 150 km, with 39 military units, 70 bunkers, 500 artillery and infantry groups, and 500 casemates (gun fortification chambers), shelters, and observation towers.

But the Maginot Line had one glaring defect: it was, in fact, half a line. It covered the French-German frontier but not the French-Belgian. In 1940 the Germans simply went around it. They invaded Belgium on May 10, crossed the Somme River, and on May 12 struck at Sedan, the French city at the northern end of the Maginot Line. German tanks and planes broke through the supposedly impassable Ardennes terrain and continued to the rear of the Maginot Line, making it useless.

On May 16 Winston Churchill flew to Paris to meet with French leaders. Churchill demanded to know the whereabouts of the strategic reserve of French troops, the *masse de manoeuvre*, to repel the German invasion. General Maurice Gamelin, "the world's foremost professional soldier," replied, "Aucune" (There isn't any).

The Wehrmacht did not capture many parts of the Maginot Line until after the French capitulated. One of the last strongholds to fall was the fortress of Marckolsheim, adjacent to the Rhine near Strasbourg. The 30 defenders fought from June 15 to June 17, 1940. Hitler came to inspect this fort after the surrender. Today the Marckolsheim fortress houses a military museum. Its casemates, guns, and armor have been carefully preserved.

Churchill, Winston. *Their Finest Hour. The Second World War*. Vol 2. Houghton Mifflin. Boston 1949.
Encyclopædia Britannica. Chicago 1998.
Michelin, Alsace Lorraine. *Guide de Tourisme*. Michelin et Cie, Propriétaires-Éditeurs 1995.
Zentner, Christian, and Friedemann Bedürftig, eds. *The Encyclopedia of the Third Reich*. English translation edited by Amy Hackett. Macmillan. New York 1991.

COMPIÈGNE

In June 1940, just after his armies had smashed France, Hitler traveled to Compiègne. Here, in a forest clearing, on November 11, 1918, Marshal Ferdinand Foch, the French commander, had humbled the kaiser's generals and accepted a humiliating German surrender, the armistice ending World War I. Foch held the fateful meeting in his railroad car, number 2419D, a dining car that the Wagon-Lits Company had converted to an office on wheels. The German delegation arrived in another train.

French officials later made the site into what they called the "Glade of the Armistice." The French architect M. Magès opened up a grand avenue, 250 yards long, leading to a broad circular center with a great granite block inscribed: "Here on 11th November 1918 perished the criminal pride of the German Empire defeated by the free people whom it set out to enslave." At the entrance to Magès's avenue stood an imposing monument in Alsatian sandstone, erected by the newspaper *Le Matin*'s public subscription, depicting the point of a sword impaling a large limp eagle. Underneath was inscribed: "To the heroic soldiers of France.... Defenders of the country and of right.... Glorious liberators of Alsace Lorraine." A statue of Marshal Foch gazing out with imperious satisfaction was added in September 1937.

Alsatian monument to French soldiers. Compiègne. Glade of the Armistice. At 3 P.M. on June 21, 1940, Hitler walked past this memorial, its skewered eagle bedecked with red Reich flags bearing black swastikas.

CBS Radio correspondent William L. Shirer arrived at Compiègne on June 19, 1940. German army engineers with pneumatic drills were feverishly demolishing the wall of the museum where Foch's railroad car was kept. Finally, they hauled the car out to the spot it occupied in November 1918.

At 3 P.M. on June 21 Hitler walked past the Alsatian monument with its skewered eagle, now bedecked with red reich flags bearing black swastikas. He wore a double-breasted gray uniform. His World War I Iron Cross First Class hung from his left breast pocket; a Jewish officer, Lieutenant Hugo Gutmann, had nominated him for this decoration. To Shirer Hitler's face looked grave, solemn, brimming with revenge and scornful inner joy. The Führer's step was springy, the step of a triumphant conqueror who had defied the world.

Surrounded by his entourage, Hitler strode up to the massive central granite block and read its inscription in silence. As he stepped off the monument, he glanced back at it, snide, angry. He swiftly snapped his hands on his hips, arched his shoulders, and planted his feet wide apart, a haughty gesture of defiance and burning contempt.

Hitler led his entourage to another smaller granite stone, 50 yards to one side. This stone marked the position of the German generals' railroad car on November 11, 1918. Hitler gave only a passing glance at the inscription, "The German Plenipotentiaries." The stone itself lay between a pair of rusty railroad tracks. Hitler appeared not even to see the nearby statue of Marshal Foch.

In Foch's railroad car Hitler gave the Nazi salute, arm raised. As his generals handed armistice terms to the defeated, dispirited French, he sat at the same table in the same position as Foch but said nothing. Twelve minutes after the French arrived, Hitler stood up, saluted stiffly, and alighted from the car. The whole surrender ceremony was over in fifteen minutes.

During the occupation (1940–44) the Germans laid waste to the entire site. They dynamited the inscribed central granite block, plowed up the avenues, cut down the trees, and took Foch's railroad car to Berlin, where in 1944 it was destroyed during a

Central granite block, Compiègne, Glade of the Armistice, inscribed: "Here on 11th November 1918 perished the criminal pride of the German Empire defeated by the free people whom it set out to enslave."

Top: Compiègne. Glade of the Armistice, granite stone marking the position of the German generals' railroad car on November 11, 1918. *Left:* Statue of Marshal Ferdinand Foch. Compiègne. Glade of the Armistice.

the Armistice. Today visitors can see a meticulous reproduction of Foch's railroad car in a shed where the original had been kept.

Codevelle, Colonel. *Armistice 1918. The signing of the armistice in the Forest Glade of Compiègne.* Translation by Jocelyne Deloroy and B. C. Cruse. Published by the Friends of the Armistice of Compiègne (undated).
Shirer, William L. *Berlin Diary. The Journal of a Foreign Correspondent, 1934–41.* Popular Library. New York 1961.

British air raid. Only Foch's statue was left untouched. Why? Hitler wanted the despised victor of 1918 to stand witness to the ruin of his work.

After the war the French used German prisoners to completely restore the Glade of

Shortly after the armistice ceremony, an adjutant telephoned Albert Speer. Speer was to come to the Führer's headquarters for a few days. Hitler had set up his temporary command post in the Belgian village of Brûly-de-Pesche, near Sedan. The Germans had cleared the village of all its inhabitants, and the generals had moved into the small houses that lined the one village street. Hitler's quarters were identical to the others.

Hitler greeted his architect ebulliently: "In a few days we are flying to Paris. I'd like you to be with us," he told Speer. The sculptor Arno Breker and the architect Hermann Giesler were also coming along.

Speer, Albert. *Inside the Third Reich.* Translated by Richard and Clara Winston. Avon Books. New York 1971.

Paris

The victorious Hitler, along with Speer, Breker, Giesler, and others proceeded to Paris, landing at Le Bourget at 5:30 in the morning.[70] Three Mercedes sedans were waiting. Hitler sat as usual in the front seat, beside the driver.

The first stop was the Opera, Charles Garnier's neobaroque masterpiece. It was Hitler's favorite example of Parisian architecture, and he carefully inspected the great stairway, resplendent in its ornamentation and sweep, the splendid foyer, and the elegant, golden parterre.

Hitler, who had made a careful study of the building, led his retinue through the deserted grand spaces, guided by a small, white-haired attendant. All of the lights burned brightly, as they would on the night of a performance. Near the proscenium box, Hitler found a salon missing and commented. Yes, the room had been eliminated during renovations many years ago, said the attendant. "There, you see how well I know my way about," said Hitler, who was fascinated by what he saw. He expostulated ecstatically about the beauty of the place, his eyes glittering with excitement.

Of course, the attendant had quickly recognized whom he was guiding through the building and was quite businesslike

and aloof. When the visit was over, Hitler whispered to his adjutant, Wilhelm Brückner, who took a 50-mark note from his wallet and offered it to the attendant. When the little white-haired man politely refused the money, Hitler asked Arno Breker to pay the attendant, but the man still refused. He was only doing his duty, he said.

The tour continued past the Madeleine, down the Champs Elysées, and on to the Trocadero, where there was another stop. Hitler posed for a famous photograph in front of the stone balustrade overlooking the Seine and the Eiffel Tower. From the Arc de Triomphe, with its tomb of the unknown soldier, the party drove on to the Invalides, where Hitler stood for a considerable time gazing down at the tomb of Napoleon.

The proportions of the Pantheon (110 meters long, 84 meters wide, and 83 meters high) greatly impressed Hitler.[71] But other classic architectural splendors left him cold: the Places des Vosges, the Louvre, the Palace of Justice, and the Sainte-Chapelle, with its exquisite stained-glass windows.

Hitler became enthusiastic again only when he visited the Rue de Rivoli. So delighted was he with this street that the German Army requisitioned part of it for their military governor of Paris, whom they installed in the Hotel Meurice (no. 228).

The three-hour tour ended with a visit to the church of Sacré Coeur on Montmartre. Surrounded by several powerful bodyguards, Hitler stood for a long time appreciating this domed building. His admiration was surprising, given his taste and the fact that Sacré Coeur had been constructed just after the Germans had soundly thrashed the French in 1870, as a symbol of French confidence in the beleaguered country's future.

By nine in the morning, the sightseeing was finished. "It was the dream of my

Hitler's Mercedes. Hitler used this black Mercedes touring car, manufactured in 1942, in processions. It weighs 4,780 kg and has bullet-proof windows. Lyon. Musée Henri Malartre (automobile museum).

life to be permitted to see Paris," Hitler told Speer. "I cannot say how happy I am to have that dream fulfilled today."

A few hours later Hitler spoke again to Speer in the small room of the peasant house in Brûly-de-Pesche. "Draw up a decree in my name ordering full-scale resumption of work on the Berlin buildings.... Wasn't Paris beautiful? But Berlin must be made far more beautiful. In the past I often considered whether we would have to destroy Paris. But when we are finished in Berlin, Paris will only be a shadow. So why should we destroy it?" Hitler spoke with great calm, Speer remembered, as though the monstrous vandalism he contemplated was the most natural thing in the world.[72]

Churchill, Winston. *Their Finest Hour. The Second World War.* Vol 2. Houghton Mifflin. Boston 1949.

Michelin. *Paris. Guide de Tourisme.* Michelin et Cie, Propriétaires-Éditeurs 1995.

Speer, Albert. *Inside the Third Reich.* Translated by Richard and Clara Winston. Avon Books. New York 1971.

LYON

Musée Henri Malartre

In this automobile museum is Hitler's armored Metcedes. The troops of General Philippe de Hauteclocque (Leclerc) found this car when they arrived at the Eagle's Nest in Berchtesgaden in 1945. The car had been given to an American general, who, according to his report, had presented it to former French prisoners of war. For a decade the car was a *bête de foire*, exhibited in city after city. Finally the soldiers forgot about the car, and the organizer of the sideshows relegated it to a garage. Henri Malartre heard about the car and after prodigious feats of diplomacy got to see it. When he did, he decided that he must have it. The owner hesitated to sell but five days later agreed. When the car arrived at Malartre's museum on June 26, 1969, many newspapers chronicled the event.

Hitler used the black Mercedes touring car, manufactured in 1942, in processions. It weighs 4,780 kg, and has bullet-proof windows. One is damaged. American soldiers with nothing better to do fired a machine gun at it. Hitler always rode in the front seat beside the driver, and in this car his seat is raised 13 cm. The doors can be locked electrically, the armored body is of manganese steel, and Hitler's banner is above the right front fender.

Malartre, Henri. *Coup d'oeil dans mon rétroviseur.* Musée Henri Malartre. Lyon 1989.

IV

UNITED STATES

New York City

189–18 184th Street, Hollis, Queens. Home of Brigid and William Patrick Hitler

When the French liner *Normandie* docked at Pier 88 on the Hudson, March 30, 1939, two of its passengers, both Hitlers, became the world's most famous sister-in-law and nephew. Brigid was a motherly looking Dubliner, age 47, with jet-black hair, blue eyes, and a thick brogue. William Patrick was 6 feet tall, handsome and athletic, and had a more attractive mustache than did his Uncle Adolf, whose own mustache, close up, resembled two big black flies perched on his upper lip.

War was approaching. For mother and son New York would be home for the duration and after. They had sailed across the Atlantic under aliases, but their anonymity evaporated as reporters stormed aboard the *Normandie* and cameras snapped.

Hitler's half–Irish nephew arrives without an O'Heil, screamed one afternoon daily. Kin of Hitler, here, are cool to Fuehrer; nephew calls Chancellor 'A Menace,' announced the *New York Times* the next morning (Rosenberg, 1999).

Brigid and Willie moved into a furnished two-story house in Hollis, Queens, but hoped to cash in across the East River, on busy Madison Ave. The William Morris Agency, with an eye for celebrity cachet, had already taken the Hitlers on; by June William Patrick had written a *Look* magazine article titled "Why I Hate My Uncle," and the Press Alliance Syndicate was trying to sell Willie's six-part tell-all series, "My Uncle, The Third Reich and I." But one newspaper editor who rejected the proposal said its title should be "Discredited relative who wasn't paid off squawks."

Brigid claimed that she met Alois Hitler Jr., Adolf's older stepbrother, at a Dublin horse show in 1910. She was 18, and he was 28.

"I won't have any foreigners in the family," her father had exclaimed. So Brigid and Alois Jr. eloped to England. Three stormy years of marriage led to one child and four separations before Alois left for good (Rosenberg, 1999).

Because the Church forbids divorce, single mother Brigid was forced into a life of

195

penury. Then the name of brother-in-law Adolf began appearing in newspapers around the world, and Brigid determined to cash in.

Learning that America's Hearst press was making offers, Adolf Hitler called Brigid and Willie to Bavaria for a stern talk on family silence. Later, as chancellor, Hitler promised his young nephew lucrative work in Germany. But after six years of boring jobs, mainly at the Opel auto works, Willie decamped for the United States.

New York City gossip columnist Leonard Lyons broke the story of Willie Hitler's plan to become a U.S. citizen. As war raged in Europe Willie's supposed knowledge of lurid Hitlerian dirt immeasurably enhanced his value as a speaker; he could expatiate endlessly on Uncle Adolf, life in Germany, prominent Nazis, and how the Gestapo spied on him. He blasted Uncle Adolf in speech after speech.

Brigid had her heart set on Hollywood. One small producer announced that he was giving her a part in "The Mad Dog of Europe," but no part ever materialized. Undaunted, she began work on a tell-all of her own. Its chief tidbit, probably entirely chimerical: Adolf's 1912 visit to Liverpool, where, she said, he'd lived off his in-laws for six months. He wouldn't find a job, Brigid wrote, he was untidy, and he slept late. "Weak and spineless," was the way she put it.

The Führer might not have been overjoyed to read Brigid's screed. But her unpublished work languished at her New York literary agent's office. "My Brother-in-Law Adolf" finally ended up on microfilm in the New York Public Library's Manuscript and Archive Division, sharing space with George Washington's Farewell Address and Thomas Jefferson's handwritten copy of the Declaration of Independence.

By June 1941 Brigid was a volunteer assistant at British War Relief on Fifth Ave. and made headlines again (IN-LAW HAS CURE FOR HITLER—SLOW TORTURE, SUGGESTS MRS. BRIGID). Willie left to join the Royal Canadian Air Force and kissed his mom good-bye at the Hotel Astor in front of a pack of photographers.

But the Canadians didn't want Willie. Neither did the U.S. Army Air Force, despite his 1-A classification. The reason may have been in the questionnaire all foreign applicants had to complete. Regarding relatives who served in foreign armed services, Willie wrote: "1. Thomas J. Dowling, uncle, England, 1923–1926, Royal Air Force. 2. Adolf Hitler, uncle, Germany, 1914–1918, corporal."

So Willie returned to the lecture circuit, at such places as Columbia University and the Marble Collegiate Church ("The Rudolph Hess Mystery," "What about Germany and the German People?").

In February 1944 Willie passed his physical at the Grand Central Palace Induction Center and on March 6 reported to the U.S. Navy recruiting station at 88 Vanderbilt Ave. for assignment to boot camp. "I have more than one score to settle with Uncle Adolf," Willie told the newspapers. He said he would write a book, "My Uncle Adolf." But he never did (Rosenberg, 1999).

Fourteen months later the war was over, and Willie became a nobody. He stayed in the New York area, changed his surname to Hiller, married a German girl, changed his surname again to distance himself even further from his late uncle, and went to work for a Manhattan urologist. He died in 1987 at age 76. His tombstone has no last name.

Willie's three sons live on Long Island and run a small business. They have also changed their surnames. "They're really scared, not only socially, as maybe being treated as some sort of pariah, but also physically, of some crazy person who's off center," their lawyer told journalist Timothy Ryback.

Rosenberg, Elliot. The In-Laws: Brigid and Willie Hitler. *New York Daily News.* August 22, 1999, p. 43.

Ryback, Timothy W. Hitler's lost family. *New Yorker.* July 17, 2000, pp. 46–57.

NOTES

I. Austria

1. Alois Hitler (1837–1903), Adolf Hitler's father, was the illegitimate son of Maria Anna Schicklgruber (1795–1847). In Linz Maria Anna had become pregnant while working as a servant in the house of a wealthy Jew named Frankenberger, and his young son might have been the father. In 1842 she married Johann Georg Hiedler, who never adopted or legitimized the stepson. Hiedler's brother, Johann Nepomuk Hüttler, executed this legal nicety in 1876, when Alois was 39 years old. The name "Hitler" probably arose through a hearing error of the pastor filling out the document. The German Hitler scholar Werner Maser has identified Hüttler as the natural father of Alois and thus the grandfather of Adolf Hitler. But Maser also asserted that Adolf Hitler fathered an illegitimate son named Jean Loret in France during World War I, a claim Anton Joachimsthaler later debunked. In fact, Joachimsthaler wrote an entire book correcting errors in Maser's Hitler biography. For a detailed account of the various theories about Hitler's paternal grandfather, see *Explaining Hitler*, by Ron Rosenbaum (Random House, New York 1998).

2. Before Hitler adopted the swastika and turned it into a symbol of racial hatred, the world regarded it as a good-luck symbol. France, Germany, Britain, Scandinavia, China, Japan, India, and the United States knew the swastika. Buddha's footprints were said to be swastikas.

Navajo blankets were woven with swastikas. Synagogues in North Africa, Palestine, and Hartford were built with swastika mosaics. *Swastika* is derived from the Sanskrit *svastika*, meaning well-being and good fortune. The earliest swastikas in Indian and Central Asia date from 2500 or 3000 B.C. A 1933 study suggested that the swastika migrated from India across Persia and Asia Minor to Greece, then to Italy and on to Germany, probably in the first millennium B.C. The German archaeologist Heinrich Schliemann made the Germanic link. From 1871 to 1875, excavating the site of Homer's Troy on the shores of the Dardanelles, Schliemann found artifacts with swastikas and associated them with the swastikas he had seen near the Oder River in Germany. As Steven Heller, the art director of the *New York Times Book Review*, writes in "The Swastika: Symbol Beyond Redemption," "Schliemann presumed that the swastika was a religious symbol of his German ancestors which linked ancient Teutons, Homeric Greeks and Vedic India." Swastikas quickly became ubiquitous, rotating both clockwise and counterclockwise. Madame Blavatsky, the founder of the Theosophical Society, included the swastika in the seal of the society. "Rudyard Kipling combined a swastika with his signature in a circle as a personal logo," Heller writes. And the swastika was part of the logo of the Bauhaus, under Paul Klee. The swastika spread to the United States, too. Coca-Cola issued a swastika pendant. Carlsberg beer etched swastikas onto its bottles. During

World War I the American Forty-Fifth Infantry division wore an orange swastika as a shoulder patch. At least one train line had swastikas on its cars. The Girls' Club published a magazine called *The Swastika*. And until 1940 the Boy Scouts gave out a swastika badge. According to Mr. Heller, the Germanen order, an anti–Semitic group that wore helmets with Wotan horns and plotted "against Jewish elements in German life," used a curved swastika on a cross as its insignia. By 1914 the Wandervogel, a militarist German youth movement, made it a nationalist emblem. The Nazi Party latched onto it around 1920. In *Mein Kampf* Hitler described "his quest to find the perfect symbol for the party" and considered the swastika. Friedrich Krohn, a dentist from Starnberg, designed the flag with a black swastika in its center. "Hitler's major contribution," Heller writes, "was to reverse the direction of the swastika" so that it appears to spin clockwise. Today the swastika is reappearing in pop culture, in punk rock, in the flying saucer cults, and in street gangs. Some teenagers wear swastikas to be fashionable or rebellious. "In the 1973 film 'Sleeper,'" Heller notes, "Woody Allen sarcastically predicted that in the distant future, the swastika would be worn as a fashion accessory." The logo for ZZ Flex skateboards looks like a swastika. The label on the heavy metal CD Sacred Reich has interlocking swastikas. "How can a symbol be guilty for the acts of a madman?" say the swastika's defenders. (Boxer, Sarah. A Symbol of Hatred Pleads Not Guilty. *New York Times*, July 29, 2000, B11.)

3. In November 1944, *Amerika* was destroyed on a Berlin railway siding during an air raid. At the time Hitler was in Wolfschanze, his East Prussian field headquarters, 560 km northeast of Berlin.

4. Krassnigg told the author of this book this story. (A *Medizinalrat* is a physician serving in an official capacity, such as a public health officer. The next step is *Obermedizinalrat*, then *Medizinaldirektor*, then *Leitender Medizinaldirektor*.)

5. In late-nineteenth-century Vienna, Karl Millöcker (1842–1899) was considered one of the three major composers of Viennese operettas, along with Franz von Suppé and Johann Strauss. He conducted at the Theater an der Wien, where he produced his own and his colleagues' works. But Millöcker lacked the melodic gift of Suppé and Strauss. Only his most popular work, *The Beggar Student*, is still recorded and occasionally performed.

6. German nationalists were Austrians, like Hitler, who wanted the German-speaking sections of the empire to become part of Germany. As Hitler wrote in the second paragraph of *Mein Kampf*: "German-Austria must return to the great German mother country, and not because of any economic considerations."

7. Hitler's two great adversaries, Winston Churchill and Dwight D. Eisenhower, were also artists who painted architectural and nature scenes similar to those Hitler produced.

II. Germany

8. One of Ley's biggest building projects was Prora, a Baltic coast resort on the island of Rügen. Prora was part of the Nazi movement "strength through joy" (KdF). At Prora 20,000 German workers were to enjoy the beaches for 10 days at minimal cost, in rooms with an ocean view. A 600-bed youth hostel, the largest in Germany, was built at Prora in 1933 and did not close until December 1999. In November 1936 work was begun on Ley's massive concrete housing colossus, five enormous block-like six-story buildings that were to cover four kilometers, along with a festival square and festival hall. Eleven architects were involved, nine building corporations, 48 contracting firms, and 5,000 workmen. The Cologne architect Clemens Klotz (1886–1969) had conceived the design. At the 1937 Paris World Exhibition Klotz's plans won the grand prize. One of Klotz's incomplete buildings occupies 180,000 square meters and was meant to hold 10,000 people. In 1939 the outbreak of war forced building to a halt. The completed space was used as a hospital and a school for lady radio operators. After 1945 Prora belonged to East Germany. The communists converted it to an army base, where 10,000 soldiers were billeted. In August 2000 a group of investors bought two of the five concrete hulks from the German government and will turn them into apartments and social dwellings. A few local museums are currently housed in another of the buildings.

9. At Langemarck, in Flanders, during World War I, a regiment of young Germans, the German national anthem on their lips, stormed an enemy position with heavy losses, October 22–23, 1914. In 1934, on the twentieth anniversary of the event, the Reich Youth Leadership created a Langemarck bureau to honor heroes

and assume the heritage of front-line soldiers. "Fulfilling the duties on the model" of Langemarck was "service to an idea that is greater than ourselves," said youth leader Baldur von Schirach, who was later sentenced at Nuremberg to 20 years in Spandau Prison (Zentner and Bedürftig, 1991).

10. Top executives of Allianz AG worked closely with the Third Reich to seize policies owned by Jews and to limit claims from riots, such as Kristallnacht in 1938, which the Nazis fomented to destroy the property of Jews. (See Johnston, David Cay. Archives yield aid for claims of Holocaust. *New York Times.* January 11, 1998, A10.)

11. Flak is an acronym of the German *Fliegerabwehrkanone*— antiaircraft gun.

12. Freisler was president of the people's court, which tried traitors and subversives. In his red robe he was a living terror. His fiendish, raucous judicial temperament is well preserved on newsreel film, showing him as he presided at the trial of the July 20, 1944, conspirators, who tried to assassinate Hitler. "Never before in the history of German justice," wrote one shorthand secretary, "have defendants been treated with such brutality, such fanatic ruthlessness, as at these proceedings" (Toland, 1976). Some defendants screamed at Freisler that the Allies would hang him after the war. But he died during an Allied bombing raid on Berlin, February 3, 1945, while conducting another treason trial. SONY's corporate headquarters is now on the site of his people's court in Berlin.

13. Not all high Nazi officials had this pro–Catholic attitude. In his cell at Nuremberg in 1946 Hermann Göring, a Protestant, told prison psychologist G. M. Gilbert, "Did you ever see one of their seminaries? There are 14, 15, 16, and 17-year-olds from all over the world, and you can see at 10 paces that they are selected pederasts. It stands to reason. You cannot go against human nature. When we arrested their priests because of homosexuality, they hollered that we were persecuting the Church. Some persecution! We had to pay them close to a billion marks a year in taxes anyway. But that Catholic clergy— don't you think I know what goes on behind drawn curtains in those confessions, or between the priests and the nuns. The nuns are 'brides of Christ' you know. What a setup!" (G. M. Gilbert. *Nuremberg Diary.* DaCapo Press. New York 1995.)

14. Silence gives consent.

15. "Warm brother" (*warmer Bruder*) is German slang for a gay man.

16. Another famous meeting, between Hitler and Mussolini, occurred in the Führerbau June 18, 1940, just after the fall of France. Although Hitler had had virtually no help from Mussolini, the two dictators discussed the French peace terms. Afterward, Hitler and Mussolini autographed postcards. Mussolini wrote on one, "Men make history." Underneath, Hitler wrote, "History makes men" (Deming and Iliff, ca. 1986).

17. One of the conspirators in the July 20, 1944, plot to assassinate Hitler, Beck was murdered by the SS.

18. On the night of April 30, 1945, news of Hitler's suicide, the flight of SS guards, and the arrival of American troops unleashed a horde of looters on the Führerbau. After carting away the cigarettes, cognac, and food stored in the cellar, they stuffed draperies, furniture, silverware and table linen into their sacks and cartons. Then they broke through heavy steel doors, leading to basement rooms full of priceless art the Nazis had plundered. Among the masterpieces, which Hitler had intended for the enormous museum he planned for Linz, were works by Canaletto, Van Dyck, Jan Steen, Rembrandt, and Ruysdael. The Nazis had confiscated many of these works from the collection of a French Jew, Alphonse Schloss. When day broke and the U.S. Army arrived, ordinary citizens of Munich had carried off 650 paintings, valued at 50 million dollars (close to a billion dollars today). In December 1945 authorities began a search for the plundered art, appealed to the populace to return it, and established a "collecting point," Haus Hubertusstrasse 20. By 1950 rueful Munich burgers had returned 150 of the paintings. Another 500 are still missing.

19. After the annexation of Austria in 1938, the Gestapo made a frantic effort to find Hitler's draft records. But they had already been removed and were published in the early 1950s.

20. Heinrich Hoffmann made a photograph of the scene. Years later, as Hitler's personal photographer, Hoffmann enlarged part of the negative, showing a jubilant Hitler in the middle of the frenzied crowd. This famous photo brought Hoffmann enormous profits.

21. Franz von Stuck (1863–1928) was Hitler's favorite Munich artist. Of Stuck's portrait *Medusa*, Hitler exclaimed, "Those eyes! Those are the eyes of my mother!" Stuck's painting *Sensuality*, showing a snake entwining a voluptuous female nude, was another Hitler ideal. (Waite, R.L. *The Psychopathic God: Adolf Hitler.* Basic

Books. New York 1977). Franz von Lenbach (1836–1904) was a Munich artist famous for his portraits of such luminaries as Bismarck.

22. Helene Bechstein, wife of the wealthy piano manufacturer, was another early Hitler patron.

23. The Nazis murdered Kahr on June 6, 1934.

24. Berliners were famous for their Führer jokes. When Hitler overran France in 1940, some of his generals called him *der grösste Feldherr aller Zeiten* (the greatest supreme commander of all time). The Berliners soon began calling Hitler *der Gröfaz.*

25. August Bebel (1840–1913) was a German Socialist, cofounder of the German Social Democratic Party, and its most influential and popular leader for more than 40 years.

26. Frederick's single exception was Judaism. The Prussian king detested Jews, declared them a menace to Christian civilization, and harassed them with anti–Jewish ordinances.

27. The bombing of Berlin also badly damaged the century-old Kroll Opera. The communist government razed it, March 27, 1951, to create their Place of the Republic. A few months earlier the East Germans had demolished the ruins of the nearby Stadtschloss, the city palace of the kaisers. Many Berliners deeply miss the Stadtschloss and have proposed plans for rebuilding it. But that would require demolishing the modernistic building that replaced it, the Palace of the Republic, a boarded-up structure dear to the hearts of other Berliners nostalgic for the good-old days of Big Brother.

28. Carl Gotthard Langhans was the father of Carl Ferdinand Langhans, who rebuilt the Berlin Opera House.

29. James Simon was sole heir to the Gebrüder Simon (Simon Brothers) textile firm, founded 1857. In 1898 Simon created the Deutsche Orient-Gesellschaft, and Kaiser Wilhelm II, an archaeology enthusiast, became a patron. Though no fan of Jews, Wilhelm developed a warm friendship with James Simon. "The Kaiser deals with me as though with an older brother," Simon remarked, and Wilhelm returned the compliment: "Every time I get together with Herr Simon, I learn something" (Wilderotter and Pohl, 1991). The two men exchanged gifts; one was a copy of Nefertiti, which Simon gave to Wilhelm, and which the exiled Kaiser had with him in Doorn, Holland, when he died in 1941. The friendship between Simon and Wilhelm withered during the First World War. James Simon is buried in Berlin's Old Jewish Cemetery, Prenzlauer Berg, Schönhauser Allee 22/23.

30. After the explosion Hitler began to complain of chronic head pain. His doctors ordered x-rays of his skull, and in 1999 a forensic odontologist, Michel Perrier, compared them with Hitler's fire-blackened remains, which Soviet soldiers found outside his bunker in May 1945. In addition, Perrier analyzed film clips of Hitler's most animated speeches during which the dictator bared his teeth. Perrier concluded that Hitler neglected his teeth during the last years of the war and was plagued by dental woes, including advanced gum disease, tooth decay and erosion, bone resorption, and missing teeth. This pathology would account for Hitler's frightfully malodorous breath, noted by many of his associates.

31. Remer was promoted to major general in January 1945 and surrendered to Americans on the River Elbe near the end of the war. In the 1950s he was highly active trying to keep Nazi values alive and helped found the Socialist Reich Party, which was banned in 1952. After fleeing to Egypt, he was amnestied in 1954 and returned to Germany. In 1994 he was sentenced to 22 months in jail for denying that the Auschwitz gas chambers existed. He fled to Spain, where neo–Nazis lionized him. Remer died in October 1997, age 85, in Marbella, Spain, unrepentant to the end and fiercely proud of his fortuitous but critical role in foiling the July 20 conspiracy.

32. Thierack committed suicide by hanging, October 26, 1946, at the Neumünster camp, while a case was being prepared against him at Nuremberg.

33. Hess is buried in Wunsiedel, a town in Bavaria. His grave is frequently a gathering place for neo–Nazis.

34. A few months after the Night of the Long Knives, Göring was late for a meeting with Sir Eric Phipps, the British ambassador. Göring excused himself, saying he had been delayed by a hunting party. Phipps replied, "Animals, I hope" (Knopf and Martens, 1999).

35. Not all SS records were in the trove the American soldiers found. The records of the Waffen SS, the military arm and largest SS branch, are in Prague, along with those of the Reichskriegsgericht (military court). Among the Waffen SS documents are records of the murder of 26,000 Jews in the Ukraine and White Russia. In the proceedings of the Reichskriegsgericht are the secret transcripts from the trials of the

July 20, 1944, conspirators in the plot to kill Hitler. In 1945 the SS had moved these archives to Czechoslovakia, where they fell into the hands of resistance fighters. The Czech government refuses to return this material, now in their military archives, to Germany.

36. According to Gerald Posner, Göth's nephew, Gerd Honsik, is a virulent anti–Semite, convicted of 14 violations of Austrian law for neo–Nazi activity, such as making speeches and publishing a magazine denying the reality of the Holocaust (crimes in Austria and Germany). Honsik is a fugitive in Spain.

37. Two former Third Reich officials in prominent postwar positions were Hans Globke (1898–1973) and Erich von Manstein (1887–1973). Globke wrote the official commentaries on the Nuremberg Laws, and critics accused him of playing a major role in writing the laws. After the war, Chancellor Konrad Adenauer retained Globke in his post as state secretary of the chancellery from 1953 to 1963. Field Marshal Erich von Manstein, the master strategist who devised the successful plan to crush France in 1940, spent 12 years in prison after the war and then became a military consultant to the West German government.

38. Persons wishing to see Nazi and Communist German records should write to the Bundesarchiv, Abt. Reich und DDR, Postfach 450 569, Berlin 12 175.

39. German information office for the next of kin of the fallen of the former German Wehrmacht.

40. The *Reichsarbeitdienst* (Reich Labor Service) was established by law in 1935 as a general obligation of all healthy males ages 18–25 to serve in self-contained units for socially useful tasks. Originally conceived to combat unemployment, the *Reichsarbeitdienst* inculcated nationalistic spirit in its members and prepared them for war.

41. Two of the best-known military figures buried in the Invalidenfriedhof are Gerhard David von Scharnhorst (1756–1813), the Prussian general who developed the modern general staff system, and Manfred von Richthofen, the famous aviator and dogfighter known as the Red Baron, who was killed in 1918, just before his twenty-sixth birthday. Part of the Invalidenfriedhof was leveled because it lay on the border between East and West Berlin, and in 1975 Richthofen's remains were transferred to the family plot in Wiesbaden. But Colonel General Max Hoffmann's grave can still be found.

Hoffmann (1868–1927) planned the 1914 Battle of Tannenberg, which resulted in the crushing defeat of the invading Russian army, the only significant German military victory of World War I. At the time, Field Marshal Paul von Hindenburg got the credit. But when Hoffmann later took visitors over the field of Tannenberg, he would tell them, "This is where the Field Marshal slept before the battle; here is where he slept after the battle; here is where he slept during the battle!" (Tuchman, 1962)

42. Alexander August Wilhelm von Pape was a Prussian colonel general of infantry. He was born in 1813 in Berlin and served in the Franco-Prussian War. In 1871 he was promoted to lieutenant general and then in 1880 to general of infantry.

43. Telephone cables still run from the abandoned underground Zeppelin bunkers to the nearby Zossen post office. The German telephone network was part of the postal service (Bundespost) until 1990, when German politicians made the phone company into a separate corporate entity, *Deutsche Telekom*.

44. The 1941 Berlin telephone book, the last until after the war, lists Krebs as living in Friedenau, Offenbacher Strasse 4. Krebs witnessed Hitler's "political testament" in the Führerbunker, April 29, 1945. In the early morning of May 1 Krebs negotiated the surrender of the Berlin garrison with General Vassily Chuikov. That evening in the Führerbunker, the 47-year-old Krebs committed suicide with a pistol shot to avoid being taken prisoner.

45. Read, Anthony, and David Fisher. *The Fall of Berlin.* Norton. New York 1992.

46. Harald Quandt, Magda Goebbels's son from her first marriage, 1921, a pilot, survived the war. Afterward he worked for his father, Günther Quandt, a textile manufacturer. Harald married in 1950 and fathered three daughters. At Günther Quandt's death in 1954 Harald and his brother took over the father's business. Harald was one of the richest men in Germany when he was killed in an alpine crash of his private plane on a flight to Nice in 1967. (Leser-Frage: Was wurde aus Magda Goebbels Sohn? *Berliner Morgenpost.* August 30, 1999.)

47. Critics accused Schliemann of buying some pieces of King Priam's supposed treasure in the local bazaars. At the end of World War II the Russians carted off the hoard, and have refused all entreaties to return it.

48. Kaltenbrunner went to the gallows at Nuremberg in 1946. *New Yorker* writer Rebecca

West described him as "resembling a particularly vicious horse."

49. Käthe Niederkirchner (1909–44) was a tailor who joined the Communist Party in 1929 and immigrated to the Soviet Union in 1933. In 1943 she parachuted from a Russian airplane into Poland and was arrested on her way to Berlin. She was incarcerated in Ravensbrück concentration camp in the summer of 1944, where she was murdered on September 22.

50. The blood type was tattooed in the SS member's armpit so that he could easily receive a blood transfusion in case of injury. A Viennese Jew, Karl Landsteiner, had identified the A-B-O blood groups in 1901. Landsteiner received the 1930 Nobel Prize in Medicine for this discovery, which made blood transfusion possible. While Eichmann was busy slaughtering other Jews, Landsteiner was out of harm's way, in the Rockefeller Institute in New York. At Rockefeller he identified the Rh blood groups, which give the blood type its characteristic positive (+) or negative (-) sign. Landsteiner also discovered that a rhesus monkey could be infected with poliomyelitis; this identification of an animal model for polio made possible the polio vaccine.

51. Adolf Eichmann traveled from Germany to Genoa to Argentina along the "route of the rats," a well-trodden path followed by thousands of Nazis and their collaborators after the war. Other émigrés were Dr. Josef Mengele, notorious for his horrifying human experiments at Auschwitz, and Erich Priebke, responsible for the massacre of 355 civilians in the Ardéatine caves north of Rome in 1944. Bishop Alois Hudal and the Argentine government under its president, Juan Perón (1946–55), were the organizers.

The Austrian-born Alois Hudal was director of the German College of Priests in Rome. When the Nazis deported more than 1,000 Roman Jews to Auschwitz in 1944, Bishop Hudal, along with Axis diplomats in Rome, had discouraged Pope Pius XII from mounting even a mild protest. Hudal, not surprisingly, had been a great proponent of the Nuremberg laws.

Convents and other Catholic religious institutions received the fleeing former Nazis. They received passports from the International Red Cross at the recommendation of the Vatican or from the Argentine government, which had issued more that 8,000 blank passports. Argentine consulates in Switzerland, Italy, or Spain processed the visas according to lists Buenos Aires had furnished.

An ex–Nazi, Walter Rauff, opened a center in Genoa for receiving the émigrés in 1945. Rauff, a former specialist in mobile gas chambers, finally immigrated to Chile in 1949.

In Buenos Aires a special division of the bureau of immigration, called the Peralta Commission, received the ex–Nazi fugitives. Three close associates of Juan Perón — Carlos Fuldner, an ex–Nazi officer; Jacques de Mahieu, a Frenchman, formerly of the Charlemagne Division; and Branko Benzon, a Croat — chose the candidates for immigration from lists the Vatican furnished. The Argentines were eager for scientists and specialists who could participate in economic expansion of the country.

52. According to Albert Speer, after Göring had renovated the villa himself, Hitler came to see it and commented, "Dark! How can anyone live in such darkness? Compare this with my professor's work. Everything bright, clear, and simple." Göring immmdiately repudiated the decorative scheme he had just completed. "Don't look at this," Göring told Speer. "I can't stand it myself. Do it any way you like. I'm giving you a free hand; only it must turn out like the Führer's place."

53. Hochtief is one of the world's largest construction companies. One recent project was the new Israeli embassy in Berlin. "We were not aware of the fact that Hochtief built that," said Israeli spokesperson Yoval Fuchs, when asked about the Führerbunker. Visit Hochtief on the Internet at www.hochtief.de.

54. Intending to escape Berlin by plane, Fegelein slipped out of the bunker April 26, 1945. An SS search party found him, quite drunk, in his apartment (10–11 Bleibtreustrasse) in civilian clothes. With him was his mistress, who may have been an English spy, and who escaped through an open window. Fegelein was brought back to the bunker, where a furious Hitler ordered him shot on April 28. His execution probably took place in a nearby Gestapo cellar.

55. Hitler's last meal, one and a half hours before his suicide, was spaghetti with a light tomato sauce. For other details of his diet and health, see Ernst Günther Schenck. *Patient Hitler. Eine Medizinische Biographie*. Droste Verlag. Düsseldorf 1989. When Schenck wrote the book, he was the only physician still alive whom Hitler had consulted.

56. Before Hitler came to power the *Berliner Morgenpost* was part of Ullstein Verlag, the giant German publisher of books, printing five daily and eight weekly newspapers. In 1934

the Nazis seized the company, and the Jewish Ullstein family immigrated to England.

57. A *Torfklo* is a toilet bowl connected to a chest filled with peat. The user pulls a lever on the chest, causing peat to plop into the bottom of the bowl, thus guaranteeing a certain standard of hygiene.

58. The architect Johann Philipp Gerlach built the baroque Garnisonkirche, 1731–35, to replace an older church that was razed because of structural instability. The soldier king Friedrich Wilhelm I commissioned the building of a carillon for the new church. For two centuries the ringing of the bells gave this quarter of Potsdam a singular charm. In 1805 King Friedrich Wilhelm III and Queen Luise met with Czar Alexander I in the Garnisonkirche to form an alliance against Napoleon. On November 23, 1943, an Allied bomb burned out the entire church. In June 1967 East German chief Walter Ulbricht visited the ruin, on the corner of Spandauer Strasse and Burgstrasse (formerly Neue Friedrichstrasse), and ordered it razed because of its association with Hitler. In 1968 the remains were brought down with explosives. Construction workers laying rails for the S-Bahn unearthed the stairway to the crypt in June 1998 and found the polished marble table altar of King Friedrich Wilhem IV.

59. Hindenburg died seventeen months later at Neudeck, his ancestral East Prussian estate, which German industrialists had bought and presented to him on his eightieth birthday. Hindenburg was initially buried at Tannenberg, the site of his great World War I victory over the invading Russians. But in 1945 the Nazis razed the Tannenberg monument, which Hindenburg had built. In January 1945 they carried the coffins of Hindenburg and his wife through Königsberg and Schleswig-Holstein to Potsdam. From there they took them to an abandoned salt mine, Bernterode, in Thuringia. In 1945 American troops found the coffins and moved them to the Marburg State Archives. Since 1946 the remains of Hindenburg and his wife have lain in the Elisabeth Church in Marburg an der Lahn.

60. On March 3, 1945, the Gestapo arrested Kurt Freiherr von Plettenberg (1891–1945), a general representative of the House of Brandenburg-Prussia, in the Cecilienhof. Accusing Plettenberg of participating in the July 20, 1944, assassination plot, the Gestapo incarcerated him. A few weeks later, Plettenberg knocked down a guard and jumped to his death from a fifth-floor jail window. "I would kill myself before I would kill anyone else," he had said (Müller, 1997). There is now a memorial plaque for Plettenberg in the Cecilienhof.

61. So many Germans and Austrians today claim to have a relative who was involved in the July 20, 1944, plot, one wonders how it could have failed.

62. When buying German or northern European Renaissance art, of which he was especially fond, Göring relied on the judgment of Max Jakob Friedländer (1867–1958). Friedländer, a Jew, was a curator of paintings at the Kaiser Friedrich Museum (now the Bode Museum) in Berlin, until the Nazis fired him, June 20, 1933. His monumental 14-volume work, *Early Netherlandish Painting*, originally published in German, 1924–37 and translated into English, 1967–76, is still a standard reference. In 1938, Friedländer immigrated to Holland after the Swiss refused to admit him. Friedländer brought with him his extensive library and archive, which was installed at the Rijksbureau voor Kunsthistorische Documentatie in The Hague. In Holland other art-world émigrés looked after the seventy-one year old Friedländer, a hopelessly impractical academic, and his elderly housekeeper. When the Germans overran Holland in May 1940, the Gestapo arrested Freidländer along with thousands of other Jews. Hearing of Friedländer's incarceration, Göring sent his curator, Walter Andreas Hofer, to the Osnabrück internment camp to procure Friedländer's release. Hofer explained that the arrest was a case of mistaken identity, and Friedländer was let out. In 1942, when the Nazis required all Dutch Jews to have the yellow star sewn to their clothing, Friedländer was declared an "honorary Aryan," exempted from wearing the star. Hofer sent a memo stating that "due to the great expertise of Professor Friedländer in German and Dutch painting, the Reichsmarschall desires that he remain in the Hague, and not be disturbed by the Delegate on Jewish Questions" (Nichols, 1995). Friedländer survived the war making appraisals of paintings for Göring and other high Nazi officials. But despite Friedländer, Göring made mistakes. One of Göring's prized works was a fake Vermeer, "Christ with the Woman Taken in Adultery," painted by the forger Han van Meegeren.

63. Curators of the documentation center complain that the space they were allotted is far too small. There is barely room for the catalogue of the exhibit, and when classes of schoolchildren troop through, the place almost bursts at the seams.

64. The 1941 Berlin telephone book lists Speer's Berlin address as Charlottenburg 9, Lindenallee 18. After Speer was released from Spandau Prison in 1966, he lived in Heidelberg. While with a woman not his wife, he died September 1, 1981, age 76, in a London hotel room. Speer's affair had devastated his wife, Margret. How had Margret found out about the young woman? Gitta Sereny asked Speer's daughter Hilde Schramm. "He used to report absent [*er meldedte sich ab*] when he went to meet her," Hilde replied bitterly.

65. In 1492 Martin Behaim (1459–1507), a merchant, commissioned this world globe, the oldest still in existence.

66. Ulrich von Hutten (1488–1523) was a Franconian knight and Humanist, famed as a German patriot, satirist, and supporter of Martin Luther's cause. His restless, adventurous life reflected the turbulent Reformation period. Hutten pursued his public and private quarrels with both pen and sword. As a supporter of the ancient status of the knightly order (*Ritterstand*), Hutten looked back to the Middle Ages; but as a writer he looked forward, employing the new literary forms of the humanists in biting Latin dialogues, satirizing the pretensions of princes, the papacy, scholasticism, and obscurantism. He was the principal contributor to the second volume of the *Epistolae obscurorum virorum* (1515–17; "Letters of Obscure Men"), a renowned assault on monkish life and letters. As a patriot he envisioned a united Germany and after 1520 wrote a series of satiric pamphlets on Luther's behalf, which were published in Latin and translated into German. Hutten fought in the knights' war (1522) against the German princes. On the defeat of the knights' cause he fled to Switzerland. Hutten was penniless and dying of syphilis when Huldrych Zwingli granted him refuge. The legend of Hutten as a warrior for freedom has been much romanticized in German literature, particularly in C. F. Meyer's *Huttens letzte Tage* (1871; "Hutten's Last Days"). *Encyclopædia Britannica.*

67. The German word *Gut* refers to a piece of land with both agricultural buildings and a home. In general, such a property is described as a *Gut*, irrespective of its size.

68. Hitler oversaw the Polish campaign from his special train rather than from a fixed field headquarters.

69. Wałbrzych (Waldenburg) is the capital of Wałbrzych Województwo (province), southwestern Poland, in the central Sudeten Mountains. Wałbrzych is the second largest town in Lower Silesia after Wrocław (Breslau) and an important rail junction. The city was first chronicled as the location of Ksiaz Castle, built by Boleslaw I in 1290 and continuously remodeled into the 1920s; with 415 rooms it is the third largest castle in Poland. The mining of silver and lead ores in the area began in the fourteenth century and continues to this day. Wałbrzych received its town rights in 1400. Since the fifteenth century it has been a dressmaking center, and in 1818 the first mechanized weaving mill in Silesia was built there. In the late nineteenth century, Wałbrzych became an industrial center with linen weaving, coke, and chemical production, based on nearby coal mines. During World War II the Gross-Rosen Nazi concentration camp was located near the city. Liberated by Soviet troops in 1945, the region was annexed to Poland (*Encyclopædia Britannica* 1998).

III. French

70. There is controversy over the exact date. Speer writes that the visit occurred "three days after the commencement of the armistice," which would be Friday, June 28. Max Domarus also gives this date, referring to newspaper reports of June 30, 1940, on the visit. (Kershaw, Ian. *Hitler. 1936–1945: Nemesis*. Norton. New York 2000).

71. Louis XV, who had fallen quite ill at Metz, had vowed to replace the crumbling abbey of Saint Geneviève if he recovered. He fulfilled his vow with the Pantheon. During the French Revolution the Pantheon became the repository of the "ashes of the great men of the epoch of French liberty," among them Honoré Mirabeau, Voltaire, and Jean-Jacques Rousseau.

72. Paris has come within a hair's breadth of destruction at the hands of the Germans five times. In December 1870, after the Prussians had defeated the French Army at Sedan, German troops surrounded Paris and began to bombard the city. But before their Krupp ordnance had done much damage, the starving, freezing Parisians, who had been reduced to eating rats, surrendered. In September 1914, had the French and British armies not been able to stop the advancing Germans at the Battle of the Marne, the Germans would have reached Paris. The Pari-

sians would have resisted, and the Germans would have destroyed Paris. In 1918 a massive German advance almost reached Paris, but was stopped with the help of fresh American troops. ("I will fight in front of Paris, in Paris, and behind Paris," Georges Clemenceau, the French premier, had said [Churchill, 1949].) In 1940, as the German armies were overrunning France, Winston Churchill demanded that Paris should be defended vigorously: "I emphasized the enormous absorbing power of the house-to-house defense of a great city upon an invading army" (Churchill, 1949). But the French commander, Marshal Henri Philippe Pétain, believed nothing would be gained by reducing Paris to a ruin and declared the city open. Paris surrendered without a shot being fired. In 1944, as General Leclerc's army was poised to liberate Paris, General Dietrich von Choltitz, the military governor, disobeyed Hitler's order to dynamite all the principal buildings, monuments, and bridges of Paris ("Is Paris burning?" Hitler had screamed over the phone to von Choltitz [Collins, Larry, and Dominique Lapierre. *Is Paris Burning?* Warner Books, New York 1965]). Anyone who visits Paris today and is overwhelmed by its incomparable beauty should keep in mind that only by a series of miracles has the City of Light survived intact.

BIBLIOGRAPHY

Adolf Hitler: Bilder aus dem Leben des Führers. Foreword by Dr. Joseph Goebbels. Herausgegeben vom Cigaretten-Bilderdienst, Altona-Bahrenfeld. [Printed J.J. Weber, Leipzig.] 1936.

Adolf Hitlers Geburtshaus als "Stätte der Versöhnung"? *Die Presse.* February 23, 2000.

Alings, Reinhard. *Die Berliner Siegessäule. Bezirksamt Tiergarten von Berlin-Gartenbauamt.* 2nd edition. Berlin 1991.

Almstedt, Jan. Innovativer Monumentalbau. Flugplatz Tempelhof: Nazi Prestigeobject für dreissigfache Passagierzahlen geplant. *Berliner Morgenpost.* September 26, 2000.

_____. Mutterrede für Bauern, barras, Bomber. *Berliner Morgenpost.* September 19, 2000.

Archaeologen präsentieren Fundstücke aus Göring-Bunker. *Frankfurter Allgemeine Zeitung.* March 18, 1995.

Arendt, Hannah. *Eichmann in Jerusalem. A Report on the Banality of Evil.* Viking Press. New York 1965.

Badewanne mit schmutziger Geschichte. *Berliner Morgenpost.* October 29, 1998.

Baecker, Brigitte. Zwangsarbeit: Die dunkle Seite der Geschichte eines Krankenhauses. *Berliner Morgenpost.* January 9, 1998.

Bahr, Christian. Keine Scheu vor der Geschichte. Verteidigungsministerium folgt auf Reichswehr und Wehrmacht. *Berliner Morgenpost.* June 20, 1998.

_____. Licht Kunst gegen die Finsternis des Hauses. Arbeitsressort zieht in frühere NS-Zentrale. *Berliner Morgenpost.* June 18, 1998.

Berlin 1856–1896. Photographien von F. Albert Schwartz mit Bilderläuterungen von Hans-Werner Klünner und einer Einführung von Laurenz Demps. Nicolaische Verlagsbuchhandlung. Berlin 1991.

Bernhard, Marianne, Madeleine Cabor, Rainer Eisenschmid. *Baedeker's Berlin.* 3rd ed. Macmillan. New York 1994.

Beyer, Beppo. Allentsteig: Waldviertler Dörfer mit Vergangenheit und ohne Zukunft. *Die Presse* (Vienna). March 19, 1997.

Bombensichere Schatzkammer der Diktatur. *Süddeutsche Zeitung.* September 26, 1997.

Bönisch, Georg, and Mathias Müller von Blumencron. Trophäen des Sieges. *Der Spiegel.* 5:50–54, 1999.

Bornhöft, Petra. Schweinkram mit blauer Kreide. *Der Spiegel.* 26:46–47, 1999.

Botstein, Leon. *Die Walküre* Analysis. Texaco–Metropolitan Opera International Radio Network. New York 1997.

Boxer, Sarah. A Symbol of Hatred Pleads Not Guilty. *New York Times.* July 29, 2000, B11.

Brecht, Bertolt. *Ausgewählte Werke in sechs Bänden.* Dritter Band, Gedichte I. Suhrkamp Verlag. Frankfurt am Main 1997.

Brühl, Carolin. Gedenktafel für Joachim Gottschalk. *Berliner Morgenpost.* November 7, 2000.

Chronik Berlin. Chronik Verlag. Munich. 3rd updated edition 199.

Churchill, Winston. *The Gathering Storm. The Second World War*. Vol 1. Houghton Mifflin. Boston 1948.

_____. *Their Finest Hour. The Second World War*. Vol 2. Houghton Mifflin. Boston 1949.

Codevelle, Colonel. *Armistice 1918. The Signing of the Armistice in the Forest Glade of Compiègne*. Translation by Jocelyne Deloroy and B. C. Cruse. Friends of the Armistice of Compiègne (undated).

Cohen, Roger. Why? New Eichmann notes try to explain. *New York Times*. August 13, 1999, p. 1.

Collins, Larry, and Dominique Lapierre. *Is Paris Burning?* Warner Books, New York 1965.

Concise Columbia Encyclopedia. Columbia University Press. New York 1995.

Craig, Gordon A. *The Germans*. New American Library. New York 1983.

Cristol, Pierre, et al. *Vienna*. Alfred A Knopf. New York 1994.

Dannenbaum, Uwe. Nazi-Bunker wird gesprengt: "Keine Gefährdung für Brandenburger Tor." *Berliner Morgenpost*. January 30, 1997.

Davis, Mike. Angriff auf "German Village." *Der Spiegel*. 41:238–243, 1999.

Deming, Brian, and Ted Iliff. *Hitler and Munich: A Historical Guide to the Sights and Addresses of Munich Important to Adolf Hitler, His Followers, and His Victims*. Verlag A. Plenk KG. Berchtesgaden, Germany ca. 1986.

Demps, Lawrence. *Zwischen Mars und Minerva. Wegweiser Invalidenfriedhof*. Verlag für Bauen und Bauweisen. Berlin 1998.

Deutschland erwacht: Werden, Kampf und Sieg der NSDAP. Herausgegeben vom Cigaretten-Bilderdienst, Altona-Bahrenfeld. 10 November 1933.

Diering, Frank. Document Center abgerissen. Nur die denkmalgeschützten Gebäude bleiben stehen. *Berliner Morgenpost*. January 29, 1999.

DRK erhält Geheimdaten über die NKWD-Lager. *Berliner Morgenpost*. May 5, 1999.

Durth, Werner. *Deutsche Architekten*. Vieweg-Verlag, Braunschweig/Wiesbaden 1989.

Eichmann Interrogated. Transcripts from the Archives of the Israeli Police. Edited by Jochen von Lang in collaboration with Claus Sibyll. Translated from the German by Ralph Mannheim. Farrar, Straus, and Giroux. New York 1983.

Eversloh, Saskia. In Bundesarchiv diente einst Hitlers Leibwache. *Berliner Morgenpost*. August 13, 1999.

Fauré, Michel. Argentine. Sur le piste des derniers Nazis. *L'Express*. April 9, 1998, pp. 44–51.

Fetscher, Irving. *Joseph Goebbels im Berliner Sportpalast 1943*. Europäische Verlagsanstalt. Hamburg 1998.

Fischer, Jan Otakar. Beating swords into suburbs in East Germany's bunker capital. *New York Times*. March 16, 2000 F1.

Fischer, Vera. Senat lenkt ein: zusätzliches Honorar für Bildhauerin. *Berliner Morgenpost*. December 19, 1997.

Flottau, Heiko. Die Bunkertrümmer bei Rastenburg wo das Attentat auf Hitler misslang. Eine Privatfirma betreibt heute die Touristenattraktion Wolfschanze. *Süddeutsche Zeitung*. July 20, 1994.

Frank, Michael. Braunau wehrt sich gegen Internet-Angebote. *Süddeutsche Zeitung*. August 12, 2000.

Frankel, Andrew. *The Eagle's Nest. From Adolf Hitler to the Present Day*. Plenk Verlag. Berchtesgaden 1985.

Friedrich, Otto. *Before the Deluge*. Harper and Row. New York 1972.

Fülling, Thomas. Ein Ehrenbürger namens Hermann Göring. Gross Schönebeck streitet um seine Vergangenheit. *Berliner Morgenpost*. March 13, 1998.

Galante, Pierre, and Eugene Silianoff. *Voices from the Bunker*. G.P. Putnam's Sons. New York 1989.

Geisler, Kurt. Aus dunkler Ferne hallt der Ton: Üb immer Treu und Redlichkeit. *Berliner Morgenpost*. October 17, 1999.

Geitner, Paul. Secret bunkers begin to see light of day. History: Architectural engineer works to ensure that Berlin's subterranean past is not forgotten. *Los Angeles Times*. February 16, 1997, p. 20.

Gilbert, G. M. *Nuremberg Diary*. DaCapo Press. New York 1995.

Goebbels, Joseph. *The Diaries of Joseph Goebbels*. Final Entries 1945. Avon Books. New York 1979.

Goebbels' bunker found at Holocaust memorial site. *Guardian*. Manchester. January 27, 1998, p. 13.

Goebbels' bunker possibly located. *Washington Post*. January 28, 1998, p. A13.

Goodman, Walter. Crime and Punishment: The Trial of Eichmann. *New York Times*, Late Edition (East Coast). April 30, 1997, C14.

Gorf, Martina. Flickwerk am Bad Fincken-steinallee. Grundsanierung der maroden Schwimmhalle gefordert. *Berliner Morgenpost.* January 26, 2000.

———. Wie geht es weiter mit dem Fincken-stein-Bad? *Berliner Morgenpost.* January 26, 2000.

"Der Griff nach dem letzten Grasbüschel." München 1938: Hitlers Triumph über die Westmächte — Der Schacher um die Tsche-choslowakei. *Der Spiegel.* 39:51–60, 1988.

Grimes, William. Capturing the man who caught Eichmann. *New York Times.* November 10, 1996, sec. 2, p. 18.

Gruber, Ruth Ellen. Standing on Hitler's Grand-stand. *New Leader.* January 26, 1998, pp. 9–10.

Gumbel, Peter. War's End (A special report): Europe — The Haunting: How should Germany deal with the crimes of its past? *Wall Street Journal.* April 24, 1995, R10.

Haddock, Charles, and Charles E. Snyder. *Trea-sure Trove. The Looting of the Third Reich.* Snyder's Treasures. Bowie, Md. 1998.

Hamann, Brigitte. *Hitlers Wien.* Piper Verlag. München 1996.

Hammes, Katharina. Wie ein Ort des Krieges zur Friedenstadt wird. Waldstadt Wüns-dorf— von Hauptquartier der sowetischen Truppen zum beliebten Wohn-und-Ar-beitsort. *Berliner Morgenpost.* January 17, 2000.

Heydrich, Lina. *Leben mit einem Kriegsver-brecher.* Verlag W. Ludwig. Pfaffenhofen, Germany 1976.

Hitler's Höllenfahrt. *Der Spiegel.* 14:170, 1995.

Höfl-Hielscher, Elisabeth. 1945 — Münchner auf Beutezug. Bei der Plünderung des "Führerbaus" kam es zum grössten Gemäl-deraub der Geschichte. *Süddeutsche Zeitung.* May 5, 2000.

Hofmann, Paul. *The Viennese: Splendor, Twi-light, and Exile.* Anchor Press and Double-day. New York 1988.

Höhling, Cornelia. Mit der Schaufel den Welt-wundern auf der Spur. Seit 100 Jahren er-möglicht die Deutsche Orient-Gesellschaft Grabungen in Ruinenfeldern. *Berliner Morgenpost.* January 24, 1998.

Holden, Constance. Teeth of Evidence. *Science* 286:1473, 1999.

Holzhaider, Hans. Grosser Andrang auf dem Obersalzberg. *Süddeutsche Zeitung.* Febru-ary 9, 2000.

Horowitz, Joseph. The specter of Hitler in the music of Wagner. *New York Times.* Novem-ber 8, 1998, sec. 2, p. 1.

Huber, Andrea. Einblicke in eine einst "ver-botene Stadt." *Berliner Morgenpost.* Octo-ber 13, 1997.

Hyngar, Michael. 12,360 Tonnen Beton: In-vestor verzweifelt gesucht. Hinterlassen-schaft Albert Speers steht unter Denk-malschutz — Wie der "Grossbelastungskörper" künftig genutzt wird, ist unklar. *Berliner Morgenpost* Janu-ary 5, 2000.

Isnard, Jacques. Le quartier général de Hitler en France est a vendre. *Le Monde.* November 22, 1995.

Jäckel, Hartmut. *Menschen in Berlin. Das letzte Telefonbuch der alten Reichhauptstadt 1941.* Deutsche Verlags–Anstalt. Stuttgart, München 2000.

Jahr-Weidauer, Konrad. Auf Schatzsuche in Göring's Refugium. *Berliner Morgenpost.* April 11, 1999.

Johnston, David Cay. Archives yield aid for claims of Holocaust. *New York Times.* Jan-uary 11, 1998, A10.

Jones, Ernest. *The Life and Work of Sigmund Freud.* Edited and abridged in one volume by Lionel Trilling and Steven Marcus. Basic Books. New York 1961.

Kahn, David. *Seizing the Enigma. The Race to Break the German U-Boat Codes.* Houghton Mifflin. Boston 1991.

Karwelat, Jürgen. Antisemit, Kriegshetzer. TAZ. October 7, 1996.

Keegan, John. *The First World War.* Alfred A. Knopf. New York 1999.

Kershaw, Ian. *Hitler. 1889–1936: Hubris.* Nor-ton. New York 1998.

———. *Hitler. 1936–1945: Nemesis.* Norton. New York 2000.

Kinzer, Stephen. Retrieve the lurid past? (Some Germans recoil). *New York Times.* Febru-ary 12, 1992.

———. Torch is passed, and the past is in German hands. *New York Times.* April 1, 1994, A4.

Kittler, Andreas. *Hermann Göring's Carinhall. Der Waldhof in der Schorfheide.* Druffel Verlag. 82335 Berg. 1997.

Kniess, Oliver. Geheimnis um roten Marmor wird gelüftet. Neue Belege: Edler Stein in der Humboldt-Uni stammt wohl doch aus der Reichskanzlei. *Berliner Morgenpost.* March 2, 1998.

Knigge, Jobst. Unbequeme Erinnerungsstätte — Vor 60 Jahren in der "Wolfsschlucht."

Deutsche Presse-Agentur (DPA) — Europa. June 25, 2000.

Knopf, Volker, and Stefan Martens. *Göring's Reich. Selbstinszenierungen in Carinhall.* Ch. Links Verlag. Berlin 1999.

Kohl von polnischem Ministerpräsidenten begrüsst. Eröffnung von Jugendbegegnungsstätte in Kreisau. AP Worldstream. June 11, 1998.

Kreiss, Stefanie. Noch Grabesruhe an Hess-Ruhestätte in Wunsiedel. AP Worldstream. August 15, 1995.

Krüger, Karl Heinz. Die Entnazifizierung der Steine. *Der Spiegel.* 4:64–81, 1989.

Krump, Hans. Die "Strassen des Führers" — eine Sackgasse? *Berliner Morgenpost.* March 23, 1997.

Kubizek, August. *Adolf Hitler, Mein Jugendfreund.* Leopold Stocker Verlag, Graz and Stuttgart. 6th ed. 1995.

Kuntz, Tom. On display in Los Angeles: Legal foreshadowing of Nazi horror. *New York Times.* July 4, 1999. sec. 4, p. 7.

_____. Word for word; the Nuremberg Laws; on display in Los Angeles: Legal foreshadowing of Nazi horrors. *New York Times.* July 4, 1999.

Lehrer, Steven. *Wannsee House and the Holocaust.* McFarland. Jefferson, N.C. 2000.

Leser-Frage. Haben Nürnberg, München und Bonn Denkmäler für Nazi-Opfer? *Berliner Morgenpost.* October 12, 1999.

_____. Stimmt es, dass vom Olympiastadion ein Tunnelsystem ausgeht? *Berliner Morgenpost.* March 6, 1999.

_____. Wann stand Bismarck vor dem Reichstag? *Berliner Morgenpost.* May 21, 1999.

_____. Wann wird ein landwirtschaftlicher Betrieb als Gut bezeichnet? *Berliner Morgenpost.* August 8, 1999.

_____. Was wurde aus dem "Kanonendenkmal"? *Berliner Morgenpost.* December 15, 1998.

_____. Was wurde aus der Berolina? *Berliner Morgenpost.* November 18, 1998.

_____. Was wurde aus Magda Goebbels Sohn? *Berliner Morgenpost.* August 30, 1999.

_____. Wer war General von Pape? *Berliner Morgenpost.* November 14, 1999.

_____. Wie wurde Hitler deutscher Bürger. *Berliner Morgenpost.* October 8, 1998.

_____. Wo befindet sich das Grab Hindenburgs? *Berliner Morgenpost.* December 9, 1999.

_____. Wo befindet sich der Kleistsaal? *Berliner Morgenpost.* April 4, 2000.

_____. Wo liegt der Betonklotz für Messungen der Nazis? *Berliner Morgenpost.* July 3, 1999.

_____. Wo war die Reichskanzlei in der Wilhelmstrasse? *Berliner Morgenpost.* May 8, 1999.

_____. Woher kommt der Name für das Reichpietschufer? *Berliner Morgenpost.* March 22, 1999.

_____. Woher kommt der Name Goldelse? *Berliner Morgenpost.* April 10, 1999.

_____. Woher kommt der Name "Speerplatte"? *Berliner Morgenpost.* August 6, 1999.

Loos, Andreas. Umzug mit 60 Jahren Verspätung. *Berliner Morgenpost.* August 10, 1999.

Lorant, Stefan. *Sieg Heil! An illustrated history of Germany from Bismarck to Hitler.* Norton. New York 1974.

MacDonald, Callum. *The Killing of Reinhard Heydrich.* DaCapo Press. New York 1998.

Makartsev, Alexei. Picknick auf dem Bunker. Kuhfladen, Betontrümmer und ein böser Fluch: Ortstermin in den Ruinen von Hitlers Hauptquartier "Werwolf" bei Winniza in der Ukraine. *Berliner Morgenpost.* July 17, 1999.

Malartre, Henri. *Coup d'oeil dans mon rétroviseur.* Musée Henri Malartre. Lyon 1989.

Mauch, Christof. *Schattenkrieg gegen Hitler. Das Dritte Reich im Visier der Amerikanischen Geheimdienste 1941–1945.* Deutsche Verlags-Anstalt, Stuttgart 1999.

Mayr, Walter. "Soll' mer'n wegsprengen?" *Der Spiegel.* 33:101–11, 1996.

McGrath, Peter. The lessons of Munich. *Newsweek.* October 3, 1988, p. 37.

Merten, Jola. Als die Uhr stehen blieb. Ausstellung zum 60. Jahrestag des Beginns des II. Weltkriegs. *Berliner Morgenpost.* September 2, 1999.

_____. Der Ort, an dem die Nazis Kunst lagerten. Gedenktafel erinnert an Depot der Goebbels-Aktion. *Berliner Morgenpost.* March 22, 1999.

_____. Erfolg der "Bunkerküsser." Die Schaustelle führt erstmals in die Unterwelt. *Berliner Morgenpost.* June 6, 1999.

_____. Gedenken an zivilen Protest gegen Fabrikaktion 1943. *Berliner Morgenpost.* March 1, 1999.

_____. Schrott — oder Zeugnis der Zeitgeschichte? Wilfried Menghin, Leiter des Archäologischen Landesamtes, zum Thema "ausgegrabene Nazi-Bunker." *Berliner Morgenpost.* February 2, 1998.

_____. Torfklo und armdicke Telefonkabel: Was Goebbels im Bunker hinterliess. *Berliner Morgenpost.* January 29, 1998.

_____. Wannsee-Idyll und Nazi Terror. Schau in

der Gedenkstätte informiert über die wechselhafte Geschichte der vornehmen Villenkolonie. *Berliner Morgenpost.* June 21, 2000.

_____. Was soll aus Goebbels Bunker werden? Verein "Berliner Unterwelten" warnt vor Zerstörung und regt Diskussion an. *Berliner Morgenpost.* January 31, 1999.

Michelin. *Alsace Lorraine. Guide de Tourisme.* Michelin et Cie, Propriétaires-Éditeurs 1995.

_____. *Paris. Guide de Tourisme.* Michelin et Cie, Propriétaires-Éditeurs 1995.

Möller, Horst, Volker Dahm, Hartmut Mehringer. *Die tödliche Utopie.* Institut für Zeitgeschichte. Munich 1999.

Moser, Erich Peter. *Salzburg. City and Countryside.* Rudolf Krey, Gmbh, Vienna (undated).

Müller, Heike. *Die Konferenz von Potsdam 1945 im Schloss Cecilienhof.* Stiftung Preussische Schlösser und Gärten. Berlin-Brandenburg. 3rd ed. 1997.

Nayhauss, Dirk von. Adressen einst und jetzt. Beten für die Verfolgten. *Berliner Illustrierte Zeitung.* September 17, 2000.

_____. Adressen einst und jetzt. Ein nackter Held für Mussolini. *Berliner Illustrierte Zeitung.* February 13, 2000.

_____. Brot und Spiele — zwischen Sport und Propaganda. *Berliner Morgenpost.* September 19, 1999.

Neues Licht für alte Laternen. *Berliner Morgenpost.* January 21, 2000.

Nichols, Lynn H. *The Rape of Europa. The Fate of Europe's Treasures in the Third Reich and the Second World War.* Vintage Books. New York 1995.

O'Donnell, James P. *The Bunker.* Houghton Mifflin Company. Boston 1978.

Opitz, Eckhardt, and Reinhard Scheiblich. *Auf Otto von Bismarcks Spuren.* Ellert and Richter Verlag. Hamburg 1998.

Pätzold, Kurt, and Erika Schwarz. *Tagesordnung: Judenmord. Die Wannsee-Konferenz am 20. January 1942.* Metropol Verlag. Berlin 1992.

Plenk, Anton. *The Obersalzberg and the Third Reich.* Verlag Plenk. Berchtesgaden 198.

Posner, Gerald. Secrets of the files. *New Yorker* 70:39–47. March 14, 1994.

Potsdam Privat. Kulturförderer. *Berliner Morgenpost.* January 19, 1997.

Potsdam-Infos. Gedenktafel erinnert an Hitler-Gegner. *Berliner Morgenpost.* July 20, 1997.

Preis, Kurt. *München unterm Hakenkreuz.* F. A. Herbig Verlagsbuchhandlung. München 1989.

Rath, Florian. Eine Zeitzeuge erinnert sich an das Leben mit den Bunkern. Immer wenn der Kuckuck schrie. *Süddeutsche Zeitung.* April 23, 1999.71, 79

Read, Anthony, and David Fisher. *Berlin Rising.* Norton. New York 1994.

_____. *The Fall of Berlin.* Norton. New York 1992.

Ritzmann, Kai. Entscheidung vor 50 Jahren: Nofretete is Berlinerin. Als die Amerikaner den Rückgabestreit um die ägyptische Skulptur beendeten. *Berliner Morgenpost.* January 29, 1997.

_____. Erstmals gezeigt: Wie die Nazis Berlin wiederaufbauen wollten. *Berliner Morgenpost.* April 20, 1997.

Rosenbaum, Ron. *Explaining Hitler.* Random House. New York 1998.

_____. Hitler's Angel. *Vanity Fair.* April 1992, p. 180.

Rosenberg, Elliot. The In-Laws: Brigid and Willie Hitler. *New York Daily News.* August 22, 1999, p. 43.

Rürup, Reinhard, et al. *Topographie des Terrors.* Verlag Willmuth Arenhövel. Berlin 1987.

Ryback, Timothy W. Hitler's lost family. *New Yorker.* July 17, 2000, pp. 46–57.

Sandvoss, Hans-Rainer. *Stätten des Widerstandes in Berlin 1933–1945.* Gedenkstätte Deutscher Widerstand. Berlin (undated).

Schauplatz Berlin. Vergangenheit, die nicht vergeht. Zum Umgang mit dem Bauerbe der NS-Zeit. *Neue Zürcher Zeitung.* March 28, 1998.

Schmemann, Serge. Where Hitler's story began: Birthplace alive with ghosts. *New York Times.* April 20, 1989, p. 1.

_____. A Munich refrain: Peals of music in Hitler's hall. *New York Times.* September 30, 1988.

_____. Landsberg Journal. The prostitutes leave, but Nazi ghosts linger. *New York Times.* July 1, 1989, p. 4.

Schmidt, Heiner. Prora-Koloss mit Zukunft. *Hamburger Abendblatt.* October 2, 2000.

Schmidt, Paul. *Hitler's Interpreter.* Macmillan. New York 1951.

Schmidt, Walter. Schweigen über dem Felsennest. *Hamburger Abendblatt.* May 20, 2000.

Schoelkopf, Katrin. Der Fall Barbarossa und der Mauerbau … oder weshalb die Telefonkabel vom Wünsdorfer Zeppelin-Bunker zur

Post in Zossen führen. *Berliner Morgenpost.* April 8, 1998.

Schönrock, Dirk. "Diese Stunde der Idiotie." Augenzeugenbericht und Analyse: Irving Fetschers Buch "Joseph Goebbels im Berliner Sportpalast 1943. *Berliner Morgenpost.* May 10, 1998.

Schubert, Peter. *Schauplatz Österreich: Topographisches Lexikon zur Zeitgeschichte in drei Bänden.* Verlag Brüder Hollinek. Vienna 1976.

_____. Baustart im künftigen Zweisitz von Minister Rühe. Bendlerblock wird jetzt saniert. *Berliner Morgenpost.* December 2, 1997.

_____. Das grösste Bürogebäude Berlins. Ex-Reichsluftfahrtministerium im Umbau zum Bundesfinanzministerium. *Berliner Morgenpost.* July 31, 1997.

_____. Umzug in ein Haus voll deutscher Geschichte(n). Denkmalschützer jetzt im "Krausenhof." *Berliner Morgenpost.* April 30, 1998.

_____. Umzug ins "Haus der Lügen." Die Last der Altbauten: Vom schwierigen Umgang mit der NS-Architektur. *Berliner Morgenpost.* June 3, 1997.

Schütz, Erhard, and Eckhard Gruber. *Mythos Reichsautobahn. Bau und Inszenierung der "Strassen des Führers" 1933–1941.* Ch. Links Verlag. Berlin 1996.

Seewald, Stefan. Buswartehäuschen erinnert an berüchtigtes Judenreferat. *Berliner Morgenpost.* December 12, 1998.

Seidler, Franz W., and Dieter Zeigert. *Die Führerhauptquartiere. Anlagen und Planungen im Zweiten Weltkrieg.* Herbig Verlag. Munich 2000.

Sereny, Gitta. *Albert Speer: His Battle with Truth.* Alfred A. Knopf. New York 1995.

Shirer, William L. *Berlin Diary. The Journal of a Foreign Correspondent 1934–41.* Popular Library. New York 1961.

Sigmund, Maria Anna. Des "Führers" Grossmutter und deren exquisite Möbel. *Die Presse* (Vienna) April 26, 1999.

Sims, Calvin. Film stirs Argentines' memories of a Nazi. *New York Times.* March 5, 1996, sec. C, p. 11.

Snyder, Louis L. *Encyclopedia of the Third Reich.* McGraw-Hill. New York 1978.

Soltis, Andy. New embassy in Berlin raises historic Führer. *New York Post.* November 24, 2000.

Spar, Jan. Gedenken an die Opfer der Köpenicker Blutwoche. *Berliner Morgenpost.* June 21, 1999.

Speer, Albert. *Inside the Third Reich.* Translated by Richard and Clara Winston. Avon Books. New York 1971.

_____. *Infiltration. How Heinrich Himmler Schemed to Build an SS Industrial Empire.* Translated from the German by Joachim Neugroschel. Macmillan, New York 1981.

_____. *Spandau. The Secret Diaries.* Translated by Richard and Clara Winston. Pocket Books. New York 1977.

Stasi im Führerbunker. *Der Spiegel.* 10:18, 1997.

Steinmetz, Greg. Some ghosts vanish as Germany relocates from Bonn to Berlin. Storied Reichsbank is typical of Nazi buildings getting an exorcising makeover. *Wall Street Journal.* January 22, 1999, p. 1.

Stengel, Mathias. Grabfelder im Schatten der Mauer. Vor 250 Jahren liess Friedrich II. den Invalidenfriedhof anlegen. 1961 mussten viele Ruhestätten dem Todesstreifen weichen. *Berliner Morgenpost.* November 10, 1998.

Taylor, Telford. *Anatomy of the Nuremberg Trials.* Little, Brown. Boston 1992.

Teile des Tischaltars Wilhelm IV. gefunden. Berolinensien sollen in diesem Jahr der Öffentlichkeit zugänglich gemacht werden. *Berliner Morgenpost.* October 7, 1998.

Terrance, Marc. *Concentration Camps. A Traveler's Guide to World War II Sites.* Universal Publishers 1999.

Toland, John. *Adolf Hitler.* Doubleday. Garden City, N.Y. 1976.

Traynor, Ian. Hitler's saviour dies unrepentant. *Guardian.* Manchester October 7, 1997, p. 1.

Tucek, J., and U. Thiede. Brisantes Erbe: Fast 90 Prozent des Archivs der Waffen-SS lagert in Prag. *Berliner Morgenpost.* October 31, 1997.

Tuchman, Barbara. *The Guns of August.* Macmillan. New York 1962.

Uhde, Michael. Historische Türen kommen zurück in den Bendlerblock. *Berliner Morgenpost.* July 6, 1998.

_____. In den Kasernen büffeln jetzt Schüler. Deutschlands Hauptstadt: Die Spandauer Wilhelmstadt und ihre militärische Vergangenheit. *Berliner Morgenpost.* October 1, 1998.

Umbau zur Eisarena. *Berliner Morgenpost.* September 17, 2000.

Vor 30 Jahren wurde die Garnisonkirche gesprengt. *Berliner Morgenpost.* June 23, 1998.

Vor Kriegsende abgerüstet. *Berliner Morgenpost.* March 15, 2000.

Waite, Robert G. L. *The Psychopathic God. Adolf Hitler.* Basic Books. New York 1977.

Walsh, Mary Williams. Berlin considers future of Hitler's field of dreams. *Los Angeles Times.* August 25, 1995, p. 5.

_____. Heirs' Angst upstages Wagner. The Bayreuth Festival, Germany's new showcase for the composer's works, has become a gothic tale of infighting. Control of the operas, new revelations of Third Reich ties figure in the generational face-off. *Los Angeles Times.* July 31, 1998, p. 1.

_____. A witness to Hitler's last stand as Germany debates sealing the Berlin bunker where the Nazi leader killed himself; one of its last occupants describes the intrigues and tension of the final days. *Los Angeles Times.* April 29, 1995, p. 1.

Webster, Paul. Nazi HQ sale raises fears of 'Hitlerpark.' *Guardian.* Manchester. November 25, 1995, p. 13.

Wehmut am Ende einer Berlin Tradition. Nach 62 Jahren die letzte Vorstellung in der Deutschlandhalle. *Neue Zürcher Zeitung.* January 3, 1998.

Weihrauch, Dieter. Vorschlag: Garnisonkirche als Ruinen — Mahnmal wiederaufbauen. *Berliner Morgenpost.* July 12, 1998.

Welles, Benjamin. *Sumner Welles. FDR's Global Strategist.* St. Martin's Press. New York 1997.

Westphal, Dirk. Das Auswärtige Amt ist enthüllt. Anbau für 150 Millionen Mark stellt früheres DDR-Staatsratsgebäude in den Schatten. *Berliner Morgenpost.* August 10, 1999.

Weyerer, Benedikt. Wie die Nazis ihren Aufstieg finanzierten. Eine Hand wäscht die andere. In der Müchner Zentrale flossen erhebliche Summen aus Industriekänalen zusammen. *Süddeutsche Zeitung.* December 4, 1998.

White, Michael, and Kevin Scott. *Introducing Wagner.* Totem Books. New York 1995.

Widmann, Carlos. Play it again, Putzi. *Der Spiegel.* 10:58–64, 1999.

Wiegrefe, Klaus. Staat von Blut und Eisen. *Der Spiegel.* 4: 70–84, 2001.

Wilderotter, Hans, and Klaus D. Pohl. *Der Letzte Kaiser. Wilhelm II.* im Exil. Bertelsmann Lexikon Verlag/Deutsches Historisches Museum. Berlin 1991.

Wistrich, Robert S. *Who's Who in Nazi Germany.* Routledge. London 1982.

"Wollt Ihr den totalen Krieg?" *Berliner Morgenpost.* December 31, 1998.

Zentner, Christian, and Friedemann Bedürftig, eds. *The Encyclopedia of the Third Reich.* English translation edited by Amy Hackett. Macmillan. New York 1991.

Zinn, Iwan. Soldatenschicksale auf vergilbten Karteikarten. Auskunftstelle am Eichborndamm verwaltet das grösste Wehrmacht-Personalarchiv. *Berliner Morgenpost.* September 26, 1999.

Zipfel, Friedrich, Eberhard Aleff, Hans Ludwig Schoenthal, Wolfgang Göbel. *Gedenkstätte Plötzensee.* Gedenkstätte Deutscher Widerstand Berlin 1972.

Zsolnay, Robert. Im Reich der Schreibtischtäter. *Süddeutsche Zeitung.* November 26, 1999.

_____. Mahnmal in Hitlers Alpenfestung. Auf dem Obersalzberg wurde eine ständige Ausstellung über die NS-diktatur eröffnet. *Berliner Morgenpost.* October 21, 1999.

Zum Schluss noch eine Party: Der Sportpalast hat ausgedient. *Berliner Morgenpost.* August 26, 1998.

Die zwei Geschicter der Militär-Geschichte in Wünsdorf. *Berliner Morgenpost.* March 30, 1997.

INDEX